THE HUMAN FUTURES SERIES

Barry N. Schwartz and Robert Disch,
General Editors

JOSEPH RYAN teaches in the Department of Sociology
at New York City Community College in Brooklyn.
He is a member of the Center for Cutural Diversity.

white ethnics:

their life in working class america

EDITED BY *Joseph Ryan*

PRENTICE-HALL, INC.   *Englewood Cliffs, New Jersey*

A SPECTRUM BOOK

Library of Congress Cataloging in Publication Data

RYAN, JOSEPH.
 White ethnics.

 (The Human futures series) (A Spectrum book)
 Bibliography: p.
 1. Minorities—United States—Addresses, essays,
lectures. I. Title.
E184.A1R82   301.45′1′0973   74–22326
ISBN 0–13–957712–2
ISBN 0–13–957704–1 pbk.

10 9 8 7 6 5 4 3 2 1

PRENTICE-HALL INTERNATIONAL, INC. (*London*)
PRENTICE-HALL OF AUSTRALIA PTY. LTD. (*Sydney*)
PRENTICE-HALL OF CANADA LTD. (*Toronto*)
PRENTICE-HALL OF INDIA PRIVATE LIMITED (*New Delhi*)
PRENTICE-HALL OF JAPAN, INC. (*Tokyo*)

to my mother and father

contents

introduction

Social phenomena, such as the resurgence of ethnicity described in this book, have their own rhythms and timetables for emerging into public view. Throughout the 1960s, as the title of Michael Novak's book "The Rise of the Unmeltable Ethnics" suggests, momentum was building up within white ethnic neighborhoods to the point where their concerns and grievances demanded the attention of the society at large. Since they were no longer willing to be silent about the social decisions others were making over their lives, white ethnic groups began asserting the right to shape the social institutions which affected their lives and their place in American society. Along with this assertion came the rediscovery of the right to be consciously ethnic. White ethnics, as well as others, began searching their backgrounds for a usable past as a basis for reformulating their ethnic identity. Writers, educators, politicians and clergymen are now beginning to speak of this as the "new ethnicity" in American life and to stress its potential for improving the quality of life not only for ethnics, but for the larger society as well.

While there are no easy explanations for the appearance of this new ethnicity in a country that has long prided itself as the world's melting pot, there are nevertheless important factors behind this rising-up of ethnicity which can be explored. Partly it is a consequence of the growing discontent among white ethnics with their socio-economic position in America, partly it is one facet of the broader movement towards self-definition on the part of many groups within American society. Blacks, women, chicanos and others are all reexamining their statuses, cultural values, and historical backgrounds in contrast to those laid down by the dominant segments of our society. Finally, it is in part a reaction to the social and political upheavals of the 1960s compounded by the inflationary economic spirals which followed.

Unfortunately it has been these later aspects of reasserted white

1

ethnicity which have dominated the mass media's coverage of this population. The media conveniently exploited such dramatic demonstrations as those between civil rights activists and white ethnics over neighborhood integration, those between construction workers and antiwar demonstrators and those whites rallying around George Wallace and his appealingly simplistic brand of politics.

While all of these confrontations served as prime time fodder for the evening news, they were often only symptomatic of the more deeply rooted causes behind white ethnic reactions. Not much was done by the media to help the rest of America understand the real sources of discontent within ethnic neighborhoods or the complex realities of white ethnic life. Instead, the media helped popularize the stereotyped images of them as hard hats, anti-intellectuals, and worse, as pigs and white racists. Whatever the context, white ethnics were portrayed as callously indifferent to the needs of the repressed urban minorities.

Subsequently, concern grew among some of society's more thoughtful observers over the lack of reasonable, balanced explanations for what was happening and the accumulating evidence that polarization was taking place between conflicting racial, class, and cultural groups. Early attempts to fully understand the real reasons behind these clashes came at such meetings as the National Consultation on Ethnic America held at Fordham University in June of 1968. Other similar gatherings followed in Chicago, Washington, D.C. and San Francisco. At each of these conferences participants from civil rights organizations, urban study centers and the social sciences met to ask themselves the harder questions: who was specifically reacting in these confrontations and to what? What legitimate complaints were being voiced? What positive values were being protected? More importantly, conference participants began to listen to the whites directly involved in such confrontations and what they had to say about their own reasons for reacting. A dialogue had begun between white ethnic Americans and interested social observers.

It was through such beginnings that the real causes behind the overt conflicts started to emerge in all of their complexity. Portraits which had been cast in stereotypes by the media gave way to clearer, more detailed pictures of these white ethnics. Many of them are second and third generation whites who have ethnic ties with the last great waves of European immigration to America in the late 1800s and early 1900s. For many of them this means that their original ethnic ties were with southern and eastern Europe—Poles, Slovaks, Italians and Greeks number largely among them as well as numerous other groups.*

* Some Irish-Americans may be included, too, but for the most part, as Glazer and Moynihan point out in *Beyond the Melting Pot,* there has been ". . . a decline of Irish identity in America . . ." not yet matched by the above groups. For a lively account of the Irish-Americans see Andrew Greeley's *That Most Dis-*

Working class status is a recurring reality for this white ethnic population, and will be brought into the discussion by many of the contributors. At times it will be difficult to separate out ethnicity from working class participation, for as Msgr. Geno Baroni states, "The ethnic factor in northern urban areas is intrinsically related to the alienated working class population."

Largely Roman Catholic, most white ethnics are concentrated in the older urban neighborhoods, first suburban rings, and milltowns of the industrialized midwest and northeast. While these descriptive characteristics represent the major share of white ethnics, they are by no means exclusive—Jews, Protestants, small town residents and non-working class members may also consider themselves ethnic. Conversely, these characteristics encompass some white Americans who would prefer not to be labeled ethnic.

In addition to exploring these major identifying characteristics of the book's white ethnic population, the contributors also refer to the historical importance of the original immigrant experiences, the sequence of ethnic groups settling in America, and the resulting socio-economic positions held by white ethnics. A sense of the historical background, then, is necessary to fully understand the current status of this population in American society.*

Further compounding the past and present complexities found in the lives of white ethnics is the inadequacy of the language used in describing the dynamics of this population. For as Nathan Glazer argues, ". . . whatever was happening to ethnic groups in the United States, we didn't have a language, a rhetoric, an ideology, that explained it." Social observers have continually played down the importance of ethnic cultural differences in our society; particularly muted are those ethnic groups which came after the original Anglo-Saxon settlements were established. These first settlers and others who arrived early on in our national development played an inordinately large role in establishing an American ethos from their own cultural roots, religious beliefs and political values. Statesmen, writers, and national leaders who subsequently shaped the dominant American culture, therefore, ignored much of what later immigrant groups had to offer.

Developing a way of speaking about the possibility of cultural diversity has been and continues to be an obstacle in defining the life styles of white ethnic Americans. It should come as no surprise to the

---

tressful Nation. (Quadrangle Books, 1972) Some Jewish Americans can also be numbered among this population, but they have mostly moved out of the working class and the inner urban areas except for occasional pockets of older, working class Jews.

* See such works as Handlin's *The Uprooted,* Hansen's *The Immigrant in American History* and Higham's *Strangers in the Land.* The bibliography contains further reference to historical materials.

reader, then, to discover that many social scientists have not yet thought out, indeed even been interested in, a more realistic social documentation of this population. Cultural anthropologists and community sociologists alike often know more about exotic island enclaves in the Pacific than they do about white ethnic neighborhoods in America.

Hence, the contributions to this book were purposefully chosen to present a variegated picture of the life of white ethnics. Some contributors are themselves ethnic and describe experientially what it means to be so in America. Others are social scientists who present more scholarly interpretations of the population. Some contributors are happily both. All of them have in common a deep concern for presenting a more complete picture of the human lives and values white ethnics hold; taken together they present a view of social reality at once both more balanced and complex than that usually given in the popular writings about this population.

Putting aside these caveats to the reader, there has been a concerted effort to present the book's materials in a coherent and comprehensive framework. Part One: "Defining White Ethnicity" introduces major definitional characteristics of the population; both from a statistical and a personal point of view, the reader is given some of the descriptive parameters necessary for a fuller understanding of white ethnic Americans.

The central core of the book evolves out of the second and third parts; here selected social institutions which play important roles in ethnic life are viewed from several perspectives. Part Two: "Private Lives" deals with the very essence of ethnic identity as it develops in the primary social institutions of family, parish, and neighborhood. "These are places," Gabriel Fackre claims, ". . . where the white worker gets back his face and his name, where he 'has a say,' where he experiences participation and community." *

"Public Lives" next demonstrates the adjustments and accommodations white ethnics must make as they come to terms with several major secondary institutions: schools, work and politics. Here they confront what is called the "larger society," implying ethnic alienation from the centers of power which decide the shape of American society. It is in their daily interactions within these secondary institutions that many ethnics have their first experience of being differently white in America.

Part Four; "A Resurgence of White Ethnicity," concludes the book with several selections on the reappearance and importance of white ethnic identity, both to ethnics themselves and to the society as a whole. The authors included here attempt to deal with ethnic di-

---

* Gabriel Fackre, *Liberation in Middle America* (Philadelphia: Pilgrim Press, 1971), p. 42.

versity in American life and show how it need not necessarily lead to divisive group conflicts, or degenerate into ethnocentrism. All would agree that some aspects of ethnic identity relate to fear and racist attitudes. As Nathan Glazer puts it in his essay, "Let me say at the outset that I do not deny there was some admixture of simple racial prejudice (in the urban confrontations of the late 1960's). . . . But there was something else. There was a sense that a valued way of life was being threatened. And that kind of motivation for that kind of behavior was different from racism and different from racial prejudice. It had to be understood—conceivably it had to be protected." It is that "something else," the positive values central to the new ethnicity which are probed here.

Those who defend the new ethnicity have to deal with the frequently heard charge that a resurgence of ethnicity is essentially reactionary, that it will only serve to further polarize American inter-group life. Judith Herman has aptly set the task facing America as ". . . how to help people maintain what is theirs and what is precious to them, but still be able to adapt to changing needs and changing conditions. It is this balance which is so difficult to strike, but it is exactly the balance which will help bring about the 'new pluralism' so many of us are talking about."

White ethnic Americans are not alone in their search for meaning in the larger society today; it is a painful time of searching for many as to what national goals and priorities ought to be, what values remain important and lasting in the fiber of American life. Hopefully, white ethnics will increasingly take part in this revaluation of our national life on many levels. Michael Novak speaks for many interested in the "new pluralism" when he states

> The task is to discover what America is, or might yet be. No one, of course, can address that larger issue without coming to terms with his own particularity. No one ethnic group speaks for America. Each of us becomes aware of his own partial standpoint. For it is in possessing our own particularity that we come to feel at home with ourselves and are best able to enter into communion with others, freely giving and receiving of each other. The point of becoming ethnically alert and self-possessed is not self-enclosure; it is genuine community, honest and un-pretending.*

* Michael Novak, *The Rise of The Unmeltable Ethnics* (New York: Macmillan Co., 1971) paperback edition, p. xxviii–xxix.

defining white ethnicity

The melting pot is a fiction. Ethnic group loyalties are a fact of life. It is a mistake to suppress ethnic communal ties and values, as the "assimilationists" have tried to do, for both are necessary to the mental health of the individual and to the stability of the community of which he is a part. It is true that most of us are still working people but whatever our occupation or income we hold our heritage in high regard. We are fearful that our children, stripped of a strong group self-identity, will become defenseless and will be unable to cope with the pressures which are a prominent part of our society today. The demagogue exploits the rootless man whose fears compel him to think and act in a manner which is inconsistent with his needs and those of his fellow-man.

You don't have to tell us we're Americans; we know that and we're proud of it, but don't forget that many of us are reminded of our "ethnicity" when we hear Polish jokes or allusions that any office seeker of Italian descent must be involved in criminal activities. Because stereotypes of this kind have been perpetuated over generations and still thrive, many of our people carry invisible wounds—to recognize our uniqueness is not to promote inter-group hostilities. On the contrary, as long as a man is without communal ties of some kind and values which guide him through difficult periods of his life he will be unable to relate to and work with others on the basis of respect and good will.

Workshop participant
Working Class & Ethnic Priorities
National Center for Urban Ethnic
Affairs, Washington, D.C.

What is ethnicity? More specifically, who can legitimately be called white ethnics? Andrew Greeley and Perry Weed look to provide definitions of both questions in the opening contribu-

tions to this section. Such definitions are difficult to formulate, for human populations change too quickly for any definition to remain constant. As Greeley notes, "Whatever definition we emerge with is likely to leave us with some very embarrassing questions." What characteristics, for instance, determine real ethnic identity? At what point can we say that a person is too assimilated to be truly ethnic? While the contributors would agree that answers to these and other questions are elusive, they would also agree that it is necessary to pursue such answers if we are to clearly locate and understand the white ethnic population.

Greeley points out that we do know something of the origins of ethnic group identity:

The ethnic group was created only when the peasant commune broke up, and was essentially an attempt to keep some of the values, some of the informality, some of the support and intimacy of the communal life in the midst of an impersonal, formalistic, rationalized, urban and industrial society.

How we explain the persistence of ethnic group identity is, however, more perplexing. It was only recently, after all, that many social observers would even admit to the possibility of continued ethnic identity. Up almost to the present, it has been fashionable to speak of the great American "melting pot" wherein all new immigrant groups would assimilate into one, larger American culture. But, as many of the following articles reveal, complete assimilation has not taken place, and is not likely to in the near future.

Milton Gordon's Assimilation in American Life *thoroughly examines the persistence of ethnic identity by analyzing two stages of the assimilation process. The first, cultural assimilation (or acculturation) involves the ethnic group's acceptance of the dominant culture's language, dress, diet, and other daily customs. This stage is often quickly accomplished because it requires only observation and daily contact with the dominant culture, though it may be virtually one-sided.*

The second stage includes the processes of structural assimilation in which the ethnic groups are assimilated into the dominant culture's primary social groupings—play and peer groups, or country clubs and neighborhoods. Being so accepted takes place much more slowly than cultural assimilation, and is one of the areas where distinct ethnic groupings still persist in American society.

While the authors in this section may not agree on precise definitions of ethnicity, all agree that we can identify distinct

white ethnic structural groupings that maintain their own pri-
mary values and social institutions while living within the larger
society.

Historically, the values and social institutions of the dom-
inant American culture slowly evolved out of the colonial settle-
ments of the late 17th and 18th centuries, and were the bases for
establishing the political structures of the newly emerging Amer-
ican nation. By the time of the Revolutionary War, about 60%
of the population was of English descent. As Perry Weed notes,
these early English settlers cannot be counted as immigrants:

John Higham, historian of American nativism, contends that the founders of a society must be excluded from the immigrant category because
as original settlers they firmly established "the polity, the language, the
pattern of work and settlement, and many of the mental habits to
which the immigrants would have to adjust."

America is not so much a "nation of immigrants" as it is a nation
in which a firmly entrenched group, Anglo-Saxon settlers, early
set the tone for American society and greatly affected the lives of
all subsequent immigrant groups.

Adjusting to this established culture presented different
problems for each succeeding immigrant group. In general, the
so-called "old immigrants"—those from northern European coun-
tries such as Sweden, Germany, Scotland and, lastly, Ireland—
were better able to assimilate than were the "new immigrants"
of the late 19th and early 20th centuries.

Predominantly Roman Catholic, these new immigrants
came mainly from eastern and southern Europe. Conspicuously
different from those who came before them in language, religion,
and cultural values, their assimilation was conspicuously slower.
Today, it is largely the descendants of these mostly Italian, Polish,
Slovak and Greek immigrants who are identified as white ethnics,
and who are the major concern of this book. Others, such as Jew-
ish and Irish city dwellers may also be included.

The reaction of the dominant population to the millions of
new immigrants was ambivalent at best. On the one hand, they
were welcomed, indeed solicited, as sources of cheap labor to man
the mills, factories, and construction gangs which were rapidly
turning America into an urban, industrial empire. On the other
hand, they were met with derisive hostility and, at times, violence
by those who felt their overwhelming numbers threatened the
very fabric of American life.

They were resented on many fronts: by laborers because
they flooded the labor market and kept wages down, by Protes-
tants suspicious of Catholicism, by native-born whites who saw

them as threats to an imagined purity of culture and race, and, finally, by many Americans for no other reason than that they were strangers.

All of these reactions, according to Greeley, provided justification for the immigrants to preserve their original cultural values, customs and mores—i.e., to maintain an ethnic identity. Confronted by a both beckoning and dangerously hostile dominant culture, the maintenance of ethnicity was an attempt to rebuild the protective social milieu of their "old world" cultures.

Another important factor that helped these new immigrants maintain their ethnic identity was the powerful influence of their religion. Most new immigrants were Roman Catholic; for their communities, the Church and its calendar of worship provided a common religious core, without which they might well have been fragmented in the face of a hostile native protestantism. Of this coupling of cultural roots and religious beliefs, Greeley writes that "both blood and belief impinge strongly on what happens to a man, his wife and his children."

As these fundamental ties of "blood, land and belief" merge, a distinctive sense of ethnic identity arises. For individual groups it emerges as an awareness of the differences which separate "us" from the rest of "them." This sense of being distinctly different both from the dominant culture and all other ethnic groups has resulted in a continuous ethnic diversity in American society.

In "Components of the White Ethnic Movement," the second essay, Perry Weed attempts to define what populations can legitimately be called white ethnics. Weed presents four indices frequently used to describe white ethnics: how many of them there are, where they live, their religion and work status. That he cannot accurately identify the boundaries of this population reveals how indifferent much of the traditional social sciences have been towards the study of white ethnic Americans. Their numbers, according to Weed, amount to over 40 million, or about one-fifth of the nation's population. A significant enough figure, one would think, to be more accurately accounted for by social scientists.

Despite the limitations of available data, Weed establishes that many white ethnics work in blue collar and lower-paid white collar occupations. (Other contributors below consider working class membership a defining characteristic of white ethnics.) They live, Weed points out, in the older industrial cities of the midwest and northeast, and are largely Roman Catholic. While these indices do not exclusively describe all American white ethnics, they are useful because they locate the socio-economic and geographic status of most of the population we look at here.

Descriptive parameters and statistical data, though, are not as immediately interesting as the actual experiences of white ethnic individuals confronting the larger society's values and mores. An exceptional writer in this vein, who celebrates his own ethnicity, is Michael Novak.

In his essay, "Confessions of a White Ethnic," Novak relates well the estrangement white ethnics experience when they interact with the dominant American life style, and the price they must pay for their success in terms of the dominant culture—undervaluing, if not altogether rejecting, their own cultural roots. From his own background, Novak makes plain many of the deceits the larger society has heaped on white ethnics, and the inevitable clashes which occur when ethnic values are tested against those of the larger society.

One crucial conflict which Novak depicts centers on white ethnics' high regard for family connectedness, their sense of being jointly involved and responsible for actions taken within the blood group; of being, in short, members of what Novak calls "network people." The "typical" American, by contrast, "makes it" only as an individual, at the cost of most if not all family ties. Such successful individuals become, in Novak's term, "atomic men," rewarded with the isolation and loneliness many find at the pinnacle of personal success. In his efforts to purge himself of such "americanisms"—or to at least understand them in relation to more personal values—Novak largely revaluates ethnicity and reveals its potential value to the larger society. An understanding of the "communion of memories" which one shares intuitively with others of his own "blood, land and belief" may provide a healthy alternative to the alienation so characteristic of contemporary American life.

what is an ethnic?

Andrew Greeley

It is very difficult to speak precisely about what an ethnic group is, but it is possible to develop a working definition somewhat empirically and to describe ethnicity by showing how contemporary ethnic groups came into existence. While there is some broad equation possible between ethnic groups and immigrant groups, it is not enough merely to say that the ethnic groups are immigrant groups. Whatever definition we emerge with is likely to leave us with some very embarrassing questions. For example: Does everyone belong to an ethnic group? Is a white Anglo-Saxon Protestant an ethnic? Are Texans or Kentuckians, for example, ethnics? And what about American intellectuals, particularly those who are not Jewish and who seem to be quite cut off from any trace of nationality background? Do they constitute a new ethnic group? Such questions do not admit of quick answers; yet we must address ourselves to them if only because there are a number of Americans who are not prepared to take ethnic issues seriously unless responses to those questions are provided.

The ancestors of the immigrants to the United States were, for the most part, peasants living in the agricultural communities of European post-feudal society. This society was post-feudal in the sense that the peasants either owned some land of their own, or at least had been emancipated from the worst rigors of the feudal system. The peasant villages of Ireland, Germany, Italy, Poland or the Balkans were not the most comfortable places in the world, and the nostalgia bordering on romance over them that is to be found in the works of some 19th-century sociological writers is misleading. Granted that post-feudal peasant society provided a great deal of stability, it did so at the price of stagnancy; and granted also that it provided a great deal of

"What is an Ethnic?" From Andrew Greeley, *Why Can't They Be Like Us?* (New York: Institute of Human Relations Press), pp. 15–22. Reprinted by permission of Institute of Human Relations, American Jewish Committee.

social support, it did so by imposing a great deal of social control. A man was, indeed, sure of who he was and where he stood and what he might become in such societies, but most men were in inferior positions and had no expectation of becoming anything more than inferior.

Nevertheless, there was a warmth and intimacy and closeness in these peasant communities. A person could be sure of the pattern of relationships and be sure that while he might have enemies, he also had friends, and the friends and enemies were defined by historic tradition. Society indeed controlled individual members, but it also rallied support, strength and resources when help was needed. It was a highly personal world, not in the sense that the dignity of the human person was respected more than it is today, but in the sense that relationships were, for the most part, between persons who knew each other, understood their respective roles, and knew what kind of behavior to expect. Family, church and community were all fairly simple and overwhelmingly important, and though mankind had evolved beyond the all-pervading intimacy of the tribe or the clan, life was nonetheless quite personal and intimate in a stylized and highly structured way.

Some time after 1800, European peasant society began to break up, partly because, as the population increased, there were more people than jobs in the agricultural communes, and partly because the emergent industrialization in the cities desperately needed new labor. Those who made the move from commune to metropolis in hope of finding a better life began a number of social trends which actually meant a better life, if not for them, at least for their children or their grandchildren. The pilgrimage from peasant village to city, and later to the cities of America, brought to many the wealth of the affluent society.

But something was also lost: the warmth and intimacy, the social support of the commune was gone. Gabriel Le Bras, the famous French sociologist of religion, remarked that there was a certain railroad station in Paris which apparently had magical powers, because any Breton immigrant who passed through that station never set foot in a Catholic church again. The church, the family, the commune which had provided the parameters of the ordinary person's life were all either destroyed or so substantially altered as to be unrecognizable. The peasant migrant was forced to spend most of his waking day with people who were strangers. This is an experience which does not seem peculiar to us at all, but to a man who had encountered few strangers ever before in his life, it was frightening and disorienting.

"OUR OWN KIND"

In the strangeness of the new environment, the individual or his battered and bedraggled family looked around for someone with whom he had something in common—hopefully a place in the big city where previous migrants from his village had settled. Because such settlers were "his kind of people," he could trust them; they knew their obligations to him and would help him to adjust to this new world in which he found himself. Thus, in the Italian neighborhoods of New York's lower east side in the early 1920s it was possible to trace, block by block, not only the region in Italy but also the very villages from which the inhabitants had come. Indeed, it is no exaggeration to say that some of these blocks were nothing more than foreign colonies of Sicilian villages.

If you weren't able to find someone from your own village, then you searched for someone from your area of the country; even though you may never have met him before, you could depend on him to have some of the same values you had, and you shared some sort of common origin. He may not have been from Palermo, but at least he was a Sicilian; he may not have been from Ballyhaunis, but at least he was from County Mayo; and these village or regional groupings, based especially on family and kinship relationships, in their turn sought protection and some power against the strange world in which they found themselves by banding together, one with another. So that for many groups, as Glazer has pointed out, the nationality became a relevant factor only when the necessities of adjusting to American experience forced the village and regional groups to band together.

The ethnic group provided a pool of preferred associates for the intimate areas of life. It was perhaps necessary in large corporate structures to interact with whomever the random possibilities of the economic system put at the next workbench or desk. But when it came to choosing a wife, a poker (and later on, bridge) partner, a precinct captain, a doctor, a lawyer, a real estate broker, a construction contractor, a clergyman and, later on, a psychiatrist, a person was likely to feel much more at ease if he could choose "my kind of people."

So then, as Max Weber[1] defines it, an ethnic group is a human collectivity based on an assumption of common origin, real or imaginary; and E. K. Francis, supplementing the Weber definition, has argued that the ethnic collectivity represents an attempt on the part of men to keep alive, in their pilgrimage from peasant village to industrial metropolis, some of the diffuse, descriptive, particularistic modes of behavior that were common in the past. The ethnic group was created only when the peasant commune broke up, and was essentially an attempt to keep some of the values, some of the informality, some of the support, some of the intimacy of the communal life in the midst of an impersonal, formalistic, rationalized, urban, industrial society.

1. Max Weber, "The Ethnic Group," in Talcott Parsons, et al. *Theories of Society*, Vol. 1, p. 305 (Glencoe, Ill.: The Free Press, 1961).

That the immigrants tried to associate with their own kind was understandable enough in the early phases of immigration, but we are still faced with the necessity of explaining why ethnic groups have persisted as important collectivities long after the immigration trauma receded into the background. Why was not social class the membership around which American city dwellers could rally, as it was in England? Why have the trade unions rarely, if ever, played quite the fraternal role in American society that they have in many continental societies? Granted that urban man needed something to provide him with some sort of identification between his family and the impersonal metropolis, why did he stick with the ethnic group when there were other groupings to which he could make a strong emotional commitment?

First of all, one must acknowledge the fact that other groups have, on occasion, provided the same enthusiasm that ethnic groups do. Some men need more of this enthusiasm than others, and by no means all who need it seek it in a nationality group. As a matter of fact, it is probably likely that for many, at least at the present stage of acculturation, religion is more important than ethnicity as a means of social definition and social support, a means of identifying ourselves in relation to others. However, religion and ethnicity are so intertwined in the United States that it is extremely difficult to separate them; an attempt to sort out this relationship is one of the major challenges facing social theorists who become concerned with ethnic groups.

PLURALISM AND GROUP SURVIVAL

It seems to me that there were two factors which made for the survival of ethnic communities after the immigration trauma was over. First of all, the United States is a society which has demonstrated considerable ability in coping with religious and racial pluralism, one way or another. A nation which was, in effect, religiously pluralistic before it became politically pluralistic, the United States had to learn a sufficient amount of tolerance for religious diversity merely to survive. It was necessary only to expand this tolerance when the new immigrant groups arrived on the scene with their own peculiar kinds of religious difference. It also seems that, even before the Revolutionary War, nationality differences were important, so the Germans and the Irish (usually meaning the Scotch Irish) were considered as a group quite distinct from the Anglo-Saxon majority. Furthermore, even though the racial relationship had deteriorated into tyranny and slavery, there was, at least until the invention of the cotton gin, apparently some possibility that even this might be peacefully settled. In other words, by the time the large waves of immigrants came, in the early and middle 19th century, America was already acquiring some skills in coping with the religiously and ethnically pluralistic society. The immigrants were not welcome, and considerable pressure was put upon them to become Anglo-Saxons as quickly as possible. Yet the pressures stopped short of being absolute; the American ethos forced society to tolerate religious and ethnic diversity even if it did not particularly like it. Under such circumstances, it was possible for the ethnic groups to continue and to develop an ideology which said they could be Irish, German, Polish or Jewish, and at the same time be as good Americans as anyone else—if not better.[2]

But why is it still important to be an Italian, an Irishman, a German or a Jew? Part of the reason, I suspect, has something to do with the intimate relationship between ethnicity and religion. But another element, or perhaps another aspect of the same element, is that presumed common origin as a norm for defining "we" against "they" seems to touch on something basic and primordial in the human psyche, and that much of the conflict and strife that persists in the modern world is rooted in such differences. If anything, the separatist nationalisms within the major nation states seem stronger today than they were a quarter of a century ago: Catholics rioting in Londonderry, Ireland; Scots electing nationalist members to Parliament; the mutterings of Welsh separatism. The Basques, and even the Catalonians, grumble about being part of Spain; the Flemings and the Walloons are at odds with each other over Louvain; the Bretons wonder if it might be possible for them to escape from France; and the French Canadians are not at all sure they want to remain part of the Canadian nation, even if they could have their own prime minister.

Most of these separatist movements make little sense in terms of economic reality. The Province of Quebec would be hard put to go it on its own; Wales and Scotland would very quickly have to form a political and economic union with England, not much different from the one that already exists; and Brittany would have to do the same with the government in Paris. Maybe tribal loyalties and tribal separatism ought not to continue in a rational, industrial world—but they do, and it is a threat to the fabric of almost any society large enough to be made up of different ethnic communities. One is almost tempted to say that if there are no differences supposedly rooted in common origin by which people can distinguish themselves from others, they will create such differences. I suspect, for example, that if Scotland did become independent of England, there would be conflict between the Highlanders and the Lowlanders as to who would run the country. Ethnic diversity seems to be something that man grimly hangs on to, despite overwhelming evidence that he ought to give it up.

2. Daniel Patrick Moynihan summarized the super-patriot syndrome beautifully when he said, "At last the time had come to investigate Harvard men, and Fordham men were going to do the investigating."

Edward Shils has called these ties primordial and suggests that, rooted as they are with a sense of "blood and land," they are the result of a pre-rational intuition. Such an assumption seems to make considerable sense, but is difficult to prove empirically. It is certainly true, however, that family, land and common cultural heritage have always been terribly important to human beings, and suspicion of anyone who is strange or different seems also to be deeply rooted in the human experience. Ethnic groups continue, in this hypothesis, because they are a manifestation of man's deep-seated inclination to seek out those in whose veins he thinks flows the same blood as flows in his own. When blood is also seen as something intimately related to belief, and both blood and belief impinge strongly on what happens to a man, his wife and his children, he is only too ready to fight to protect the purity of that belief, or the purity of his blood, or the purity of his family when it is threatened by some strange outside invader.

This view of ethnicity, it must be confessed, is essentially a negative one. But one can make a more positive case for it. It could be said that the apparent inclination of men, or at least of many men, to consort with those who, they assume, have the same origins they do, provides diversity in the larger society and also creates sub-structures within that society that meet many functions the larger society would be hard put to service. And while the demons of suspicion and distrust prove very hard to exorcise from inter-ethnic relationships, such suspicion and distrust are not, I am convinced, inevitable. If they can be eliminated, ethnicity enriches the culture and reinforces the social structure.

To sum up, ethnic groups have emerged in this country because members of the various immigrant groups have tried to preserve something of the intimacy and familiarity of the peasant village during the transition into urban industrial living. These groups have persisted after the immigrant experience both because American society was not basically hostile to their persistence and because of an apparently very powerful drive in man toward associating with those who, he believes, possess the same blood and the same beliefs he does. The inclination toward such homogeneous groupings simultaneously enriches the culture, provides for diversity within the social structure, and considerably increases the potential for conflict. It may some day be possible to isolate ethnicity from suspicion and distrust, but no one has yet figured out the formula for doing so.

components of the white ethnic movement

Perry Weed

INTRODUCTION

Most first-, second-, and third-generation Americans of European ancestry are Catholics and residents of the older industrial cities of the North. As white ethnics, they are developing a new sense of self-awareness. They are reacting to the black and affluent student revolutions of the 1960s and to the economic stagnation and the social and cultural disruptions that have recently affected their lives. Moreover, they are becoming increasingly positive about their own ancestral cultural traditions, confused toward American culture, and in many ways negative toward Anglo-Protestant dominance. White ethnics are becoming a distinct minority. They have recently been described as alienated, forgotten, troubled, disillusioned, frustrated, and angry. Their shared grievances, coupled with their recent immigrant experiences, have drawn them together, both into their separate nationality groups and into the larger category of "white ethnics."

Most of the growing attention paid since the mid-1960s to the "backlash," "white ethnics," "blue-collar" Americans, and the "lower-middle class" has been too vague and simplistic to foster understanding. Was the backlash only against racial groups or against other groups as well? Who was lashing back at whom? Is a white ethnic a "hard hat" or a "blue-collar" worker, is he a Wallaceite, a racist—is he a member of the "little people," the "silent majority," or "middle America"? Are non-Roman Catholic Americans such as Orthodox Greeks and German Protestants also to be considered white ethnic? Are Irish and Ger-

"Components of the White Ethnic Movement." Excerpted from Perry Weed, *The White Ethnic Movement and Ethnic Politics* (New York: Praeger Publishers, Inc., 1973) Reprinted by permission of Praeger Publishers, Inc.

man Americans, who are more thoroughly assimilated than Americans from Southern, Central, and Eastern Europe, less likely or more likely to identify with their ancestral heritage? Are racial minorities part of the "white ethnic" category?

NUMERICAL SIGNIFICANCE

A United States Census Bureau survey conducted in November 1969 showed that 75 million Americans identified themselves with one of the seven major ethnic groups in Table 1. The survey found that 11

TABLE 1 POPULATION BY ETHNIC ORIGIN

Group	Millions
German	20.0
English	19.1
Irish	13.3
Spanish	9.2
Italian	7.2
Polish	4.0
Russian (mostly Jews)	2.2

Source: U.S. Census, *Current Population Reports*, Series P-20, No. 221, "Characteristics of the Population by Ethnic Origin: November 1969."

million Americans were foreign-born and that one-third of them said they usually spoke the language of their homeland in the home. This was the first time the Census Bureau had collected information on questions that specifically required identification as to origin or descent. Until then, the Census Bureau had to infer ethnic origin from information as to place of birth, country of origin, mother tongue, surname, etc. A later survey, in March 1971, found that 60 percent of the population sample identified themselves as having a single ethnic origin.

The 1960 census lists more than 33 million Americans in the "foreign white stock" category, which is defined by the Census as either foreign-born or children of at least one foreign-born parent. Of this figure, more than 9 million were themselves foreign-born. Table 2 shows the 1960 figures of foreign white stock for the eleven largest groups.

In 1960 foreign white stock made up 18.4 percent of America's total population of nearly 180 million. Italian foreign stock constituted 2.5 percent of the total, German 2.4 percent, and Canadian 1.8 percent. In its definition of foreign stock population, the census excludes third and subsequent generations, which means that the ethnic population exceeds the census figures. Since the Irish, Germans, and

TABLE 2 FIGURES AND PERCENTAGES OF FOREIGN WHITE STOCK

	Total (in thousands)	Percent	1969 Estimates
Italian	4,540	13.7	4,531
German	4,313	13.0	4,118
Canadian	3,154	9.5	
Polish	2,778	8.4	2,777
Russian	2,287	6.9	2,164
English and Welsh	1,955	5.9	
Irish	1,771	5.4	1,487
Mexican	1,725	5.2	
Austrian	1,098	3.3	1,035
Swedish	1,046	3.2	976
Czechoslovakian	917	2.8	885

Source: "Foreign White Stock by Country of Origin, Statistical Abstract of the United States," 1969, Table 34; and Pierre de Vise, "A Demographic Survey of Chicago's Ethnic Groups," unpublished paper presented to the Chicago Consultation on Ethnicity, November 1969.

Scandinavians entered the United States in large numbers during the latter half of the nineteenth century, they here appear to constitute a far smaller portion of the total foreign stock than they would have earlier, while the Italians, Poles, Russians, and Mexicans, whose peak immigration occurred later, now take on much large proportions.

If we define "ethnic" as "any individual who differs by religion, language, and culture from the white Protestant Anglo-Saxon settlers," the figure would exceed 65 percent of the total population. Aside from "whites," America has no majority group. The largest minority is the so-called "WASP-NN," that is, White Anglo-Saxon Protestant Native-born of Native Parents. These account for less than a third of the population, but though they are a minority, it is misleading to think of them as such.

When Oscar Handlin in the introduction to his book *The Uprooted,* writes, "Once I thought to write a history of the immigrants in America. Then I discovered that the immigrants were American history," he overemphasizes the influence of immigration between 1845 and 1924. John Higham, historian of American nativism, contends that the founders of a society must be excluded from the immigrant category because as original settlers they firmly established "the polity, the language, the pattern of work and settlement, and many of the mental habits to which the immigrants would have to adjust." In 1790 the English constituted approximately 60 percent of the white population of the United States. Thus while white America is a nation of immigrants, it is more practical to consider the original immigrant group as natives, since they early became dominant and effectively pre-empted the crucial levers of economic and political power.

RESIDENCY

According to the 1960 census, the largest concentration of European immigrants and their children is in the Northeast and comprises 34 percent of its total population. The Northeastern states with the largest concentrations of foreign stock were Connecticut (Italian, Canadian, Polish), Massachusetts (Canadian, Italian, Irish), New Jersey (Italian, German), New York (Italian, Russian), Pennsylvania (Italian, Polish), and Rhode Island (Italian, Canadian, British). In the Midwest, large foreign stock populations were found in Illinois (German, Polish), Michigan (Polish, German), and Ohio (German, Italian). Massachusetts had the highest percentage of foreign stock in relation to the total state population—40 percent. Rhode Island was second with 39.5 percent, New York third with 38.7 percent.

Most white ethnics reside in the older industrial cities of the Northeast and Great Lakes regions, as is illustrated by the two largest American cities. In 1960, New York had a total population of 7,781,984, consisting of 19 percent white foreign-born, 28 percent native white with at least one foreign-born parent, 8 percent first- and second-generation Puerto Rican, and 14 percent black. The overwhelming majority of other New Yorkers who were the grandchildren and great grandchildren of immigrants still thought of themselves, on some occasions and for some purposes, as Jews, Italians, Germans, and Irish. Immigrants and their children thus comprised nearly one-half of the city's total population in 1960. In Chicago, according to the 1960 census, more than one person out of three was an immigrant or child of an immigrant.

According to the Census Bureau's Congressional District Data Book (April 1964), of the 50 Congressional districts with the highest percentage of foreign stock, 39 were in the East (21 in the New York City area), 30 were urban, 9 suburban, 9 mixed, and only 2 rural. In 1960, of the ten cities over 500,000 population with the highest percentage of foreign stock, all except San Francisco and Los Angeles were in the North, only Seattle was in the Northwest, and all had more than 30 percent foreign stock—excluding Puerto Ricans. New York was the highest (48.6 percent), followed by Boston (45.5 percent), then San Francisco (43.5 percent), Chicago (35.9 percent), and Buffalo (35.4 percent).

RELIGION

In the Northeastern and Northcentral United States, which include more than 58 large cities, the Roman Catholic population is more than one-third of the total population of 90 million. The 50 Congressional districts with the highest percentage of immigrants and their children sent thirty-one Catholics and six Jews to the House of Representatives in 1964, which indicates the strong Catholic and Jewish affiliations of these largely Eastern constituencies (39 of the 50). In his book, *The Population of the United States,* Donald J. Bogue writes, "The outstanding fact . . . is that Roman Catholics comprise a disproportionately large share of the population in the most heavily industrialized areas" and "have an excess of the urban working-class persons."

THE BLUE-COLLAR DIMENSION

White ethnics constitute a disproportionately high percentage of the blue-collar labor force. Close to one-half of all male workers of Irish, Polish, and Italian origin are, according to a November 1969 survey by the Bureau of the Census, employed in blue-collar occupations. This survey found that for males, 44.8 percent of the Irish, 49.1 percent of the Poles, and 50.2 percent of the Italians were blue-collar workers. For females, the proportion of Italian and Polish women employed as blue-collar operatives (25.3 for Italians and 19.2 for Poles) was substantially higher than the 15.37 average for all ethnic groups. The same survey showed that in educational attainment the Irish, Poles, and Italians lagged behind Jews, English, and Germans.

The Bureau of Labor Statistics defines blue-collar occupations to include the following census occupational categories: craftsmen, foremen, and kindred workers; operatives and kindred workers; and laborers, except farm- and mineworkers. Some analysts also include service workers and private household workers. Operatives—that is, those employed in mechanical industries such as manufacturing and mills—are the largest blue-collar occupational group in the private economy. According to the report of Assistant Secretary of Labor Jerome M. Rosow, entitled *The Problem of the Blue Collar Worker,* "forty percent of American families—including 70 million family members—have incomes between $5,000 and $10,000 per year and might be termed 'lower middle income.'" Sar Levitan, editor of *Blue-Collar Workers,* published in late 1971, agrees that 70 million persons living in families headed by blue-collar workers have annual incomes concentrated between $5,000 and $10,000. While precise numbers are not known, white ethnics represent a large part of this group. The November 1969 survey of the Census Bureau found that the following family heads by ethnic origin had median family incomes below $10,000:

Irish	66.4
Italians	62.4
Poles	61.7

Of the 21 cities over 500,000 population in 1960 ranked by the percentage of families with incomes of $10,000 a year or more, all but two,

ranked within the $11–21,000 range, were in the Northeast and Midwest.

In 1971 the Bureau of Labor Statistics reported that the labor force in 1970 consisted of the following:

	Number (in millions)	Percentage of Total
Blue-collar	27.8	35.3
White-collar	38.5	48.3
Service		12.4
Farm		4.0

Analysis of the 1960 census reveals the heavy concentration of blue-collar workers in the industrial Northeast and Midwest states. New York City, Detroit, Chicago, Cleveland, Boston, Gary, Buffalo, and Pittsburgh all have disproportionately high percentages of blue-collar workers. Of the 21 cities over 500,000 population, only New York City (ranked sixth), Washington (seventh), and Cincinnati (eleventh), figured in the first eleven by percentage of employed persons in white-collar occupations. The last ten were all in the Northeast and Midwest with Detroit (32.1 percent), Milwaukee (31.5 percent), Buffalo (30.4 percent), and St. Louis (30.2 percent), with Cleveland (24.8 percent) the lowest. Blue-collar workers are strategically located in America and the prominent segment of this group are the white ethnics.

SUMMARY AND DEFINITION

White ethnics easily number more than 40 million Americans. They live in the Northeast and Great Lakes regions, generally in the larger cities rather than rural areas, are predominantly Catholic, but with large numbers of Jews in New York City and other Northern urban areas, and lastly are heavily represented, except for Jews, in blue-collar occupations. Irish-Americans, German-Americans, and Jews are less likely to be a part of this broadly defined group than Americans of Eastern, Central and Southern European descent.

To the extent that a white American thinks and acts in terms of his European origins, to that extent he is a "white ethnic," that is, the child, grandchild, great grandchild, of European immigrants, thus still regarding himself, on some occasions and for some purposes, as a German, an Irishman, an Italian, a Pole, or a Jew. Also, of course, as an American.

A final note: there are more poor whites in the Northern metropolitan areas than poor blacks, and a disproportionately high number of them are first-, second-, and third-generation ethnic Americans of European descent.

confessions of a white ethnic

Michael Novak

1. NEITHER WASP NOR JEW NOR BLACK

Growing up in America has been an assault upon my sense of worthiness. It has also been a kind of liberation and delight.

There must be countless women in America who have known for years that something is peculiarly unfair, yet who only recently have found it possible, because of Women's Liberation, to give tongue to their pain. In recent months I have experienced a similar inner thaw, a gradual relaxation, a willingness to think about feelings heretofore shepherded out of sight.

I am born of PIGS—those Poles, Italians, Greeks, and Slavs, those non-English-speaking immigrants numbered so heavily among the workingmen of this nation. Not particularly liberal or radical; born into a history not white Anglo-Saxon and not Jewish; born outside what, in America, is considered the intellectual mainstream—and thus privy to neither power nor status nor intellectual voice.

Those Poles of Buffalo and Milwaukee—so notoriously taciturn, sullen, nearly speechless. Who has ever understood them? It is not that Poles do not feel emotion—what is their history if not dark passion, romanticism, betrayal, courage, blood? But where in America is there anywhere a language for voicing what a Christian Pole in this nation feels? He has no Polish culture left him, no Polish tongue.[1] Yet Polish feelings do not go easily into the idiom of happy America, the America

---

"Confessions of a White Ethnic." From Michael Novak, *The Rise of the Unmeltable Ethnics* (New York: MacMillan Publishing Co.,), Reprinted by permission of MacMillan and Curtis Brown LTD.

1. See Andrew R. Sisson's chapter "Our Kooky English Language" in his *Applehood and Mother Pie* (Peterborough, N.H.: Orchard Press, 1971), pp. 1–16, for a discussion of the ways in which Continental languages differ from English according to their respective cultural divergencies.

of the Anglo-Saxons and yes, in the arts, the Jews. (The Jews have long been a culture of the word, accustomed to exile, skilled in scholarship and in reflection. The Christian Poles are largely of peasant origin, free men for hardly more than a hundred years.) Of what shall the young man of Lackawanna think on his way to work in the mills, departing his relatively dreary home and street? What roots does he have? What language of the heart is available to him? [2]

The PIGS are not silent willingly. The silence burns like hidden coals in the chest.

All four of my grandparents, unknown to one another, arrived in America from the same county in Slovakia. My grandfather had a small farm in Pennsylvania; his wife died in a wagon accident. Meanwhile, Johanna, fifteen, arrived on Ellis Island, dizzy from witnessing births and deaths and illnesses aboard the crowded ship. She had a sign around her neck lettered PASSAIC. There an aunt told her of a man who had lost his wife in Pennsylvania. She went. They were married. She inherited his three children.

Each year for five years Grandma had a child of her own. She was among the lucky; only one died. When she was twenty-two and the mother of seven (my father was the last), her husband died. "Grandma Novak," as I came to know her many years later, resumed the work she had begun in Slovakia at the town home of a man known to my father only as "the Professor"; she housecleaned and she laundered.

I heard this story only weeks ago. Strange that I had not asked insistently before. Odd that I should have such shallow knowledge of my roots. Amazing to me that I do not know what my family suffered, endured, learned, and hoped these last six or seven generations. It is as if there were no project in which we all have been involved, as if history in some way began with my father and with me.

The estrangement I have come to feel derives not only from lack of family history. Early in life, I was made to feel a slight uneasiness when I said my name.[3]

Later "Kim" helped. So did Robert. And "Mister Novak" on TV. The name must be one of the most Anglo-Saxon of the Slavic names. Nevertheless, when I was very young, the "American" kids still made something out of names unlike their own, and their earnest, ambitious mothers thought long thoughts when I introduced myself.

Under challenge in grammar school concerning my nationality,

2. Royko wrote in his *Chicago Daily News* column: "I imagine that the ethnic in Buffalo is thinking the same thing that the white Southerner in Birmingham is thinking, or the Okie oil workers in Tulsa: Another day, another dollar. In fact, that's probably what the guy in Warsaw is thinking on his way to work." There is at least one point Royko overlooks: the bottled-up anger of workers in America.

3. See Victor R. Greene's "Sons of Hunkies: Men with a Past?" *Slovakia,* vol. XVI, No. 39, 1966, pp. 85–86.

I had been instructed by my father to announce proudly: "American."
When my family moved from the Slovak ghetto of Johnstown to the
WASP suburb on the hill, my mother impressed upon us how well we
must be dressed, and show good manners, and behave—people think
of us as "different" and we mustn't give them any cause. "Whatever
you do, marry a Slovak girl," was other advice to a similar end: "They
cook. They clean. They take good care of you. For your own good." I
was taught to be proud of being Slovak, but to recognize that others
wouldn't know what it meant, or care.

When I had at last pierced the deception—that most movie stars
and many other professionals had abandoned their European names in
order to feed American fantasies—I felt only a little sadness. One of my
uncles, for business reasons and rather late in life, changed his name,
too, to a simple German variant—not long, either, after World War II.

Nowhere in my schooling do I recall any attempt to put me in
touch with my own history. The strategy was clearly to make an American of me. English literature, American literature, and even the history books, as I recall them, were peopled mainly by Anglo-Saxons from
Boston (where most historians seemed to live). Not even my native
Pennsylvania, let alone my Slovak forebears, counted for very many
paragraphs. (We did have something called "Pennsylvania History"
somewhere; I seem to remember its puffs for industry. It could have
been written by a Mellon.) I don't remember feeling envy or regret: a
feeling, perhaps, of unimportance, of remoteness, of not having heft
enough to count.

The fact that I was born a Catholic also complicated life. What is
a Catholic but what everybody else is in reaction against? Protestants
reformed "the whore of Babylon." Others were "enlightened" from it,
and Jews had reason to help Catholicism and the social structure it was
rooted in fall apart. The history books and the whole of education
hummed in upon that point (for during crucial years I attended a public school): to be modern is decidedly not to be medieval; to be reasonable is not to be dogmatic; to be free is clearly not to live under ecclesiastical authority; to be scientific is not to attend ancient rituals, cherish irrational symbols, indulge in mythic practices. It is hard to grow
up Catholic in America without becoming defensive, perhaps a little
paranoid, feeling forced to divide the world between "us" and "them."

English Catholics have little of the sense of inferiority in which
many other Catholic groups tend to share—Irish Catholics, Polish
Catholics, Lithuanians, Germans, Italians, Lebanese, and others. Dan-
iel Callahan (*The Mind of the Catholic Layman, Generation of the
Third Eye*) and Garry Wills ("Memories of a Catholic Boyhood," in
Esquire) both identify, in part, with the more secure Catholicism of an
Anglo-Catholic parent. The French around New Orleans have a social
ease different from the French Catholics of Massachusetts. Still, as

Catholics, especially vis-à-vis the national liberal culture, nearly all have felt a certain involuntary defensiveness. Granted our diverse ethnic circumstances, we share a certain communion of memories.

We had a special language all our own, our own pronunciation for words we shared in common with others (Augústine, contémplative), sights and sounds and smells in which few others participated (incense at Benediction of the Most Blessed Sacrament, Forty Hours, wakes, and altar bells at the silent consecration of the Host); and we had our own politics and slant on world affairs. Since earliest childhood, I have known about a "power elite" that runs America: the boys from the Ivy League in the State Department as opposed to the Catholic boys in Hoover's FBI who (as Daniel Moynihan once put it) keep watch on them. And on a whole host of issues, my people have been, though largely Democratic, conservative: on censorship, on communism, on abortion, on religious schools, etc. "Harvard" and "Yale" long meant "them" to us.

The language of Spiro Agnew, the language of George Wallace, excepting its idiom, awakens childhood memories in me: of men arguing in the barbershop, of my uncle drinking so much beer he threatened to lay his dick upon the porch rail and wash the whole damn street with steaming piss—while cursing the niggers in the mill below, and the Yankees in the mill above—millstones he felt pressing him. Other relatives were duly shocked, but everybody loved Uncle George; he said what he thought.

We did not feel this country belonged to us. We felt fierce pride in it, more loyalty than anyone could know. But we felt blocked at every turn. There were not many intellectuals among us, not even very many professional men. Laborers mostly. Small businessmen, agents for corporations perhaps. Content with a little, yes, modest in expectation, and content. But somehow feeling cheated. For a thousand years the Slovaks survived Hungarian hegemony and our strategy here remained the same: endurance and steady work. Slowly, one day, we would overcome.

Yet more significant in the ethnic experience in America is the intellectual world one meets: the definition of values, ideas, and purposes emanating from universities, books, magazines, radio, and television. One hears one's own voice echoed back neither by spokesmen of "middle America" (so complacent, smug, nativist, and Protestant), nor by the "intellectuals." Almost unavoidably, perhaps, education in America leads the student who entrusts his soul to it in a direction which, lacking a better word, we might call liberal: respect for individual conscience, a sense of social responsibility, trust in the free exchange of ideas and procedures of dissent, a certain confidence in the ability of men to "reason together" and adjudicate their differences, a frank recognition of the vitality of the unconscious, a willingness to protect workers and the poor against the vast economic power of industrial corporations, and the like.

On the other hand, the liberal imagination has appeared to be astonishingly universalist and relentlessly missionary. Perhaps the metaphor "enlightenment" offers a key. One is *initiated into light*. Liberal education tends to separate children from their parents, from their roots, from their history, in the cause of a universal and superior religion. One is taught regarding the unenlightened (even if they be one's uncles George and Peter, one's parents, one's brothers, perhaps) what can only be called a modern equivalent of *odium theologicum*. Richard Hofstadter described anti-intellectualism in America (more accurately, in nativist America rather than in ethnic America), but I have yet to encounter a comparable treatment of anti-unenlightenment among our educated classes.

In particular, I have regretted and keenly felt the absence of that sympathy for PIGS which simple human feeling might have prodded intelligence to muster, that same sympathy which the educated find so easy to conjure up for black culture, Chicano culture, Indian culture, and other cultures of the poor. In such cases one finds the universalist pretensions of liberal culture suspended; some groups, at least, are entitled to be both different and respected. Why do the educated classes find it so difficult to want to understand the man who drives a beer truck, or the fellow with a helmet working on a site across the street with plumbers and electricians, while their sensitivities race easily to Mississippi or even Bedford-Stuyvesant?

There are deep secrets here, no doubt, unvoiced fantasies and scarcely admitted historical resentments. Few persons in describing "middle Americans," "the silent majority," or Scammon and Wattenberg's "typical American voter" distinguish clearly enough between the nativist American and the ethnic American. The first is likely to be Protestant, the second Catholic. Both may be, in various ways, conservative, loyalist, and unenlightened. Each has his own agonies, fears, betrayed expectations. Neither is ready, quite, to become an ally of the other. Neither has the same history behind him here. Neither has the same hopes. Neither lives out the same psychic voyage, shares the same symbols, has the same sense of reality. The rhetoric and metaphors proper to each differ from those of the other.

There is overlap, of course. But country music is not a polka; a successful politician in a Chicago ward needs a very different "common touch" from the one needed by the county clerk in Normal. The urban experience of immigration lacks that mellifluous, optimistic, biblical vision of the good America which springs naturally to the lips of politicians from the Bible Belt. The nativist tends to believe with Richard Nixon that he "knows America, and the American heart is good." The ethnic tends to believe that every American who preceded him has an angle, and that he, by God, will some day find one, too. (Often, ethnics complain that by working hard, obeying the law, trusting their political leaders, and relying upon the American dream, they now have only their own naiveté to blame for rising no higher than they have.)

It goes without saying that the intellectuals do not love "middle America," and that for all the good, warm discovery of America that preoccupied them during the 1950s no strong tide of respect accumulated in their hearts for the Yahoos, Babbitts, Agnews, and Nixons of the land. Willie Morris in *North Toward Home* writes poignantly of the chill, parochial outreach of the liberal sensibility, its failure to engage the humanity of the modest, ordinary little man west of the Hudson. The Intellectual's Map of the United States is succinct: "Two coasts connected by United Airlines."

Unfortunately, it seems, the ethnics erred in attempting to Americanize themselves before clearing the project with the educated classes. They learned to wave the flag and to send their sons to war. They learned to support their President—an easy task, after all, for those accustomed to obeying authority. And where would they have been if Franklin Roosevelt had not sided with them against established interests? They knew a little about communism—the radicals among them in one way, and by far the larger number of conservatives in another. To this day not a few exchange letters with cousins and uncles who did not leave for America when they might have, whose lot is demonstrably harder than their own and less than free.

Finally, the ethnics do not like, or trust, or even understand the intellectuals. It is not easy to feel uncomplicated affection for those who call you "pig," "fascist," "racist." One had not yet grown accustomed to not hearing "hunkie," "Polack," "spic," "mick," "dago," and the rest. A worker in Chicago told reporter Lois Wille in a vividly home-centered outburst:

> The liberals always have despised us. We've got these mostly little jobs, and we drink beer and, my God, we bowl and watch television and we don't read. It's goddamn vicious snobbery. We're sick of all these phoney integrated TV commercials with these upper-class Negroes. We know they're phoney.
>
> The only time a Pole is mentioned it's to make fun of him. He's Ignatz Dumbrowski, 274 pounds and 5-foot-4, and he got his education by writing into a firm on a matchbook cover. But what will we do about it? Nothing, because we're the new invisible man, the new whipping boy, and we still think the measure of a man's what he does and how he takes care of his children and what he's doing in his own home, not what he thinks about Vietnam.[4]

4. Lois Wille, "Fear Rises in the Suburbs," a reprint from the *Chicago Daily News,* in *The Anxious Majority* (New York: Institute on Human Relations, 1970), p. 8.

At no little sacrifice, one had apologized for foods that smelled too strong for Anglo-Saxon noses; moderated the wide swings of Slavic and Italian emotion; learned decorum; given oneself to education, American style; tried to learn tolerance and assimilation. Each generation criticized the earlier for its authoritarian and European and old-fashioned ways. "Up-to-date" was a moral lever. And now when the process nears completion, when a generation appears that speaks without accent and goes to college, still you are considered "pigs," "fascists," and "racists."

Racists? Our ancestors owned no slaves. Most of us ceased being serfs only in the last two hundred years—the Russians in 1861. Italians, Lithuanians, Slovaks, Poles are not, in principle, against "community control," or even against ghettoes of our own.

Whereas the Anglo-Saxon model appears to be a system of atomic individuals and high mobility, our model has tended to stress communities of our own, attachment to family and relatives, stability, and roots. Ethnics tend to have a fierce sense of attachment to their homes, having been homeowners for less than three generations: a home is almost fulfillment enough for one man's life. Some groups save arduously in a passion to *own;* others rent. We have most ambivalent feelings about suburban assimilation and mobility. The melting pot is a kind of homogenized soup, and its mores only partly appeal to ethnics: to some, yes, and to others, no.

It must be said that ethnics think they are better people than the blacks. Smarter, tougher, harder working, stronger in their families. But maybe many are not sure. Maybe many are uneasy. Emotions here are delicate; one can understand the immensely more difficult circumstances under which the blacks have suffered; and one is not unaware of peculiar forms of fear, envy, and suspicion across color lines. How much of this we learned in America by being made conscious of our olive skin, brawny backs, accents, names, and cultural quirks is not plain to us. Racism is not our invention; we did not bring it with us; we had prejudices enough and would gladly have been spared new ones. Especially regarding people who suffer more than we.

When television commentators and professors say "humanism" or "progress," it seems to ethnics like moral pressure to abandon their own traditions, their faith, their associations, in order to reap higher rewards in the culture of the national corporations. Ethnic neighborhoods usually do not like interviewers, consultants, government agents, organizers, sociologists. Usually they resent the media. Almost all spokesmen they meet from the world of intellect have disdain for them. It shows. Do museums, along with the "Black art" and "Indian art," have "Italo-American" exhibitions or "Lithuanian-American" days? Dvorak wrote the *New World Symphony* in a tiny community of Bohemian craftsmen in Iowa. All over the nation in print studios and metal foundries when the craftsmen immigrants from Europe die, their crafts will die with them. Who here supports such skills?

2. A CUMULATIVE POLITICAL AWAKENING

Such a tide of resentment begins to overwhelm the descendant of "the new immigration" when he begins to voice repressed feelings about America that at first his throat clogs with despair. Dare he let resentment out? Shouldn't he keep calm? Can he somehow, out of anything available, put together categories and words, and shoot them aloft, slim silver missiles of despair? The incoming planes are endless. The illusions of Americans are vast.

Allies are foes; foes are friends. A language for ethnic divergence does not exist. Prejudices are deep in social structures and institutions; deep, too, in moralities and philosophies; not shallow in families and close relationships. American politics is going crazy because of a fundamental ignorance. Intellectuals, too, are blind.

The battle is partly in one's own soul. On the one hand American, enlightened, educated; on the other, stubbornly resistant, in love with values too dear to jettison, at home neither in the ethnic community nor in any intellectual group, neither with theorists nor with practical politicians, convinced of a certain rightness in one's soul and yet not confident that others will see, can see, the subtle links in a different way of life. It is the insecurity of certainty: the sense that something of value is not likely to be understood. The planes keep droning on and on.

A Slovak proverb: When trees are blown across the road in front of you, you know a tornado's coming.

It is impossible to define people out of existence, or to define their existence for them. Sooner or later, being free, they will explode in rage.

If you are a descendant of southern and eastern Europeans, everyone else *has* defined your existence. A pattern of "Americanization" is laid out. You are catechized, cajoled, and condescended to by guardians of good Anglo-Protestant attitudes. You are chided by Jewish libertarians. Has ever a culture been so moralistic?

The entire experience of becoming American is summarized in the experience of being made to feel guilty.

For southern and eastern Europeans, there is one constant in their experience of America—abated and relieved for perhaps the decade of the fifties only. They are constantly told to gear up for some new morality. Even in being invited to give a speech on ethnic problems (as the token ethnic), one is told chummily by the national organizer: "As far as I'm concerned, the white ethnics are simply a barrier to social progress." Catching himself, he is generous: "Though I suppose they have their problems, too."

The *old* rule by which ethnics were to measure themselves was the WASP ethic. The *new* rule is getting "with it." The latter is based on new technologies and future shock. The latter could not have existed without the family life and social organization of the former. Parent and child are now at war. In the middle—once again—are southern and eastern Europeans. We are becoming almost Jewish in our anticipation of disaster. When anything goes wrong, or dirty work needs doing, we're *it*.

I never intended to think this way. I never intended to begin writing—ye gods!—as an *ethnic*. I never intended to dig up old memories.

What began to prod me were political events. The anomaly in American publishing and television of William F. Buckley, Jr., had long troubled me: a Catholic who was making a much-needed criticism of American "enlightenment," but from a curiously Anglo-Saxon and conservative point of view. I hoped he was not a dotted line which a larger Catholic movement would fill in.

By the time of the Goldwater campaign of 1964 and the Wallace campaign of 1966, I was alarmed by the cleavage between the old WASP and the new technological consciousness. Catholics might be driven to choose, and might choose the older ways. Worse still, I began to be irritated by the controlled, but felt, anti-Catholic bias among journalists and intellectuals. Despite myself, I disliked the general American desire to believe that ethnic groups do not exist, or if they do, should not. I had nothing to do with ethnic groups myself, and no intention of linking myself to them. I was neither ashamed of them nor hostile to them; it simply seemed to me important, even from their point of view, for me to live the fullest life and to do the best work I could.

But then interpretations of the Wallace vote among Catholics in Wisconsin and Maryland seemed to me grossly false and unfair. I wasn't about to *identify* with the pro-Wallace voters. But I felt increasingly uncomfortable with the condescension and disdain heaped upon them.[5] So I found myself beginning to say "we," rather than "they," when I spoke of ethnics. It is not an entirely comfortable "we," for many ethnics have not been to college, or travelled, or shared the experiences I've had. I wasn't sure I wanted to defend them, or whether I was entitled to do so after too many years of separation from them. I couldn't

5. One of my first published writings was on the gap between intellectuals and people in *The Nation*, October 1960; I included it in my *A New Generation, American and Catholic* (New York: Herder & Herder, 1964). See also my *Politics: Realism and Imagination*.

be sure whether in the next decade the ethnics or the intellectuals would first abandon the path of community, diversity, integrity, and justice. Despite their internal diversity, intellectuals are by and large as capable of minority rule and a relatively narrow ideology as any other group. Meanwhile, the despair and frustration of ethnic groups might become so great that they will think only of their own survival and welfare, and close their hearts to everybody else. American life sometimes hardens. It has not yet hardened, but the present decade is (as usual) crucial.

Which group offers a better chance for social progress—the intellectuals or the ethnics? The sixties have convinced me. The intellectuals cannot do it alone. Arrogance is their principal defect, an arrogance whose lash everybody else in America has felt. A Boston policeman gave Robert Coles the picture:

> I think the college crowd, the left-wing college crowd, is trying to destroy this country, step by step. They're always looking for trouble. They're never happy, except when everyone pays attention to them— and let me tell you, the ordinary people of this country, the average workingman, he's sick and tired of those students, so full of themselves, and their teachers who all think they're the most important people in the human race.[6]

Then a gas station attendant gave Coles some advice to pass along to Daniel Berrigan in jail:

> And tell him he's wasting his time, because this country is run by the big industrialists, and the politicians who do what they're told to do, and the big-mouthed professors (they're all so swellheaded) who are always whispering advice to people—as if they know how the world works! That's what I say: tell the poor father to mind his own business and get out of prison and speak honestly to his flock, but stay away from politics and things like that—or else he'll start sounding like a crook himself. All politicians learn to sugarcoat the truth; they just don't talk straight from the shoulder. I guess they look down on the ordinary American workingman. I guess they don't trust us. I guess they figure they can con us, all the time con us.[7]

3. THE ITCH TO MODERNIZE

In recent years, the scientist has faced Reformers. Theses have been nailed upon his laboratory doors. The stole of sacred power has fallen on the shoulders of the social scientist or program organizer, who will

6. Daniel Berrigan and Robert Coles, *The Geography of Faith* (Boston: Beacon Press, 1971), p. 9.
7. *Ibid.*, pp. 12–13.

reconstruct society. Take it apart, put it back together. In love with change, the new social activist dreads apathy and inertia, is excited by "breakthroughs." He likes things that are "forward-looking." "Liberation" is his banner.

Imagine, then, an uncertain Slovak entering an Introductory Course in the Sociology of Religion at the nearby state university. Is he sent back to his Slovak roots, led to recover paths of experience latent in all his instincts and reflexes, given an image of the life of his grandfather that suddenly, in recognition, brings tears to his eyes? Is he brought to a deeper appreciation of his Lutheran or Catholic heritage and its resonances with other bodies of religious experience? On the contrary, he is secretly taught disdain for what his grandfather *thought* he was doing when he acted or felt or imagined through religious forms. In the boy's psyche, a new religion is implanted: power over others, enlightenment, an atomic (rather than a communitarian) sensibility, a contempt for mystery, ritual, transcendence, soul, absurdity, and tragedy; and deep confidence in the possibilities of building a better world through scientific understanding. Or, by way of reaction, the new myths of the counterculture, the new hopes of radical politics. He is led to feel ashamed for the statistical portrait of Slovak immigrants, which shows them to be conservative, authoritarian, not given to dissent, etc. His teachers instruct him with the purest of intentions, in a way that is value-free.

To be sure, certain radical writers in America have begun to bewail "the laying on of culture," and to unmask the cultural religion implicit in the American way of science.[8] Yet radicals, one learns, often have an agenda of their own. What fascinates *them* about working-class ethnics are the traces, now almost lost, of *radical* activities among the working class two or three generations ago. Scratch the resentful boredom of a classroom of working-class youths, we are told, and you will find hidden in their past some formerly imprisoned organizer for the CIO, some Sacco-Vanzetti, some bold pamphleteer for the IWW. All this is true. But suppose a study of the ethnic past reveals that most ethnics have been, are, and wish to remain culturally conservative? Suppose, for example, they wish to deepen their religious roots and defend their ethnic enclaves? Must a radical culture nonetheless be "laid on" them?

According to the sense of reality of educated people, we are living in a new age which demands a new kind of man and woman. It is *better, liberated, more advanced,* and *more mature* to fall in behind the avant-garde. Such is the modern but invisible religion.

One tenet of the new sense of reality (for that is what a religion

8. I especially cherish John McDermott's "The Laying on of Culture" in *The Nation,* 10 March 1969.

is) is that each person is an individual; his body is his property, his personal behavior is his business. Another tenet is that society is *put back together again* rationally, cognitively, bureaucratically.

Becoming modern, then, is a matter of learning to be solitary—assuming it is normal to be alone—and dreaming of reconstruction. "New," "alone," and "alienated" are words of moral status. Those to whom they apply are to be commended. (My own name, "Novak," means newcomer, stranger, the new man who comes alone; I do not think the ancient connotations were of commendation.)

Many today express the invisible religion in their behavior. Their fundamental metaphor is atomic: they exist alone, apart. If they *join* something, the association is extrinsic. They remain encapsulated in their own hard center. Thus loyalties are temporary, marriages are contingent. Warren Bennis characterizes the most radical image for the new religion: "the temporary society." We are instructed to think about ourselves in a new way, to imagine ourselves in a different relationship to the universe and to others. Nothing permanent, everything discardable. Being temporally later in human history is assessed as being morally higher. The younger the person, the more likely he is to be pure.

So pervasive is the new sense of reality, in its conservative as well as in its radical expression, that one hardly knows how to call attention to it. We are so much *in* it; it is so much a part of the texture of our language, our distinctions, our stories, and our learned responses that we have very little distance from it. Except . . .

Except that many of us do have wives and husbands: children; close friends; sets of people with whom we spend seventy or eighty percent of our free time; relatives; and autobiographies. We have roots. A certain elite, it is true, has fewer roots than others: those who know no neighborhood, who move a great deal—the mobile ones, the swinging atoms, the true practitioners of the new religion. Others worship only occasionally from afar.

Some people in America today are network people, not atoms; socially textured selves, not individuals; persons described more accurately as "we" than as "I." They live, no not they, but their neighbors live in them. It is the natural, normal, ordinary way of life. And in fact, the liberated, mobile ones, the atomic ones, imitate it far more than pure doctrine would allow. Like tends to marry like, to bring up children in the new way, to seek out employment with and residence near like-minded people. The patterns of freely chosen association come to resemble somewhat the closely knit communities of the sociological past. *Gesellschaft* is not, after all, so utterly different from *Gemeinschaft*. The children of the atomic ones manifest a pronounced communal spirit.

The network people, among whom are the white ethnics, find it hard to think of themselves as atoms, or of their neigborhoods as mere pieces of geography. Into their definition of themselves enter their family, their in-laws, their relatives, their friends, their streets, their stores, familiar smells and sights and sounds. Those things are not, as they are for the atomic people, extrinsic. For the network people these things are identity, life, *self*. It is not that the network people are *attached* to such things. They *are* such things. Take away such things, and part of them dies.

It is, of course, part of Americanizing the Indian, the slave, or the immigrant to dissolve network people into atomic people. Some people resisted the acid. They refused to melt. These are the unmeltable ethnics.

private lives: the family, parish and neighborhood

Tenth Avenue, open all the way to the river at Twelfth, with no intervening wall to give shade, was lighter than the other avenues of the city and hotter during the day. Now it was deserted. The enormous midday Sunday feast would last to four o'clock, what with the nuts and wine and telling of family legends. Some people were visiting more fortunate relatives who had achieved success and moved to their own homes on Long Island or in Jersey. Others used the day for attending funerals, weddings, christenings, or—most important of all—bringing cheer and food to sick relatives in Bellevue.

The more Americanized might even take their families down to Coney Island, but they would not do this more than once a year. The trip was long, and the size of families demanded great expenditures for frankfurters and sodas, even though they took their own food and drink along in paper bags. The men hated going. These Italians had never stretched idle on a beach. They suffered the sun all week working on the tracks of the railroad. On Sunday they wanted the cool of a house or garden, they wanted their minds occupied and alert over a deck of cards, they wanted to sip wine, or listen to the gossip of women who would not let them move a finger. They might as well go to work as go to Coney Island.

Best of all was a Sunday afternoon without duties. Children at the movies, mother and father took a little nap together after the heavy meal and made love in complete privacy and relaxation. It was the one free day a week and was jealously treasured. Strength was restored. Family bonds healed. Not to be denied, it was a day set aside by God himself.

Mario Puzo,
The Fortunate Pilgrim

"My life as a child," Paul Wrobel writes, *"centered on three separate but related spheres: family, parish and neighborhood."* This section of the book will depict the private lives of white ethnics as lived within these institutions. For if a sense of ethnicity is still important to the lives of many white Americans, it can be traced back to these wellsprings of ethnic identity.

It is in the family, the most fundamental unit, that a personal scheme of behavior is learned and the threads of ethnic cultures are transmitted to succeeding generations. For many American youths the family experience is to some extent still ethnic, and precedes involvement in *"American culture."* Since the family is the most important of all primary groups, customs and values learned in an ethnic family context will most likely influence the ways in which individuals relate to the larger society throughout their lives.

In his article, "La famiglia: *Four Generations of Italian-Americans,"* Richard Gambino poignantly captures the primacy of ethnic family ties through a personal account of growing up Italian-American in the 1940s and 50s. Through his famiglia, he absorbed a set of norms, customs, beliefs and values with specific ethnic content. And, as his account makes clear, his ethnic identity was firmly established before he had to confront the dominant culture of the larger society.

Through early childhood experiences, Gambino learned the norms governing respect for elders and parents, the importance of family loyalties, the need for supportive sharing with siblings and peers, and the joys of family and religious feasts.

Gambino also makes clear the changing nature of the struggle within succeeding ethnic generations. It is to continuously define and redefine themselves in relation to the original immigrant experience and related ethnic values. The children are often caught up in the ambivalent wishes of the older generation to *"get an education, but don't change,"* and to *"go out into the larger world, but don't become a part of it."* In other words, they are simultaneously expected to succeed as Americans, but to also retain strong ties with their ethnic heritage.

Hence the white ethnic child must inevitably learn to accommodate the conflicting claims of both ethnic and American cultures. As Paul Wrobel relates, the child soon becomes aware of two Americas: one, the world of *"authentic"* ethnic Americans known in childhood; the other, the *"preferred"* image of idealized Americans offered by the schools and the media. The painfulness generated by this conflict is deepened by the evaluation that American culture provides: the ethnic culture is distinctly inferior, while the dominant culture is just as clearly superior.

It is, Wrobel claims, just such discontinuities which the white ethnic child must live with in coming to terms with American society.

Such perceptions of the relative values placed on these two worlds present white ethnic youths with several predicaments. Ethnic parents may attempt to shield their children from the pain of discovering that a hostile reception awaits them in the outside world. This protectiveness may inhibit the young adult from full participation in the opportunities offered by the larger society; paradoxically, if these inhibitions prevent many youths from successfully competing, then the ethnic community may, in turn, disparage the dominant society for excluding their children from the "good American life." On the other hand, white ethnic youths receive many signals that tell them they are neither wanted nor capable of participating in the highly competitive stakes of the larger society. In point of fact, Wrobel argues, many ethnics feel that "a traditional ethnic family does not fit in with what is desirable in the dominant American culture."

After the family, another social institution which has been and is of great importance to white ethnics is the local, most often Roman Catholic parish. Frequently, as Joseph Lopreato shows, it was difficult for the new immigrants to adopt the religious customs and practices established by the Irish-American clergy, who were dominant in American Catholicism in the late 19th century. In comparison with Italian religious practices, centered on saints' festas, Irish religious expression was restrained and foreign. From their dominant position in the hierarchy, the Irish saw the Church as a tool for the Americanization of each subsequent immigrant group.

Out of the inevitable struggles which ensued over these conflicting modes of religious expression emerged a series of compromises and adaptations. The formation of ethnic parishes with services in native languages and often schools which taught ethnic values and culture is balanced against a slow process of assimilation of many groups of new immigrants into an Americanized version of Catholicism.

Today, as Bill Moyer's article relates, the Catholic Church contains a number of priests who combine—as does Fr. Paul Asciolla—a strong sense of ethnic identity with a solid grasp of the larger socio-economic issues which affect his parishioners, whatever their ethnic backgrounds. Working in Melrose Park, Illinois, Father Asciolla attempts to form coalitions among diverse ethnic groups around shared community needs—whether for more police patrols, better garbage collection, or improved public schools.

Worried about the distance he sees between the affluent middle and upper classes and the working class, Father Asciolla believes

. . . the politicians and the clergy are the people today who really have to do something about this class gap. It's hard for people in neighborhoods like this to identify with big government. They identify with the local ward politician who does them favors. What a burden— what an opportunity—this is for the politician. Things can happen if he begins to identify the real anxieties of people and tries to bring them together to work on everyday matters like street repairs and health services and schools.

By taking into account the cultural backgrounds of his parishioners and helping them act together to achieve beneficial social change, Father Asciolla's efforts are helping to weld a mixed ethnic neighborhood into a community with considerable political clout.

In the concluding contributions the authors examine the importance of local neighborhoods, like Father Asciolla's, in the lives of white ethnic Americans. The large urban centers of the northeast and midwest contain surprising numbers of functioning, if weathered, white ethnic neighborhoods. The residents of these neighborhoods usually feel a strong sense of belonging, of community, for here they can find shops with their favorite provisions, a local social club, political ward house, parish church and often parochial school. Here, too, are reliable neighbors who can be counted on for support and friendship.

Furthermore, it is within the boundaries of the ethnic "urban village"—as Herbert Gans has called it—that extended "peer group societies" develop and perform a variety of important functions for community members. Typically recruited from among friends and relatives of similar age, sex, and ethnic background, the group helps the individual deal with the conflicts that inevitably result when the primary values of the ethnic community interact with those of the dominant culture. Gatherings of the "peer group society" are most often concerned with discussions of possible solutions or compromises to be made in meeting the demands of the larger society.

As Herbert Gans points out in "Ethnicity and the Peer Group Society," the individual white ethnic has little control over the national and local institutions that determine his "opportunities for income, work and standard of living," but the neighborhood "peer group society" provides him with both the cohesion and continuity necessary to start dealing with them. "It dominates his entire life," Gans states, "and structures his relationships with the community and the world" from childhood to old age. Through this concept of "peer group society," Gans has given many other social observers a valuable way of perceiving social interactions within closely knit ethnic neighborhoods.

Unfortunately, the significance these neighborhoods hold for their inhabitants has been misunderstood or severely undervalued by government bureaucrats, urban planners, and social observers. Beyond the specifics of peer group dynamics, Richard Krickus and Stephen Adubato provide a larger picture of what is at stake when white ethnic neighborhoods across America are threatened by the bulldozer, or continually pressured to alter their forms and functions.

Ironically, at the same time these neighborhoods battle for survival, many Americans are discovering in them the very qualities of community life that they miss in their highly mobile, suburban life styles. Close to urban centers, convenient to public transportation, within walking distance of shops and schools— all of these are qualities of urban life found in ethnic neighborhoods.

While Krickus and Adubato readily admit that it is impossible to place a monetary value on the advantages of living in an ethnic neighborhood, they do make it absolutely clear why residents of these neighborhoods react in rage when bureaucrats force them to move out for yet another highway, factory, or urban renewal project. Their well researched documentation chronicles the insensitive ways in which public and private agencies destroy the integrity of ethnic neighborhoods in the name of progress. Property condemnation, compulsory relocation, blockbusting and redlining are displayed in all their sordid reality as tools used for dismantling such neighborhoods.

When taken together, the contributors to this section help explain why white ethnics are so protective of these primary institutions that define and contain their private lives, why they often react in anger when labeled as "old fashioned," "reactionary," or worse, "racist" by outsiders. Clearly there are positive reasons demonstrated herein why white ethnics value these spheres of their private lives. These are the kind of values that the larger society must learn to respect if America is indeed to become a truly pluralistic society.

the family

4

la famiglia: four generations of italian-americans

Richard Gambino

To understand the special identity problems of Italian-Americans, we must begin with a very popular Sicilian proverb quoted by Leonard Covellio in his pioneering work, "The Social Background of the Italo-American School Child": *"Chi lascia la via vecchia per la nuova, sa quel che perde e non sa quel che trova"*—"Whoever forsakes the old way for the new knows what he is losing, but not what he will find."

In Sicily, *la via vecchia* was family life. The Sicilian immigrants to America were mostly *contadini* (peasants) to whom there was one and only one social reality, the peculiar mores of family life. *La famiglia* and the personality it nurtured was a very different thing from the American nuclear family with the personalities that are its typical products. The *famiglia* was composed of all of one's "blood" relatives, including those relatives Americans would consider very distant cousins, aunts and uncles, an extended clan with a genealogy traced through paternity. The only system to which the *contadino* paid attention was *l'ordine della famiglia,* the unwritten but all-demanding and complex series of rules governing one's relations within, and responsibilities to,

"La Famiglia: Four Generations of Italian-Americans (editor's title)." From Richard Gambino, "Twenty-Million Italian Americans," *The New York Times Magazine* (April 30, 1972). Reprinted by permission of the New York Times Company, New York.

his own family and his posture toward those outside the family. All other social institutions were seen within a spectrum of attitudes ranging from indifference to scorn and contempt.

One had absolute responsibilities to family superiors and absolute rights to be demanded from subordinates in the hierarchy. All ambiguous situations were arbitrated by the *capo di famiglia* (head of the family), a position held within each household by the father, until it was given to—or taken away by—one of the sons, and in the larger clan, by a male "elder." The *contadino* showed calculated respect to members of other families which were powerful, and haughtiness or indifference toward families less powerful than his own. He despised as a *scomunicato* (pariah) anyone in any family who broke the *ordine della famiglia* or otherwise violated the *onore* (honor, solidarity, tradition, "face") of the family.

Thus, Sicily survived a harsh history of invasion, conquest and colonization by a process of tribes and nations.* What enabled Sicilians to endure was a system of rules based solely on a phrase I heard uttered many times by my grandparents and their contemporaries in Brooklyn's "Little Italy": *sangu du me sangu,* Sicilian dialect for "blood of my blood." (As is typical of Sicilian women, my grandmother's favorite and most earnest term of endearment when addressing her children and grandchildren, and when speaking of them to others, was *sangu mio*— literally, "my blood.")

It was a norm simple and demanding, protective and isolating, humanistic and cynical. The unique family pattern of Sicily constituted the real sovereignty of that island, regardless of which government nominally ruled it.

As all of us are confronted with the conflicts of our loyalty to a sovereign state *vs.* our cosmopolitan aspirations, so the Italian-American has found himself in the dilemma of reconciling the psychological sovereignty of his people with the aspirations and demands of being American. Most Italian-Americans are derived from areas of Italy south of Rome, about 25 per cent of them from Sicily. In his book "The Italians," Luigi Barzini reminds us that "Goethe was right when he wrote: 'Without seeing Sicily one cannot get a clear idea of what Italy is.' Sicily is the schoolroom model of Italy for beginners, with every Italian quality and defect magnified, exasperated and brightly colored."

This background illustrates the confused situation of Italian-Americans. It would not be an exaggeration to say that to Middle America the Chinese character is more scrutable than that of the Italian-American. Although the problems of Italian-Americans are less des-

---

* Including the Phoenicians, Carthaginians, Greeks, Romans (Sicily was the first province of ancient Rome), Vandals, Goths, Byzantines, Saracens, Arabs, Normans, the French, the Spanish, the Savoians and various northern Italian powers, the Sardinians and the Allies of World War II.

perate than those of groups whose fate in this country has been determined by color, they are no less complicated. And they are rising to a
critical point.

The solutions have been too long delayed, and we have thus
lagged behind other large groups of European "ethnics," notably Jews
and Irish-Americans, in social and economic terms. We live in a time
of ethnic consciousness, when each group asserts its presence and insists
on determining its character and destiny. It remains to be seen how the
20 million Italian-Americans, many of them third- and fourth-generation citizens, will determine theirs—and how much upset it will bring.

To the immigrant generation of Italians, the task was clear: Hold
to the psychological sovereignty of the old ways and thereby seal out
the threats of the new "conqueror," the American society that surrounded them. This ingrained disposition was strongly reinforced by
the hatred and insult with which the Italian immigrant was assaulted
by American bigots who regarded him as racially inferior—a "dago," a
"wop," a "guinea." Although one might assume that such indignity has
altogether disappeared, we need only recall well-known tests used to
identify these prejudices. In one study, American college students were
shown photographs of members of the opposite sex with what pur-
ported to be the name of each person on the photograph. The students
were asked to evaluate the attractiveness of the person in the photograph. Then, some time afterward, names were changed and the procedure repeated with the same students. The result was that those people who were regarded as "handsome" or "pretty" when they had
names like "Smith" were found not attractive when their names were
changed to Italian ones. (The same result was found using names commonly thought of as Jewish.)

As a blond, blue-eyed American who was never spotted as Italian,
I was sometimes exposed to gibes and jokes such as the one I was told
by one of my teachers (a non-Italian, like almost all the staff), "You're
not *real* Italians." When I went home that day, I asked my immigrant
grandfather what the teacher meant. He sat there, looked me level in
the eye, shook his head slowly and said simply, *"gl'Americani!"* (To
Italian immigrants, all other people in this country were "Americans,"
whatever their ethnic background.) The prejudice of the Northerners,
experienced by my grandfather in the old land, had been transplanted
to his new home and visited upon his grandchild. For this reason,
among others, the mores the immigrants brought with them from the
old land gave them psychological stability, order and security, and were
held to tenaciously. But in the United States, the price was isolation
from the ways of the larger society.

The immigrants' children, the "second generation," faced a challenge more difficult to overcome. They could not maintain the same degree of isolation. Indeed, they had to cope with American institutions,

first schools, then a variety of economic, military and cultural environments. In so doing, what was a successful social strategy for their parents became a crisis of conflict for them. Circumstances split their personalities into conflicting halves. Despite parental attempts to shelter them from American culture, they *attended* the schools, *learned* the language and confronted the culture.

It was a rending confrontation. The parents of the typical second-generation child ridiculed American institutions and sought to nurture in him *la via vecchia*. The father nurtured in his children (sons especially) a sense of mistrust and cynicism regarding the outside world. And the mother bound her children (not only daughters) to the home by making any aspirations to go beyond it seem somehow disloyal and shameful. Thus, outward mobility was impeded. Boys were pulled out of school and sent to work at the minimum legal age, or lower, and girls were virtually imprisoned in the house. Education, *the* means of social and economic mobility in the United States, was largely blocked to the second generation, because schools were regarded not only as alien but as immoral by the immigrant parents. When members of this generation did go to school the intrinsic differences between American and Southern-Italian ways was sharpened even further for them. The school, the employer and the media taught them, implicitly and often perhaps inadvertently, that Italian ways were inferior, while the immigrant community constantly sought to reinforce them.

Immigrants used "American" as a word of reproach to their children. For example, take another incident from my childhood: Every Wednesday afternoon, I left P.S. 142 early and went to the local parish church for religious instruction under New York State's Released Time Program. Once I asked one of my religious teachers, an Italian-born nun, a politely phrased but skeptical question about the existence of hell. She flew into a rage, slapped my face and called me a *piccolo Americano*, a "little American." Thus, the process of acculturation for second-generation children was an agonizing affair in which they had not only to "adjust" to two worlds, but to compromise between their irreconcilable demands. This was achieved by a sane path of least resistance.

Most of the second generation accepted the old heritage of devotion to family, and sought minimal involvement with the institutions of America. This meant going to school but remaining alienated from it. One then left school at the minimum legal age and got a job that was "secure" but made no troubling demands on one's personality, or the family life in which it was imbedded. This explains why so many second- and even third-generation Italians fill civil service, blue-collar and low-echelon white-collar jobs—many of those in the last category being employed in more static, low-growth industries, for example utilities like Con Edison, where my father worked for 40 years. So we see in New York City that the Fire Department, Police Department and Sanitation Department are filled with Italians. The top positions in these services and in their counterpart private corporations remain conspicuously and disproportionately free of Italian-Americans.

Another part of the second-generation compromise was the rejection of Italian ways which were not felt vital to the family code. They resisted learning the Italian culture and language well, and were ill-equipped to teach it to the third generation.

Small numbers of the second generation carried the dual rebellion to one extreme or the other. Some became highly "Americanized," giving their time, energy and loyalty to schools and companies and becoming estranged from the clan. The price they paid for siding with American culture in the culture-family conflict was an amorphous but strong sense of guilt and a chronic identity crisis not quite compensated for by the places won in middle-class society. At the other extreme, some rejected American culture totally in favor of lifelong immersion in the old ways, which through time and circumstance virtually dissipated in their lifetimes, leaving underdeveloped and forlorn people.

The tortured compromise of the second-generation Italian-American thus left him permanently in lower middle-class America. He remains in the minds of Americans a stereotype born of their half-understanding of him and constantly reinforced by the media. Oliver Wendell Holmes said a page of history is worth a volume of logic. There are, with very few exceptions, no serious studies of the history of Italian-Americans. It is easy to see why this has left accounts of their past, their present and their future expressed almost exclusively in the dubious logic of stereotypes.

The second-generation Italian-American is seen as a "good employe," i.e., steady, reliable, but having little "initiative" or "dynamism." He is a good "family man," loyal to his wife and a loving father vaguely yearning for his children to do "better" in their lifetimes, but not equipped to guide or push them up the social ladder. He maintains his membership in the church, but participates in it little beyond ceremonial observances; while he often sends his children to parochial schools, this represents more his social parochialism than enthusiasm for the American Catholic Church, which has very few Italian-Americans at the top of the hierarchy and has never had an Italian-American cardinal. (Since the Irish immigrants who controlled the Church in its earlier years often discriminated against them, the Italian-Americans tended to view it as an alien "Irish institution.")

He is a loyal citizen of America, but conceives of his political role as protecting that portion of the status quo which he has so painfully carved out by his great compromise. Thus, his political expressions are reactive rather than active. He tends to feel threatened by social and political change, and he is labeled "conservative" or "reactionary" by the larger society. His political reactions are usually to *ad hoc* situations and individual candidates. A bloc of Italian-American voters has not been identified. And with few exceptions, Italian-Americans have not achieved visible positions of major political power. There was not an Italian-American in a Cabinet post until 1962 and none in the Senate until 1950. And even on state and local levels, this ethnic group remains under-represented, although it constitutes perhaps 11 per cent of the national population.

Clearly the most prominent—and pernicious—element in the Italian-American stereotype is that of the Mafia. The Italian immigrant carried with him a memory of the Mafia in Sicily as a kind of ultimate family. Formed in feudal times, the organization began with bands of men who were secretly organized on *ad hoc* bases to protect families (and their customs), from foreign oppression. According to an unlikely legend, the term Mafia is thought to be an acronym of the 13th-century Sicilian battle cry, *"Morte ai Francesi gl'Italiani anelano!"* ("Death to the French in Italy"), part of a violent rebellion against French oppression that began in Palermo on Easter Sunday, 1282, and spread to all of Sicily. Almost all of the French on the island were in fact killed. With characteristic sarcasm, Sicilians dubbed their bloody insurrection "Sicilian Vespers."

The early Mafia bands defended the people by appropriating two old Sicilian institutions: a) they adopted as their own code the traditional family code, and b) they adopted the *vendetta,* i.e., revenge against the enemy by deadly violence and terrorism. These were not just political wars. They were struggles of honor, demanding total allegiance and sacrifice. By the late 19th century, the Mafia had become an institutional force in the life of Western Sicily. But by this time it had lost its role of defender of the Sicilian morality and people. The code of family honor had become hopelessly corrupt. With its members bribed by alien rulers and growing in greed, the Mafia became, over the years, a federation of gangs controlling Western Sicily largely for its own profit and power. To the Italian immigrant in America, the Mafia was both feared in its present form and respected in its archaic ideal as the supreme representative and protector of the family morality. *Rispetto* (respect in the sense of awe of this ideal) was expressed in colloquialisms he brought from Sicily. The immigrant used the word *mafioso* as an adjective synonymous with "good" and "admirable." For example, he would speak of a *mafioso* horse, meaning the animal was strong and spirited. Similarly, he would say of a fine specimen of a man, *"Che Mafioso!"*

Every group living in poverty in this country—or any country—has spawned crime. The poor Italian ghettos spawned criminals whose inherited Southern-Italian morality led them naturally to band together into groups that combined both elements of that morality and their own criminal bent. This amalgam is what the so-called Mafia was, and perhaps still is, in America. *The common characteristic of the at most 5,000 to 6,000 Italian-American gangsters claimed by governmental agencies, and the 20 million other Italian-Americans, is the family morality, a noncriminal morality. The distinguishing characteristic that separates the relatively few gangsters from the millions of law-abiding Italian-Americans is that the gangsters have turned that morality to serve criminal ends.*

The responses to this by Italian-Americans of the second generation have fallen into several categories:

1. Some have adopted as the lesser of two evils the "Uncle Giovanni" image. Interestingly, Italians have a contemptuous word for this kind of vulgar fool, *cafone.*

2. Some have sought to get some public-relations mileage out of what has today become a kind of "Mafia chic" by half-jokingly adopting the Mafia myth. For example, I arrived at a plush restaurant at the Plaza Hotel recently and gave my name to the maitre d' in charge of reservations. He looked at me and said hello in Italian, and we exchanged a few words in the language. Then, searching for something else in our common background, he said, jokingly, referring to my name: "I expected somebody from 'The Godfather.' "

   At least the *Mafioso* is taken seriously as an individual of some importance, an improvement over being considered a buffoon, or being ignored. Moreover, the myth of an extrasocietal, almost omnipotent power has great appeal to people in a complex society who are exasperated by feelings of confusion, impotence and defeat.

3. Some have patiently repeated, "We are not criminals. . . . The percentage of racketeers among us is small." In the scream of the public media-exploitation of Mafia chic, such voices are, year after year, all but lost. Through the power of the media, Mafia chic has even crossed the Atlantic to Italy itself. In bookstores in Italy, I saw copies of a translation of "The Godfather," called *"Il Padrino,"* a very popular book there. And even in Florence I was asked, as I have been for years in the United States, whether I am related to the reputed boss of the American Mafia, Carlo Gambino. (I am not.)

4. Some recently have begun denying that the Mafia exists in this country at all. This hyperdefensive reaction is in reality an expression of rage, a reaction to years of abuse. The fact that some racketeers attempt to exploit the outrage for their own ends is beside the point. There is opportunism in every social expression.

   Most recently, the media have gone beyond their role in transforming a difficult social problem of organized crime into a romantic myth of fantastic proportions. Just as many media people found that the creation and exploitation of the fantasy was lucrative, so many are discovering that ridiculing overstatements of denial of the fantasy is also lucrative. (At the height of the Italian Civil Rights League's campaign to deny that the Mafia exists, New York magazine ran a parody of a fictional gangster named Salvatore Gambino who kept insisting there is no such thing as the Mafia.)

But the Mafia issue must be kept in perspective. The myth has become an example of an interesting expression I heard used in Italy, *americanata*, meaning something spectacular, wild, exaggerated. We are in danger of focusing only on this side show, which merely diverts attention from the larger issues. So far, none of the responses of Italian-Americans to the old Mafia myth and the new Mafia chic have been effective in improving either their image or their real, complex problems.

We come at last to the compound dilemma of the third- and fourth-generation Italian-Americans, who are now mostly young adults and children with parents who are well into their middle age or older. (The number of those in the third and fourth generations is estimated as at least 10 million, compared to more than 5 million in the second generation.) The difference between the problems of the second and those of the third generation is great—more a quantum jump than a continuity.

Perhaps a glimpse at my own life will serve as an illustration. I was raised simultaneously by my immigrant grandparents and by my parents, who were second generation, notwithstanding my father's boyhood in Italy. So I am both second and third generation at one time. I learned Italian and English from birth, but have lost the ability to speak Italian fluently. In this, my third-generation character has won out, although I remain of two generations, and thus perhaps have an advantage of double perspective.

My grandfather had a little garden in the back yard of the building in which we all lived in Brooklyn. In two senses, it was a distinctly Sicilian garden. First, it was the symbolic fulfillment of every *contadino's* dream to own his own land. Second, what was grown in the garden was a far cry from the typical American garden. In our garden were plum tomatoes, squash, white grapes on an overhead vine, a prolific peach tree, and a fig tree! As a child, I helped my grandfather tend that fig tree. Because of the inhospitable climate of New York, every autumn the tree had to be carefully wrapped in hundreds of layers of newspaper. These in turn were covered with waterproof linoleum and tarpaulin. The tree was topped with an inverted, galvanized bucket for final protection. But the figs it produced were well worth the trouble. Picked and washed by my own hand, they were as delicious as anything I have eaten since. And perhaps the difference between second- and third-generation Italian-Americans is that members of the younger group have not tasted those figs. What they inherit from their Italian background has become so diluted as to be not only devalued but quite unintelligible to them. It has been abstracted, removing the possibility of their accepting it or rebelling against it in any satisfying way.

I was struck by this recently when one of my students came to my office to talk with me. Her problems are typical of those I have heard from Italian-American college students. Her parents are second-generation Americans. Her father is a fireman and her mother a housewife. Both want her to "get an education" and "do better." Yet both constantly express fears that education will "harm her morals." She is told by her father to be proud of her Italian background, but her consciousness of being Italian is limited to the fact that her last name ends in a vowel. Although she loves her parents and believes they love her, she has no insight into their thoughts, feelings or values. She is confused by the conflicting signals given to her by them: "Get an education, but don't change"; "go out into the larger world but don't become part of it"; "grow, but remain within the image of the 'houseplant' Sicilian girl"; "go to church, although we are lacking in religious enthusiasm." In short, maintain that difficult balance of conflicts which is the second-generation's life-style.

Her dilemma becomes more widespread as unprecedented numbers of Italian-Americans enter colleges today. The nineteen-seventies are bound to see a sharp increase in the number of Italian-American college graduates. (In New York City only 5 per cent of native-born Italian-Americans graduated from college during the nineteen-sixties. One reason the figure is bound to jump during this decade is that large numbers of Italian-Americans, along with other lower middle-class whites, have taken advantage of the open-admissions policy of the City University of New York.) Moreover, my impression is that Italian-American college students are more inclined to move into areas of study other than the "utilitarian" ones preferred by their predecessors, which for boys were chiefly engineering, music for entertainment, and occasionally pharmacology or medicine, and for girls, were teaching and nursing.

When the third-generation person leaves school and his parents' home, he finds himself in a peculiar situation. A member of one of the largest minority groups in the country, he feels isolated, with no affiliation with or affinity for other Italian-Americans. This young person often wants and needs to go beyond the minimum security his parents sought in the world; in a word, he is more ambitious. But he has not been given family or cultural guidance upon which this ambition can be defined and pursued. Ironically, this descendant of immigrants despised by the old WASP establishment embodies one of the latter's cherished myths. He sees himself as purely American, a blank slate upon which his individual experiences in American culture will inscribe what is to be his personality and his destiny.

But it is a myth that is untenable psychologically and sociologically. Although he usually is diligent and highly responsible, the other elements needed for a powerful personality are paralyzed by his pervasive identity crisis. His ability for sustained action with autonomy, initiative, self-confidence and assertiveness is undermined by his yearning for ego integrity. In addition, the third generation's view of itself as a group of atomistic individuals leaves them politically unorganized, isolated, different and thus powerless in a society of power blocs.

The dilemma of the young Italian-American is a lonely, quiet crisis, so it has escaped public attention. But it is a major ethnic group crisis. As it grows, it will be more readily recognized as such, and not merely as the personal problem of individuals. If this is to be realized sooner rather than later, then these young people must learn whence they came and why they are as they are. A "page of history" will expose the logic of their problems and thus make them potentially solvable. *How* they will solve them is unpredictable.

They may opt for one of the several models that have served other ethnic groups. For example, they may choose to cultivate their Italian culture, pursue personal careers and fuse the two into an energetic and confident relationship—which has been characteristic of the Jewish-Americans. They may also turn toward the church, revive it and build upon its power base a political organization and morale, as Irish-Americans did. Or, they may feel it necessary to form strictly nationalistic power blocs, as some black-Americans are doing. On the other hand, they may forge their own models of individual and group identity out of an imaginative use of their unique inheritance.

Peter L. and Brigitte Berger, in an intriguing article called "The Blueing of America," write, "As the newly greened sons of the affluent deny the power of work, blue-collar class youth quietly prepare to assume power within the technocracy." No group of young people surpasses Italian-American youth in its sense of the power of work, which although derived from the old notion of labor for the family, is now, in the third generation, independent of it. It now remains for young Italian-Americans to root their sense of work in broader identity—and to take their proportionate share of what America has to offer. The dream denied their immigrant grandparents, sacrificed by their culture-conflicted parents, can be realized by them. It can be achieved by adding consciousness, knowledge and imagination to the legacy of courage, work and fortitude inherited from past generations.

becoming a polish american: a personal point of view

Paul Wrobel

Ethnicity has become an important dimension of American life in the 1970's. White ethnic Americans are clamoring to be heard as they express displeasure with being viewed as unintelligent hard-hats who spend their time drinking beer, waving the flag, and planning a move to the suburbs to escape their black neighbors. These same individuals are now beginning to articulate their growing alienation from the larger society—a society in which they are relatively powerless with many unmet social and economic needs. Yet it is the ethnic Americans who have been asked to shoulder the blame for what is wrong with America, a country they love with a passion that is neither understood nor appreciated by their government, their fellow citizens, and sometimes even their children.

Polish Americans are among those who are challenging the myth of the melting pot and drawing attention to the fact that Polish communities exist both in our cities and in the suburbs, despite what social planners and others might say.

What do we know about these communities? Very little. Indeed, we know more about the Ik in Uganda than we do about the Poles in Detroit. This is why I am currently engaged in an anthropological study of an urban Polish American community. But this article is not about anthropology, at least in a scientific sense. Nor does it deal with a contemporary community as it exists today. Rather it is an autobiographical statement, an attempt to share what it means to grow up in an urban Polish American community, and to show how that experience relates to encountering the larger society.

Let me begin by saying that I am a third-generation Polish American. Both my father and mother were born of parents who emigrated here from Poland in the late 19th century. I grew up in Detroit, which is second only to Chicago as a center for Americans of Polish descent in

Reprinted and retitled by consent of Paul Wrobel and the Association for Childhood Education International, 3615 Wisconsin Ave., Washington, D.C.

the United States. My father worked for the Ford Motor Company until his retirement a few years ago, and mother worked for several years at the Chrysler Corporation. Thus I was raised in a working-class family, the kind of family most familiar to the majority of Polish Americans. I have an older sister who was trained as a medical technologist and a younger brother who is a teacher and college basketball coach.

My early years in Detroit were spent learning to be an American. While both my parents speak excellent Polish we children were not taught the language nor did we hear it spoken in the home except on rare occasions: when our relatives came over or our parents wanted to converse without us knowing what they were saying. I can remember vividly that when Christmas time came near we could expect to hear Polish spoken more than usual, for my parents would be discussing our Christmas presents.

It is important to point out that my parents were not being rude by neglecting to teach us Polish. They were instead preparing us to be successful in this society; and they were perceptive enough to know that learning Polish was more of a liability than an asset. This was so because to speak Polish was to call attention to the fact that you were indeed of Polish descent. My father knew that very few management positions at Ford's were held by Polish Americans. He also knew that those few individuals who had advanced had done so in part because they changed their names. Thus my parents took no chances; we would not learn Polish nor would we identify with our cultural heritage. We could become Americans, hopefully non-hyphenated Americans.

There is another point to be made in discussing the process of becoming Americanized. This is that it was (and sometimes still is) very difficult for the sons and daughters of Polish immigrants to identify with the homeland of their parents. When my parents were young children they heard their parents criticize Poland for not providing opportunities for advancement. And as children of immigrants they also heard many stories about the difficulties of life on the farm in Poland. So America was seen by my grandparents as the land of opportunity, a place to make good regardless of class and ethnic background. Whether working on an assembly line for thirty years is the good life is of course debatable. But to many Polish immigrants in the early 1900's it represented something better than struggling for survival on a meager plot of land in Poland. The point I want to make, however, is that my parents and many other second-generation Polish Americans feel little attachment to Poland. Thus in my situation the saying "what the father wished to forget the son wants to remember" is certainly the case.

Even though my parents realized that Polish Americans were being discriminated against in this society, they still believed that

America was the land of opportunity. No matter that Poles held very few management positions in the factory and virtually no executive jobs; this would all change with my generation. In fact, there have been some changes, but the reality of the present situation is that the number of Polish Americans in executive positions in the Detroit area in no way corresponds to their representation in the local population.

So what I learned at home and in school about equality of opportunity was in conflict with what I later learned about the realities of life in our society.

While attending my parish school I also learned that Polish names were never found in the textbooks we used in class, just in the teacher's attendance records. The roll call included names from Andrzejewski to Zakrzewski, but it never occurred to me until later why we were studying about Mr. Adams or the Green family.

Recently, as a seventh grade teacher in a Polish parish school, I asked my students whether they noticed anything about the names of individual characters in their readers. "Sure," one of the girls responded, "none of them are Polish." I asked her why she thought this was the case. "Simple," she said, "if they had Polish names everybody would laugh." Indeed they would. And while I don't think we were conscious of this fact as young students, I do feel that a very subtle lesson was taking place. We were learning, perhaps unconsciously, that our Polish names were not prized possessions. Moreover, we were beginning to develop feelings about ourselves. However subtle the lesson, we learned that perhaps there was something wrong with us for having Polish names.

This example demonstrates how the school is a unique institution in any society. Teachers perform many of the same functions as parents by inculcating norms and values and thereby training children to become the kind of adults a society desires. In short, a school is a place where a child acquires an identity, a process of internalizing the values, norms, and expectations of others into his own behavior and self concept. The problem is, however, that this identity is based on what society considers desirable. And what society considers desirable is determined by what the dominant group in that society feels is best regardless of individual or cultural differences.

But attending school is not the only way a child learns feelings about himself and his family. When I watched TV as a young child I often wondered why fathers on the shows always worked in offices and wore shirts and ties on jobs. My dad worked in a factory and wore heavy shoes reinforced with steel to protect his feet in the foundry. But there was no protection from flying sparks of molten metal which made holes in his trousers and burned his legs.

Why was it, I wondered, that fathers on TV always had breakfast with their families before going off to work. I never had breakfast with my dad except on Saturdays and Sundays. During the week he left the house at 5:30 a.m. to be on time for the morning shift.

And grandmothers. They always looked so young and beautiful on TV, and they spoke English so well. My grandmother was older, partly because she had children in her 40's, but also because she worked cleaning offices late into the night in order to help support her family. Sure, she could speak English, but when anything important or interesting was said she said it in Polish. Moreover, I had a difficult time understanding her English, and liked it better when she spoke Polish. For then at least I didn't have to pretend that I was listening while she discussed the goings-on in her parish and neighborhood.

The point I am trying to make by citing the above examples is that nothing I saw on the screen or heard in the classroom resembled what I knew to be true about my own family. So we were different; and in America being different meant we did not represent what was desired in this society. Unfortunately, this demonstrates that our society is built on the myth of the melting pot; we are taught that people should be alike, and diversity is discouraged rather than celebrated.

This is why the anthropologist Sapir is quite right when he argues that American culture is spurious rather than genuine.[1] For according to the distinction he makes a genuine culture is built as an expression of individual differences—individual cultures, if you will—while a spurious culture is one that is imposed on individuals as an inhibition of their own or their group's uniqueness. American culture is therefore a spurious one because we have failed to recognize ethnic diversity as a reality of life in this society. To become a genuine culture in Sapir's terms, a desirable goal to my mind, we must insure that a child's early education is not in conflict with what he already knows and what he will learn later on in life. This important point is the key to understanding the relationship between ethnicity and education, for in our spurious culture there are discontinuities between what an ethnic child learns in his home and neighborhood, and what he learns from attending school or watching TV.[2] The child experiences these discontinuities as conflicts within himself, conflicts between what he knows he is and what he learns society wants him to be. Yet it seems to me that if we are to have a genuine culture in which each individual

1. See Edward Sapir, "Culture, Genuine and Spurious," in David Bidney, ed., *Edward Sapir: Culture, Language and Personality,* Berkeley: University of California Press, 1966.

2. For an excellent discussion of discontinuities in American child-rearing practices see Ruth Benedict, "Continuities and Discontinuities in Cultural Conditioning," in Clyde Kluckhohn and Henry Murray, eds., *Personality in Nature, Society, and Culture,* New York: Alfred A. Knopf, 1949.

has the opportunity to fulfill his human potentialities we must see to it that the educational process, including what we learn from the media, represents a continuous and integrated experience for every child.

This brief analysis of American society has been a digression from the main focus of this article, but I thought it important because we need to relate what we experience as individuals to the society in which we live. Now I will return to a consideration of what it means to be a Polish American by focusing on the community.

My life as a child centered on three separate but related spheres: Family, Parish, and Neighborhood. We didn't entertain often, and when we did our guests were usually relatives. The home was a place for the nuclear family, a kind of private place that deserved to be kept spotlessly clean and tidy. Though my mother denies it, and my wife expresses disbelief, I do remember scrubbing and waxing the floors on Saturday morning before I could go out and play ball. But fortunately for my brother and me, most of the cleaning was done by my sister and mother. I mention the cleanliness of the home only because it seems to be an important element of Polish American culture. The home is like a shrine, and disorder and uncleanliness are seen as disrespectful.

We did many things together as a family, as do many of the families I am studying in a similar community. We all had our friends, but often we involved them in family activities rather than going off on independent excursions. It has been argued, of course, that the close family so representative of Polish Americans and other ethnic groups hinders the ability of individual family members to succeed in our society. But when scholars argue this point they are really saying that a traditional ethnic family does not fit in with what is desirable in dominant American culture, a culture that stresses the independence and self-reliance of the individual as criteria for his success. Individuals in our society make it; families don't. Yet our achieving society, as the psychologist David McClelland calls it, is filled with lonely people asking the questions "who am I" and "what should I become." It may well be, therefore, that the ethnic family represents one of the last vestiges of folk culture in a society which Jules Henry says "is as highly developed in psychopathology as in technology." [3]

Next to the family my life as a child revolved around the Roman Catholic parish in our neighborhood. One could receive communion or attend mass at any parish, but ours was a Polish parish which performed important social functions above and beyond its canonical requirements. The parish was the center of community life, and the social life of its parishioners was based on the numerous parish clubs,

3. Jules Henry, *Culture Against Man*, New York: Random House, Inc., 1963, p. 322.

events, and activities. Parishioners were also neighbors, so the social life of the parish helped to strengthen friendships and solidify what was indeed an ethnic community. The role of the parish has not changed that much over time, for things are pretty much the same in the community which serves as the focus of my current study. People here choose their friends from the parish and neighborhood, not from their place of employment. And masses in Polish are still offered to the delight of many parishioners.

My own neighborhood was first of all a place. It grew up around the parish, which soon added a school to accommodate the children of its parishioners. The neighborhood itself consisted mainly of one-story wood frame houses which glistened from their frequent, sometimes annual paint jobs. The lawns were a prized possession, neatly cut and trimmed, and the gardens were numerous and colorful. Statues and shrines of the Blessed Virgin, often adorned with freshly cut flowers, were a common sight in the small backyards. These, then, are some of the more visible characteristics of a Polish American community.

But the neighborhood was also people, people who worked long hours in the factory during the day, and kept to themselves at night. Neighbors conversed from their porches, or over the fence, but they rarely entered one another's homes. There were no coffee klatches in my neighborhood. This is not to say that the people weren't friendly. They were; but seemingly their reserve and attitudes toward their homes resulted in what could be called a latent kind of neighborliness. If you needed help the neighbors were there, but there was very little socializing on a day to day basis. Neighbors, after all, were not as close as relatives.

Together the neighborhood and parish formed what one sociologist has termed an urban village. Everybody knew everybody else, perhaps too well, for gossip and rumor were regular events of the day. The community was suspicious of outsiders, regardless of their ethnic background. Strangers were strangers, even if they did speak Polish. These attitudes would cause problems later when they would be misinterpreted as a blatant form of racism. At any rate, the point here is that together the parish and neighborhood formed a community, something which is sadly missing in late 20th century America. The experience of growing up in such a community is discontinuous with living in other American settings or becoming a participant in the larger American society.

It has been ten years since my departure from an urban Polish American community. During that time I have lived in West Africa, the West Indies, and various American settings, both urban and rural. Still, I feel a strong desire to understand what an urban Polish American community means both for its residents and members of the larger society. This article has explored those topics. But it is just a beginning. We have much to learn about all the ethnic groups in our society, including Polish Americans. So we need to go beyond personal recollections and focus our attention on studying contemporary urban ethnic communities. Only then will we begin to understand ourselves and the society in which we live.

the parish

6

religion and the immigrant experience

Joseph Lopreato

The family has traditionally been *the* core institution of Italian society and culture. Consequently, it has received heavy emphasis because its role is essential to an understanding of the adjustment of the Italian immigrant and his children to American society and culture. Next to the family, the Catholic religion has been the most critical institution for the Italians. Even so, its importance has been distinctly secondary to that of the family. To understand this fact, one must first understand the nature of religious life in the Italian South.

The people in southern Italy have never been pious. Barring special occascions—the Christmas and the Easter holidays plus various feasts of the patron saints and the many manifestations of the Virgin Mary—churches in the agricultural villages are quite likely to be empty. Religious services are customarily attended by a score of old ladies and spinsters and a handful of very old gentlemen working diligently toward salvation in view of their imminent Confrontation. Young and middle-aged males will go to church only on very special occasions. But even then they are likely to congregate outside the

"Religion and the Immigrant Experience (editor's title)." From Joseph Lopreato, "Social Institutions and Change, *Italian Americans* (New York: Random House, Inc.). Reprinted by permission of Random House, Inc.

church and chat about various secular matters instead of attending
the services inside.

The religiosity of southern Italians is undermined by their relation to the priest. In the first place, the Catholic church has traditionally either exploited the peasants or sided with the large landowners
in their exploitation of them. There were times and places in the South
where the Catholic church owned as much as 75 percent of the local
land. The figure of the priest, in whose person Christ is presumably
reflected, was thus associated with the figure of the avaricious and cruel
landlord. Were Catholicism a religion to emphasize man's direct relation to his god, such a conception of the priest might leave a man's religious feeling undamaged. But the Catholic church represents the
priest as no less than the mediator between man and God—indeed,
under certain circumstances he is an *alter Christus* (another Christ).
The result is that a man's sense of distance from his priest is to some
extent generalized to God himself.

Second, for a long time, in some places the priest was the only
"educated" individual in the village. Isolated, lonesome, and bored,
he did not find it particularly easy to have compassion and respect for
his parishioners. When he did not exploit the peasants, he was likely
to treat them with considerable haughtiness. Even when he displayed
no obvious contempt for the humble peasant and his uneducated
world view, he was likely to anger him by real or imagined amorous
interests in his wife and daughter. In short, through the centuries, a
chasm—spiritual, social, intellectual, economic—developed between
the church, as represented by the local priest, and the working masses.

The preceding portrayal of the priest is at direct variance with
one offered by Lawrence Pisani, who argues that the Italian "small-
town priest was revered by his parishioners as one of themselves" and
"understood and loved his people." Nothing could be further from the
truth. At least in southern Italy, although the typical priest has indeed
had peasant kinsfolk, he has characteristically proceeded to take on
the demeanor of the signorial class, with all the arrogance, desire for
domination, and contempt for the people that this entails. As a result of
this and of the contempt traditionally bred by familiarity, Italians,
"the church's guardians," have long had a remarkable capacity to distinguish between the will of the Lord and the will attributed to Him
by mortals, whatever their ecclesiastical title. The spiritual influence of
the priest, therefore, was never great among the people who came to
America. It was much easier to frighten the poor peasant into submis-
sion than to evoke his religious piety.

The peasant believed in God and the various saints. Indeed he
readily availed himself of the church at critical periods of his life: birth,
marriage, and death. But his private conception of religion was nevertheless heavily strewn with all sorts of beliefs in the forces of good and

evil and included faith in various sorts of magical practices. At the heart of such beliefs and practices was the religious *festa*, which basically was a social occasion for merrymaking or an excuse for a special meal and a few hours off from hard work. The festival—this light-hearted expression of godliness—*was* religion for the masses. It gave a concrete indication of heaven. It was ever so joyful. It gave respite from the endless toil.

When the peasants came to America and settled in the ghettoes of the big cities, they found a church organization and culture that was totally outside their experience. In the words of Oscar Handlin:

> Arriving toward the end of the century, they moved into residential districts that in most cities had formerly been occupied by the Irish. . . . They were Catholics, but the Catholic churches they found in the neighborhoods they occupied were Irish and not Italian—as different from what was familiar to the newcomers as the chapels of the Episcopalians or Methodists. They were not content, and sought to recapture the old authenticity. The result was a struggle, parish by parish, between the old Catholics and the new, a struggle that involved the nationality of the priest, the language to be used, the saints' days to be observed, and even the name of the church.

The Catholic church in America was then as now dominated by the Irish hierarchy, whose conception of religion was markedly different from the Italian version. Irish religiosity was accompanied by a fervor and a faith difficult for Italians to understand. The sight of grown men taking communion on Sunday and counting the beads of a rosary was shocking to the Italian man, accustomed as he was to thinking of religion as an activity for women and children. The Irish, moreover, tended to mix religion in America with politics in the old country. To be an Irish Catholic was not merely a question of pure religious faith. This status also had a political component; it involved being anti-Protestant, and anti-English particularly. Among Italians, religion and politics did not complement each other so well. Indeed, at least for the educated few and those who became active in the various political movements and the trade unions, the Catholic church was to the Italian immigrant as Protestantism and the English had been to the Irish. Many Italians in this country could not help but remember the church's opposition to Italian unification. For these reasons, the Italian Catholics in America felt overwhelmed and alienated by the Irish attitude.

Matters were made worse by the fact that the Irishman's conception of religion tended to undermine the Italian's special interest in the religious festivals and in the social occasions that they represented. Nothing about religion was more important to Italians than the *festa*. Without it, religion was cold, formal, and lacking significance. They fought hard for it, and eventually in many cases they either organized their own church or had their own way despite the Irish hierarchy's accusations of paganism. A study in 1938 pointed out that the factor that distinguished the Italian religious life from that of other national minorities was its folk quality. The writers give descriptions of various religious festivals of New York, such as this one of the festival of Our Lady of Mount Carmel, held on June 16th.

> On this occasion Little Italy becomes completely transformed. The streets are decorated with flags, banners and flowers. Beautifully illuminated multi-colored arches extend from sidewalk to sidewalk across the roadway. Innumerable stands with pastries, fruits, and souvenirs line the thoroughfares. Worshipers of all classes and ages mill about in dense, jostling crowds. Among the devout Italians who come to the sanctuary to pay homage to Our Lady of Mount Carmel are many living in the remoter parts of the city, and some even from neighboring states who have journeyed here for this occasion. Many of them bring huge, ornate candles to light at the altar. Others bring offerings of gold and silver plaques to the church as tokens of gratitude for favors received at the hands of the Blessed Virgin.

Such festivals exist even today in the few ghetto areas where the immigrants and the in-groupers of the second generation continue to live. But they lack the pageantry and the intense carnival atmosphere of years gone by. Moreover, as the old-timers grow old and die, the festivals no longer perform their previous function. The southern Italian peasantry traditionally had few or no public recreational facilities. Church festivals filled this gap, in the Old World and, for a while, in the New World as well. In American society, however, there never has been a scarcity of public recreational opportunities. As the immigrants' children grew up, they took advantage of public recreation, all the more so because it aided in the process of cultural adaptation. The colorful religious festivals thus gradually began to disappear.

In the church as in the family, "intergenerational" conflict inevitably developed. If the old-timers felt the church in America was not old-fashioned enough—in the sense that it did not devote itself fully to maintaining the colorful folk rituals of old—the new generations viewed it as "backward" and tainted by superstition. Such divergent values created grave problems of adjustment for the church. If it attempted to reach the old folks by cultivating an atmosphere reminiscent of old times, the younger generation was estranged, tending to regard the church as "foreign" and lacking in sobriety. If the church sought to reflect urban realities and organize itself along lines that were suitable to the new generation, the old folks stayed away. Time and the capacity for compromise eventually solved the dilemma. The ultimate success of the Catholic church among the Italians in America owes much to its capacity to abandon those characteristically Italian practices that in the eyes of the younger generation marked it as "foreign" while at the same time retaining enough of the old atmosphere to make the old people feel that the church belonged to them.

Since the 1930s, there has been no "religious problem" to speak of. Indeed, as the Italians have adapted themselves to American society, the Catholic church has succeeded not only in winning their loyalty but also in gaining their respect. Nelli considers 1945 the year in which the Catholic church assumed a position of social importance among the Italians in America. That occurrence, it might be added, roughly marks the beginning of the final stage of their social assimilation. Religiosity is often a symbol of social respectability. In Italy, religious participation is predominantly a characteristic of the poor and the lowly. In America, it is an important sign of social propriety in the working and middle classes. In keeping with national criteria of social respectability, Italian Americans have found that membership in the ethnically mixed Roman Catholic church of the suburbs is an important expression of their new middle class status. Moreover, the rising Italian middle class that adopts American Roman Catholicism as a token of its new status adopts the parochial school as an equivalent symbol. As Nathan Glazer and Daniel Moynihan point out "in the third generation, the influence of Catholicism among Italian Americans has become formidable . . . the student body of Fordham University, for example, has become half Italian." There is a degree of irony in all this. The Italians, for two thousand years the chief trustees of Roman Catholicism, have adopted in America a form of Catholicism that socially and ritually bears little resemblance to what they knew in Italy, illustrating once again the drive toward assimilation generated in ethnic groups by American society.

Italians are no longer greatly concerned that their churches be run by Italian priests. In any case the desire was never realistic, for the Italians do not now (and never did) provide enough priests. Instead, the Italians join in prayer their Polish, German, and, especially, Irish co-religionists and send their children to the same schools. It is in school and in church that the melting pot is beginning effectively to do its work. As Glazer and Moynihan observed, "The Irish and Italians, who often contended with each other in the city, may work together and with other groups in the Church in the suburbs, and their separate ethnic identities are gradually being muted in the common identity of American Catholicism."

The Italians' tradition of secularism and skepticism toward church authority, however, has not disappeared and remains ingrained in the younger generations of the suburbs. Superficially, religious beliefs and practices seem to differ little between Irish Americans and Italian Americans. Closer scrutiny, however, reveals certain distinctive attitudes and beliefs. Nothing indicates the difference between the two groups more effectively than their respective stands on the use of contraceptive devices—an issue that has generated stormy dialogue within the Roman Catholic church in recent years. In late 1965 a national survey showed that only 37 percent of wives who came from Irish families used artificial means of contraception and thereby flouted church authority. By contrast, 68 percent of wives from Italian backgrounds used such means, showing thereby a higher degree of independence from the church in one of the most sacred areas of its doctrine (Potvin *et al.*).

melrose park: home of father paul asciolla

Bill Moyers

Old myths die stubbornly, and the myth of the melting pot—the boiling caldron pouring forth its uniform ingots of assimilated Americans —is no exception. The concept that "All men are created equal" has often been interpreted to mean that to be different is to be un-American. I was quite along in years in East Texas before I realized that Catholics were not citizens of a sovereign foreign state, the Vatican. There were always rumors in Marshall that the handful of Lebanese and Syrians who found their way to "our town" kept their eyes shut during public salutes to the flag lest they be unfaithful to the colors "of their own countries." And I remember once hearing the elders at my church—and this was in the early fifties—discuss whether "real Americans" would be separated in heaven from "foreign Americans." They never resolved the issue, but the idea persisted: to be a "good American" one should be as much like everyone else as possible. But of late there has been a resurgent emphasis on the ethnic differences that give the American character discernible variety and vitality. I was then only a few minutes from Melrose Park, a Chicago suburb. From Italian-American friends in New York I knew this to be the home of Father Paul J. Asciolla, C.S., a young priest who works closely with ethnic Americans. I wanted to meet him. Instead of continuing to Milwaukee I turned off the toll road and followed the signs into Melrose Park. The first policeman I hailed, himself an Italian-American, said, "Oh, yes, I know Father Paul. Follow me and I'll show you how to get there."

On the walls of the office of Father Paul J. Asciolla are stickers promoting "Italian Power" and "Schillebeecky for Pope." There are

"Melrose Park: Home of Father Paul Asciolla (editor's title)." From Bill Moyers, *Listening to America* (New York: Harper and Row, Publishers, Inc.), pp. 69–77. Reprinted by permission of Harper and Row, Inc. and the International Famous Agency.

also pictures of celebrities—Jimmy Durante, Angela Lansbury, Ron Santos, Gwen Verdon—who have helped to raise money for Villa Scalabrini, the home for the Italian aged which Father Paul serves as assistant administrator. The average age of its 152 residents is 85½; he is 36, an informal, enthusiastic man who, I am sure, will one day resemble in appearance the late Pope John XXIII. He grew up in Bristol, Rhode Island, the home of many Americans of Italian and Portuguese descent. "We swam on the same beach with the Kennedys," Father Paul said. "They were at one end and we were way down at the other."

Young Asciolla came to Chicago to attend seminary but his father, a restaurant cook, was almost totally blinded as the victim of a robbery. His son went home to work in a shoe factory to help support the family. He worked his way through Providence College, taught in the Bristol public schools, received his master's degree from Fordham, and served as principal at Sacred Heart Seminary in Chicago. Since 1965 he has been deeply involved in the life of Melrose Park, an old community of some twenty-three thousands residents, mostly Italian-Americans, on the west side of Chicago. He works closely with Father Amando Pierini, the administrator of Villa Scalabrini, an extraordinary man of sixty-three, who since 1933 has risen at four o'clock every morning to work, in Father Paul's words, "at helping our people to become good Americans with a deep and rich tradition in their own Italian past."

The three of us dined together, after which Father Paul and I talked into the morning hours. I sought his reaction to demonstrations then being staged by Italian-Americans in front of the FBI office in New York.

"This was inevitable. For a long time people have been yelling and screaming that just because they're Italian doesn't mean they're connected to the Mafia. Innocent people have been harassed on occasions, I know that. Most of the people in organized crime in this country, especially in the Italian-American community, grew up side by side with very respectable citizens. A lot of Italians made it in the system, others didn't and formed their own system, a subculture of crime, by performing services and delivering services that nobody else would give.

"I remember as a kid delivering fish and chips to a place behind the barbershop where a huge bookies ring operated. They used to lift me up and say, 'O.K., kid, point to a number on the chart,' and then they'd play that as the daily double. I didn't know what was going on until later. It was organized crime, all right, but the odd thing is they felt they were performing a service for the little guy who couldn't get to the track. Over the years these guys rubbed shoulders with the legitimate people in the neighborhood, and I think most people who aren't

Italian secretly suspect that anyone with an Italian name is somehow connected with the underworld. Guilt by association. Like—I guess most of the Ku Klux Klan were white Protestants but that doesn't mean most white Protestants belonged to the Klan. I think the decent people out in front of the FBI headquarters—and not all of them were decent—were saying, 'Look, judge me for what *I* am, not for what some other guy is.'

"I think there is something else, too. All these years Italian-Americans have known who they are. They've had pride and self-awareness for a long time. But they've also known that in the scheme of things they were supposed to suppress their differences—you know, 'Americans aren't like that.' When the blacks started reacting to their own suppressed identities—the 'Black is Beautiful' thing—ethnic Americans decided they could bring their own values right out in the open, too. People have been defining America for us in the wrong way, trying to drive a wedge between our loyalties—'You can't be Italian and be a good American.' Who says? We've got to know who we are. You can't make friends with a paranoid. You can't make friends unless *you* know who *you* are.

"Take the Italian-American family. They feel very strongly that they're Americans; they don't want to go back to Italy. But their Italian roots have given them very special characteristics as a family. The father does one thing, the mother does another, the children are expected to do certain other things. One of the most important factors in that family is the sense of who the whole family is. It extends past his brother and sister into the wider community. Ask an Italian about his family and he will tell you about his cousins, and not just his blood cousins. The family reaches beyond the blood line to the neighborhood, to their turf, to the larger community. And not only is this true of Italian-Americans. Let's say you go into a center-city situation and find an enclave of third-generation Polish-Americans. You have to understand why they came to that particular place. Usually the church was there, the industry in which they could work was there, relatives were there. In Poland they weren't property owners, but America gave them the opportunity to own land. They immediately began to identify with their neighborhood. It was their land. I don't care how small it was, they would sit in front of it with a gun if they thought it necessary. Look at Tony Imperiale in Newark. He's a symbol of the guy who says, 'This is my turf and nobody is going to take it away from me.'

"I think the politicians understand this, but the social-service agencies do not. Here is a neighborhood. We call it deteriorating, but the people who live there think it's a very nice place to live. There's a little local grocery store—it's part of the family—the church is part of the family, the ward politician, the milkman, everybody there is part of the larger family. A man's house, all of his equity, is locked into that system. Then urban renewal comes and says, 'You've got to move.' They tell him to do an awful lot of things without understanding why he is there in the first place. They don't factor his sense of family ties, his sense of blood, his idea of turf, into making social change. Without even explaining what they're trying to do, they will take the intransigence of this group of people as racism, obstructionist, reactionary. Perhaps the people should move, but there has to be some mediation between the man and his cultural ties. Even in the most optimum circumstances change is difficult.

"This is why ethnic Americans and blacks need to understand how hard it has been for each of them to make it in America and to realize that they really want the same thing. They want good jobs, they want good housing, they want a good education, and they want the freedom to do their own thing in their own way. They have to see that the progress of one group doesn't have to be at the expense of the other.

"This can happen. It happened in a part of Detroit where a friend of mine is the priest, Father Daniel Bogus. He's Polish-American and for a time this district was heavily Polish. Now it's largely black. This priest realized as the blacks started moving in that they had exactly the same needs as the Poles: jobs, good schools, and political power. In Detroit the councilmen are elected at large, which means that somebody who lives twenty-five miles from you may be your councilman. Somebody said that the Poles and the blacks ought to get together on the same meeting ground. Congressman John Conyers, the black congressman from that district, said he thought that would be a challenge because the Poles didn't know any more about blacks than blacks knew about Poles. So they had a meeting, and they discovered very quickly that they didn't know much about each other's history. It took more than six months to arrange for 300 people—150 blacks, 150 Poles—to get together, and they were tense about it. But it went well and now Poles and blacks are not so willing to believe all the bad publicity about each other. They're fighting together on all kinds of things. Like some alderman wanted to build a school in an area that would have meant knocking a lot of people out. These Poles and blacks got together and said, 'No, we don't want this high school if it's going to displace people. We want to keep our neighborhood.' That's integration. I don't know if they love each other or go to each other's churches, but that's integration.

"I can give you an illustration closer to home. There's a polyglot community in northwest Chicago—Mexican, Puerto Rican, Polish, Italian, Ukrainian, Lithuanian—where the garbage wasn't being collected. The alderman was just going to the party people to collect their garbage. All these people suffered who weren't subscribers to the political philosophy of the alderman. The streets weren't even being cleaned regularly. Now the people didn't talk about brotherhood and they didn't talk about integration. They happened to be living in the same neighborhood next to each other, black and white, although they had practically nothing to do with each other. All of a sudden somebody decided they had a common problem—garbage. It seems very mundane but it was their problem. So they all got together, they worked together, they collected all of the garbage themselves in hired trucks, they went to the alderman's wife, who owns a bar in the neighborhood, and dumped it *all* in front of the bar. Within half an hour it was all cleared up.

"This alderman had been very happy because those people were fighting each other. Politicians survive by playing blacks against Irish, Poles against Puerto Ricans, because then they're kept from understanding their real needs, their common needs. So these people finally got together and said, O.K., we're not going to be played against each other. You keep your political philosophy, we'll keep ours, but let's work at our common problem, whether it's garbage or juvenile delinquency. And they're doing it, but they don't sit around holding each other's hands and singing 'We Shall Overcome.'

"The media very seldom gets this kind of thing. With ethnic Americans the media has tended to pick up people who are reacting—reacting to their own awareness of their identity for the first time. It hasn't been very long since people were 'wops' or 'polacks'—you know, stereotypes. The media keeps trying to shove them into some new category—hardhat or racists or beefy clods—everybody has to fit into a mold. They come in and ask, 'Are you for Wallace? Are you for Wallace?' It's the old Biblical thing—the media tries to pit the Sons of Light against the Sons of Darkness. That's where the action is, and action is what the cameras record.

"When you see the hardhat, who's become the ethnic symbol today, he's beating up students. You're seeing the reaction, not what led up to it. I admire Walter Cronkite a lot, but when he says 'That's the way it is' at the end of his broadcasts, I have to smile, because very often that's not the way it is. That's only the way it seems to be. You're getting part of the effect, maybe nothing of the cause. How many television stations paid serious attention to the Indian until the Indians took over Alcatraz? Television looks at people in a pejorative way. It looks at them as if they were categories. On the *Carol Burnett Show* on CBS someone told a joke about the Polish airlines and played the Polish national anthem for comedy and the Chicago station was flooded with protests. We've got a lot of Poles here. Why were the people who put that show together so insensitive? Because there are no Poles in New York. The people who blue-pencil television shows lead very isolated lives.

"I think Agnew mistakenly tripped against a truth. Which is not only that the media has been a little bit to the left but that in general it tends to oversimplify. I doubt that they do it consciously. The very nature of television is to look for struggle that can be capsuled in one minute.

"The problem with Agnew now is that in going from city to city raising funds and saying the well-turned phrases, he's doing exactly what he criticized the media for doing. He's giving simplistic answers to very complex social problems. He's polarizing. George Wallace was right when he said he should have all his speeches copyrighted because Agnew is repeating them. Wallace appealed to people because he spoke of gut issues, a kind of barroom talk, knocking down the liberal establishment and the liberal press, but in the end they wouldn't go all the way with him because he was—he was Wallace. Agnew is saying the same thing and they like it because it gives high-level approval to their fears and prejudices—he is the Vice President, after all. Agnew makes it respectable to hate. He makes all the blacks into bad guys and all the whites into good guys, which is as bad as saying all students are bums and all white workers are right. He also makes the silent majority all white. It isn't. It's not even silent. It's the anxious majority.

"The working class that belongs to that majority has all the anxieties churned up by city living. They thought they had it made in America—'Work hard,' they were told, 'pull yourself up by your bootstraps, be industrious, and you'll make it.' So they toiled and struggled, only to discover that they haven't made it at all. Suddenly there's an inflationary economy and they have to have two jobs, which really tears at the old family structure and disrupts the familiar habits. They're making between $5,000 and $10,000 a year but their buying power is the buying power of 1948. They're 1948 Americans. The 1969 statistics in Chicago said an average family of four needs $11,400 to live moderately. But the people I'm talking about don't have any way to escape from that system. No tax benefits. Where are they going to invest, and what?

"Most of the people out here were Southern Italians and land meant very much to them. They wanted to plant and see things grow; they loved flowers. Now they're told they're living on the edge of a deteriorating neighborhood, it's going to take twenty years to pay for their house, and all the time the real-estate people are whispering, 'The blacks are coming, you've got to move. The blacks are coming, you've got to move,' and they're faced with the threat, real or imagined, of the blockbuster. They're terribly anxious. They're arming themselves with guns because they're anxious. They're being defined by everybody as a social problem. 'Me? A social problem?' And they're anxious about it. They're beginning to believe all the publicity.

"If you talk to the average guy in Melrose Park, he doesn't feel responsible for racism. He may have accepted the American dream so much by osmosis that he really is intransigent to social change; he's got it made and he doesn't want to give it up. He doesn't have anything against blacks—he has something against anybody who poses a real or imagined threat to his alleged security. And he certainly doesn't feel part of the power structure that perpetuated the slavery system that committed psychological genocide on the blacks. During all the time the black man was trying to get free the Italian was doing his damnedest in America just to survive. He didn't understand the language; he was breaking his back digging ditches and pushing wheelbarrows; he didn't even know there were blacks down there suffering worse hell than he was. All of a sudden, two or three generations later, he's in competition with the blacks who are immigrating from the South looking, he thinks, for his job. He's called a racist because he doesn't want to give up his job.

"He finds himself pressured by the upper class, the monied class, the privileged class to be the fall guy for correcting institutional racism, something he doesn't feel he created. There are no Italians in the major executive suites of the big corporations in this country. There are no Poles. Only two or three showcase blacks. The people who run the big corporations and the people who talk about brotherhood from their high-rise apartments expect this guy living in the nitty-gritty deteriorating neighborhood to take the rap for them. They needed a repressed group—a 'noble savage'—to justify their own guilt over being so well off and over being a part of the power structure that made the rules of the game, so they decided to save the blacks. Now I believe the blacks need help, although I don't think they like to be patronized, but in going to help the blacks, the liberals, the government, the establishment didn't factor in this whole middle belt of people. And you can't look at the problem of the blacks without looking at the reaction of the whites. What the liberal establishment should be telling the white working class and the blacks is: You have much more in common with each other than you think. In the history books of the country you've both been left out. You're getting short-changed right now the way things are going. Get together. Work to change things.

"But that's not what is happening. Agnew is playing to their prejudices, making them relish their bitterness, and the liberals are going around them directly to the blacks. Both groups are being driven apart. I don't want to romanticize the workingman—he can be a real slob—but I am convinced that you can't program for a revolution unless you program for the reaction to the revolution. That's the only way to keep a social order in stress from flying apart.

"There are visibly deprived people and there are relatively deprived people. We don't like to talk about class in America because everybody's supposed to be equal. We've hidden a lot of neglect, a lot of sins, under *that* myth. If everybody's equal in theory, you don't have to worry if they're not equal in fact. Well, the terrible thing is that the most unequal of all Americans are being exploited and played off against each other.

"The kids of the working class have a lot more in common with the black kids than they do with the children of the middle and upper classes. The working-class kid is starting at the same point his father did—he's got to survive in the system, beat the system, just like the black kid does. You know the pattern: 'Get your house, raise your family, be a good citizen even though it's not the best system, O.K., but get a certain amount of psychological and economic security and you will have it made in America.' The affluent kids, on the other hand, don't have these needs. Somebody is paying their bills through college; they don't have to work. They have no roots, no goal; they think history is going to end tomorrow. They have spent a lot of time watching television and they believe in the instant answer. They drift. They get bored, they move on. They can worry about the large social problems. They're worried about Vietnam. They're worried about the 'noble savages' in the ghettos. But they're terribly unhappy; they are really a mixed-up bunch of kids. What's happened to the Peace Corps? To VISTA? These were the programs of middle-class kids. Where has the great generosity of the young people gone in the last five years? At least the working-class kid has a specific goal—security. He's got to do the fieldwork so the liberal affluent kid can worry about the world.

"I think the politicians and the clergy are the people today who really have to do something about this class gap. It's hard for people in neighborhoods like this to identify with big government. They identify with the local ward politician who does them favors. What a burden—what an opportunity—this is for the politician. Things can happen if he begins to identify the real anxieties of people and tries to bring them together to work on everyday matters like street repairs and health services and schools. I believe very much in the neighborhood. I think that neighborhood organizations that cut across racial, ethnic, and class lines can be the salvation of this country. If only the politicians will see this and stop playing one group against another, stop giving the impression that if one group advances, another has to fall back. That only divides the working people and the blacks.

"I believe in introspection, but people who criticize themselves too much are usually in mental institutions—they're people who can't get out of themselves, who isolate themselves from the rest of society. I'm for criticism, but criticism and radical rhetoric, if you'll pardon the grammar, ain't social action. The heck with talking, let's do something."

Few people are doing more than Father Paul Asciolla, I thought at four o'clock in the morning as I crawled into the hospital bed he had provided me in a ward of the Villa. At dinner his superior, Father Pierini, had spoken of the importance of "enlarging the provincial mentalities of people and giving them respect and a sense of community without losing pride in their heritage." Through courses in culture, Italian civilization, and Italian-American history, through radio programs, a newspaper, seminaries, and programs featuring the food and costumes and customs of Italy, the Fathers Pierini and Asciolla are enriching the special heritage of their people and enhancing their ties to America simultaneously.

the neighborhood

ethnicity and the peer group society

Herbert Gans

Generally speaking, the Italian and Sicilian cultures that the immigrants brought with them to America have not been maintained by the second generation. Their over-all culture is that of Americans. A number of Italian patterns, however, have survived, the most visible ones being food habits. In all European ethnic groups, traditional foods and cooking methods are retained long after other aspects of the immigrant culture are given up. This is true also among West Enders. Most of the women still cook only Italian dishes at home, and many of them still make their own "pasta," especially for holiday dishes. They do not care for what they call the "American" types of spaghetti, macaroni, and other pasta products.

The pattern of heavy eating and light drinking, found in most Latin and Mediterranean cultures, also persists among the West Enders. Thus, rich food rather than alcohol is used to counteract deprivation or to celebrate. Entrees are strongly spiced, and desserts are very sweet. Even so, the food is milder and less spicy than that eaten by their parents. Moreover, West Enders have also given up the immigrant pat-

"Ethnicity and the Peer Group Society (editor title)." Excerpted from Herbert J. Ganz, "The Italians of the West End," *The Urban Villagers* (New York: Mac-Millan Publishing Co.). Reprinted by permission of MacMillan Publishing Co.

tern of preparing olive oil and wine at home, and buy the weaker commercially made ones.[1]

The durability of the ethnic tradition with respect to food is probably due to the close connection of food with family and group life. Indeed, food patterns are retained longer than others because they hold the group together with a minimum of strain. Also, there seems to be some association between food and the home. Food preparation serves as an example of the woman's skill as a housewife and mother. When company is present, it enables her to display her skills to relatives and peers.

Another pattern that has persisted into the second generation is language. Most of the West Enders I met could speak Italian—or, more correctly, the special patois of their locality—because they had learned it from their parents, and had to use it to communicate with them. Their children—that is, the third generation—are not being taught the language, however. Also, Italian names are slowly being Anglicized. Surnames are changed by people whose work brings them into contact with Americans, so that their names will be more easily understood. Given names are being changed for esthetic reasons, English ones being described as "nicer" than Italian ones. Thus, second-generation West Enders named Giuseppe by their parents introduce themselves as Joseph, and give only the English name to their children.[2]

There is little, if any, identification either with Italy or with the local areas from which the immigrants came originally. Second-generation people know their parents' birthplace, but it is of little interest to them. Excepting a handful of Italian intellectuals and artists, I encountered no identification with Italian culture or Italian symbols. Even those Italians who had made a name for themselves in sports or in entertainment were not praised solely because of their ethnicity. In fact, when a local Italian boxer lost a fight to his Negro opponent, I was told scornfully about a West Ender who had mourned this as a loss of Italian pride. Likewise, there seemed to be no objection to a Jewish singer who had made several hit records of bowdlerized Italian folk songs. "After all," people said, "most of us work for a Jewish boss." Whereas West Enders were more likely to vote for an Italian politician than any other, this was so only because they felt all politicians to be crooked. An Italian, being one of their own, would perhaps be less

1. These and other changes in Italian eating and drinking practices in America are described in detail in G. Lolli, E. Serianni, G. Golder, and P. Luzzatto-Fegiz, *Alcohol in Italian Culture,* New York: The Free Press of Glencoe and Yale Center of Alcohol Studies, 1958.

2. In a lower-middle-class suburb near Philadelphia that I studied after the West End, people of Italian background sometimes gave their children names such as Lynn or Mark.

evil, and, if not, he at least would be more accessible to them than others.

Acculturation thus has almost completely eroded Italian culture patterns among the second generation, and is likely to erase the rest in the third generation.[3] In fact, the process seems to have begun soon after the arrival of the immigrants. One West Ender told me that his Italian-born mother had saved for years for a visit to Italy, but that when she was finally able to go, came back after a month, saying that she could not live among these people because she was not like any of them. The woman, even though she had never learned to speak English properly, had become Americanized in the West End. Such rapid acculturation is not surprising, for the Italians who came to America were farm laborers whose life had been an unending round of much work and little leisure. As the patterns associated with rural poverty that they brought to America were jettisoned quickly, the ensuing vacuum was filled by things American.

Assimilation, however—the disappearance of the Italian social system—has proceeded much more slowly. Indeed, the social structure of the West End is still quite similar to that of the first generation. Social relationships are almost entirely limited to other Italians, because much sociability is based on kinship, and because most friendships are made in childhood, and are thus influenced by residential propinquity. Intermarriage with non-Italians is unusual among the second-generation, and is not favored for the third. As long as both parties are Catholic, however, disapproval is mild.

The relationship to the church is also similar to that of the immigrant generations. West Enders are religious, but they minimize their ties to the church. And while the traditional Italian emphasis on the Virgin Mary and the local saint continues, the superstitions based on the anthropomorphizing of nature have faded away.

Judging by the nostalgia of the West Enders for the past, it would appear that the Italian group is no longer as cohesive as it was in the previous generation. They say that in those days, people were friendlier and more cooperative, and that there were fewer individual wants, especially on the part of children. But while they mourn the loss of cohesion, they do not pursue it. For example, the redevelopment gave West Enders an opportunity to return to a more cohesive community in the nearby North End, which is still entirely Italian.[4] None of the West Enders seemed to be interested, however, largely because of the poorer quality of the housing. The ethnic homogeneity and cohesion of the North End were never mentioned either positively or negatively;

3. For a similar description of second-generation Italian ethnicity, and how it is changing, see Child, *op. cit.*, especially Chap. 2.
4. This is the society described in William F. Whyte, Jr., *Street Corner Society*, Chicago: University of Chicago Press, 1943; 2nd ed., 1955.

for most people it was a place to shop for Italian food, and to visit relatives.

Relationships with members of other ethnic groups are friendly but infrequent. These groups are characterized by traditional stereotypes, to which exceptions are made only in the case of specific individuals. For example, the fact that the Irish husband of an Italian woman was an alcoholic occasioned no surprise, because all Irishmen were suspected of being drunkards. The social distance between ethnic groups was illustrated by one West Ender, who was on friendly terms with her Jewish neighbor. When she spoke of the woman, however, she did not use her name, but called her simply—and entirely without malice—"the Jew."

THE STRUCTURE OF WEST END SOCIETY:
AN INTRODUCTION TO THE PEER GROUP SOCIETY

While residence, class, and ethnicity may locate the West Ender in ecological and social space, they tell us little about how he lives his daily life. As has already been noted in passing, life for the West Ender is defined in terms of his relationship to the group.

The life of the West Ender takes place within three interrelated sectors: the primary group, the secondary group, and the outgroup. The primary group refers to that combination of family and peer relationships which I shall call the *peer group society*. The secondary group refers to the small array of Italian institutions, voluntary organizations, and other social bodies which function to support the workings of the peer group society. This I shall call the *community*. I use this term because *it*, rather than the West End or Boston, is the West Ender's community. The outgroup, which I shall describe as the *outside world*, covers a variety of non-Italian institutions in the West End, in Boston, and in America that impinge on his life—often unhappily to the West Ender's way of thinking.

Although social and economic systems in the outside world are significant in shaping the life of the West Ender, the most important part of that life is lived within the primary group. National and local economic, social, and political institutions may determine the West Ender's opportunities for income, work, and standard of living, but it is the primary group that refracts these outside events and thus shapes his personality and culture. Because the peer group society dominates his entire life, and structures his relationship with the community and the outside world, I shall sometimes use the term to describe not only the primary relationships, but the West Enders' entire social structure as well.

The primary group is a peer group society because most of the West Enders' relationships are with peers, that is, among people of the

same sex, age, and life-cycle status. While this society includes the
friendships, cliques, informal clubs, and gangs usually associated with
peer groups, it also takes in family life. In fact, during adulthood, the
family is its most important component. Adult West Enders spend
almost as much time with siblings, in-laws, and cousins—that is, with
relatives of the same sex and age—as with their spouses, and more time
than with parents, aunts, and uncles. The peer group society thus continues long past adolescence, and, indeed, dominates the life of the
West Ender from birth to death. For this reason I have coined the
term "peer group society."

In order to best describe the dominance of the peer group principle in the life of the West Ender, it is necessary to examine it over
a typical life cycle. The child is born into a nuclear family; at an early
age, however, he or she—although girls are slower to do this than boys
—transfers increasing amounts of his time and allegiance to the peers
he meets in the street and in school. This transfer may even begin long
before the child enters school. Thus, one West Ender told me that
when he wanted his two-year-old son to attend an activity at a local
settlement house, bribery and threats were useless, but that the promise
that he could go with two other young children on the block produced
immediate assent.

From this time on, then, the West Ender spends the rest of his
life in one or another peer group. Before or soon after they start going
to school, boys and girls form cliques or gangs. In these cliques, which
are sexually segregated, they play together and learn the lore of childhood. The clique influence is so strong, in fact, that both parents and
school officials complain that their values have difficulty competing
with those being taught in the peer group. The sexually segregated
clique maintains its hold on the individual until late adolescence or
early adulthood.

Dating, the heterosexual relationship between two individuals
that the middle-class child enters into after puberty—or even earlier—
is much rarer among West Enders. Boys and girls may come together
in peer groups to a settlement house dance or a clubroom. Even so,
they dance with each other only infrequently. Indeed, at the teenage
dances I observed, the girls danced mostly with each other and the
boys stood in the corner—a peer group pattern that may continue
even among young adults. A West End girl in her twenties described
her dates as groups of men and women going out together, with little social contact between individual men and women during the evening. Individual dating takes place not as part of the group activity, as in the
middle class, but only after the group has dispersed. Judging from the
descriptions given by young West End men, the relationship then is
purely sexual—at least for them.

The hold of the peer group is broken briefly at marriage. During courtship, the man commutes between it and his girl. Female peer groups—always less cohesive than male—break up even more easily then, because the girl who wants to get married must compete with her peers for male friends and must be at their beck and call. At marriage, the couple leaves its peer groups, but after a short time, often following the arrival of the first child, they both re-enter peer group life.

Among action-seeking West Enders, the man may return to his corner, and the woman to her girl friends. But most often—especially in the routine-seeking working class—a new peer group is formed, consisting of family members and a few friends of each spouse. This group meets after working hours for long evenings of sociability. Although the members of the group are of both sexes, the normal tendency is for the men and women to split up, the men in one room and the women in another. In addition, husband and wife also may belong to other peer groups: work colleagues or childhood friends among the men, informal clubs of old friends that meet regularly among the women. In the West End, friendship ties seem to be formed mainly in childhood and adolescence, and many of them last throughout life.

But the mainstay of the adult peer group society is the *family circle*.[5] As already noted, the circle is made up of collateral kin: in-laws, siblings, and cousins predominantly. Not all family members are eligible for the peer group, but the rules of selection—which are informal and unstated—are based less on closeness of kinship ties than on compatibility. Family members come together if they are roughly of the same age, socio-economic level, and cultural background. How closely or distantly they are related is much less important than the possession of common interests and values. Even among brothers and sisters only those who are compatible are likely to see each other regularly.

This combination of family members and friends seems to continue to function as a peer group for the rest of the life cycle. Thus, each of the marriage partners is pulled out *centrifugally* toward his or her peers, as compared with the middle-class family in which a *centripetal* push brings husband and wife closer together.

The West End, in effect, may be viewed as a large network of these peer groups, which are connected by the fact that some people may belong to more than one group. In addition, a few individuals function as communicators between the groups, and thus keep them informed of events and attitudes important to them all.

As will be shown in detail in later chapters, the hold of the peer group on the individual is very strong. Some illustrations of this can be given here. Achievement and social mobility, for example, are group

5. I have borrowed this term from Michael Young and Peter Willmott, *Family and Kinship in East London,* London: Routledge and Kegan Paul, 1957.

phenomena. In the current generation, in which the Italian is still effectively limited to blue-collar work, atypical educational and occupational mobility by the individual is frowned upon. Children who do well in school are called "sissies," and they cannot excel there and expect to remain in their peer group. Since allegiance to any one group is slight at this stage, however, the good student can drift into other peer groups until he finds one with compatible members. Should such peers be lacking, he may have to choose between isolation or a group that does not share his standards. Often, he chooses the latter. This is well illustrated by children who have intellectual skills but who find that out of fear of peer group pressures they cannot summon the self-control to do well in school.

Life in a peer group society has a variety of far-reaching social and psychological consequences. For example, the centrifugal pressure on man and wife affects the family structure, as does the willingness— or resignation—of the parents in relinquishing their children to their own peer group at an early age. The fact that individuals are accustomed to being with—and are more at ease with—members of their own sex means that their activities are cued primarily to reference groups of that sex. This may help to explain the narcissistic vanity among West End men, that is, their concern with clothes, and displays of muscular strength or virility.[6] It also may help to explain the chaperoning of unmarried women, in fear that they will otherwise indulge in sexual intercourse. Not only does the separation of the sexes substitute for the development of internal controls that discourage the man from taking advantage of the woman, but they replace, as well, those controls that allow the woman to protect herself.

The peer group principle has even more important consequences for personality organization. Indeed, the role of the group in the life of the individual is such that he exists primarily in the group. School officials, for example, pointed out that teenagers were rough and active when they were with their peers, but quiet and remarkably mild and passive when alone. Their mildness is due to the fact that they exist only partially when they are outside the group. In effect, the individual personality functions best and most completely among his or her peers—a fact that has some implications for independence and dependence, conformity and individualism among the West Enders. In some ways the individual who lives in a peer group society is more dependent than the middle-class person. This is true, however, only on a superficial level.

My emphasis on the role of the peer group should not be taken to mean that it is distinctive to the West End, or even to second-genera-

---

6. It is thus not necessary to use explanations invoking latent or manifest homosexuality, although latent homosexuality is also present. Vanity is not limited, however, to the latently homosexual.

tion Italians. Other studies have suggested that it is a fairly universal phenomenon in working-class groups. Nor does its influence end at this point. Peer groups are found in all classes, but in the middle and upper-middle-class, they play a less important role, especially among adults. In the lower-middle-class, for example, peer groups are made up of neighbors and friends, and exist alongside the nuclear family, but usually they do not include members of the family circle. Moreover, dependence on the peer group for sociability and mutual aid is much weaker. Also, there is much more interaction among couples and groups of couples. Nevertheless, social gatherings usually do break up into male and female enclaves, and voluntary associations are segregated by sex. In the upper-middle-class, social relationships take place primarily among couples, and voluntary associations are less frequently segregated by sex. Even so, social gatherings and activity groups may break up into male and female subgroups. Upper-middle-class women often resent the fact that concentration on the mother role creates handicaps to job or organizational activities in which the sexes work together.

In the lower-middle-class, and more so in the upper-middle-class, people move in a larger number of peer groups, often formed to pursue specific interests and activities. The West End pattern, in which people spend most of their spare time within the confines of one peer group, is not found here. Consequently, the influence of the peer group on the life of the middle class is much less intense.

stabilizing white ethnic neighborhoods

Stephen Adubato & Richard Krickus

I

It has escaped urban strategists that there is an ethnic dimension to the urban crisis and it must be taken into account in urban planning. Millions of people still reside in viable white ethnic neighborhoods in the Northeast and mid-West. Like healthy working-class neighborhoods elsewhere, a large proportion of homes are owner-occupied, most purchased after years of toil and sacrifice. They may be old and not much to look at but they are structurally sound and offer living space which cannot be found in the suburbs at comparable prices. They are not merely a composite of brick and mortar providing shelter, but a physical manifestation of a bitter/sweet legacy which began when European immigrants left the "old country" at the turn of the century to build a new life in America.

Social life revolves around the family and close friends. There is a well balanced mix of old and young. Senior citizens still enjoy full lives, sharing the family's joy and sorrow. They are rarely committed to nursing homes or exiled to "plush landscaped villages" which isolate lonely old folks from the bracing companionship of young people. Tightly knit family networks and the adhesive of an ethnic subculture contribute to neighborhood stability and foster warm community life.

No one makes a lot of money; but unemployment until recently has not been a source of great concern. There are, furthermore, hidden economic assets which have escaped the sophisticated eye of orthodox economists. Irving Levine of the American Jewish Committee found in a study of white ethnic neighborhoods such tangible economic activi-

"Stabilizing White Ethnic Neighborhoods." An unpublished article by Stephen Adubato and Richard Krickus. Printed by permission of Richard J. Krickus.

ties as "casual employment and labor" in the form of "child care, mechanical maintenance and repair, house painting, snow removal, and sub-tenancy for neighbors' relatives." He also discovered "community owned recreational equipment and communal meals, bazaar sales, and fund-raising efforts in behalf of the communal sponsors."

Here the people you want to spend time with are usually within walking distance of your home, and there are friendly acquaintances on the street you can chat with. The local merchants know you by name and they take time to ask you about your family or how things are going at work. You can still find butcher shops, bakeries, and markets which sell a variety of well-prepared meats—Italian sausages or Polish kielbasa—delicious pastries and breads—gnolis, struddler, hearty ryes, black pumpernickel and crusty white bread—and unprocessed cheeses, commodities which, elsewhere in America, are only available at specialty stores which serve affluent customers. Social clubs, fraternal associations and taverns are the focus of social life outside the home; here you meet people you can talk to in a leisurely manner, purchase inexpensive drinks and play cards and shuffleboard.

We cannot quantify the economic value of "community" but it's a scarce commodity in America and it's something of value. The hippies who live in communes in the hinterlands of the U.S., the suburban youngsters who inundate Washington's Georgetown or Chicago's Old Town, and the corporation executives and middle-class housewives who do their thing at Esalen are all looking for it. Counter-culture theorists searching for authentic community life would be well advised to search out ethnic neighborhoods where the residents enjoy intimate contact not based on a contractual arrangement or exchange of commodities but rooted in unstated acceptance of others because they "belong."

Many white urban ethnics, however, are now finding it necessary to flee center city; others are holding tight; and still others would stay if our urban policy included their neighborhoods in urban redevelopment schemes. Ethnic communal ties have served as an adhesive enabling these urbanites to endure physical deterioration, racial discord, declining schools and services, street crime, and high taxes—the things which have pushed city dwellers elsewhere in the United States to the suburbs. If we are going to check white outmigration resulting in the flight of tax revenues, jobs, and the human resources which our cities cannot afford to lose, we must stabilize these viable neighborhoods.

It is against this background that we urge adoption of a residential neighborhood strategy. We focus on the white ethnic neighborhoods we know best and which, because of ethnic communal ties, are uniquely qualified to fit this strategy, but much of what follows pertains to residential communities across the United States.

II

After World War II, the highway program, the FHA mortgage insurance and VA mortgage guarantee programs facilitated suburbanization. Bankers, builders, insurance underwriters, and land speculators encouraged home building in the outer reaches of our metropolitan areas. These measures were necessary to meet the pressures of population growth and the rising demand for housing. Unfortunately, while Washington was making it possible for potential homeowners to relocate in the suburbs, very little was done to encourage redevelopment of inner-city neighborhoods. FHA discouraged the purchase of homes in the city and so did lending institutions and insurance companies. At the same time, urban redevelopment programs bulldozed sound housing and destroyed viable neighborhoods—because they were designated "gray areas." The conceptual basis for this conclusion reflected the physical determinism of planners who viewed slums in terms of unsightly dwellings, who abhorred mixed land uses, and who ignored their own strictures about viewing the city as a "system."

Today old dwellings—those made of wood or others which violate the aesthetic sensibilities of middle-class planners—are often designated sub-standard even though they are structually sound and conform to housing codes and safety regulations. High density (but not overcrowded) neighborhoods and those situated where mixed land uses prevail are declared urban renewal areas. Urban experts who tour older urban white ethnic communities are often inclined to describe them as slums when every freshman student of sociology knows that the defining feature of a slum is social disorganization—settlements where unemployment is high, family fragmentation common, and crime and other forms of social pathology pandemic—not physical decay. Despite all the rhetoric one hears in planning circles about "urban systems"—that is, changes in one part of the system will affect other components of the system—our urban policy has ignored the importance of white residential neighborhoods in urban restoration. It has even escaped the attention of many hardnosed investors.

In cities across America, billions are being spent on "downtown projects" usually involving high rise office buildings, apartments, hotels, shopping malls and occasional townhouses in which only the wealthy can afford to live. As the reinforced concrete is being poured, residential communities in proximity to downtown are being bulldozed. As potential customers and workers flee, their exodus prompts businessmen who are considering other commercial ventures to pause and take stock. "With so many people moving, where will my customers come from?" Because many small businesses and restaurants are being destroyed, "will people have sufficient incentive to travel downtown as they once did?" And because of the subsequent rise in social dislocation caused by the decline of residential communities, "will people feel it's safe to eat, shop, or attend a downtown theatre?" And "how am I going to get employees to work here?" Many businessmen have been unable to provide answers to all these questions and much downtown office space goes unrented, business ventures are halted or are never started and corporation executives quietly plot to follow the well beaten path to the suburbs. Yet, the "downtown project" approach is the basis for much of what passes for urban redevelopment and it will no doubt continue as long as Washington makes it profitable to construct these white elephants mushrooming in urban America. The restoration of blighted commercial areas is certainly a necessary part of salvaging our "urban systems," but such measures must be taken in conjunction with the revitalization of residential neighborhoods. Washington has all but neglected this facet of urban redevelopment.

White lower-middle-class neighborhoods have been excluded from most Federal housing programs. Those designed to meet the needs of the poor represent mere tokenism, or often, because of poor administration, indifference, or corrupt collusion on the part of local officials, have been a windfall for unethical businessmen. And few "urban experts" have bothered to acknowledge that ill-designed housing programs for the poor have expedited the destruction of stable working-class communities. A case in point is the FHA-sponsored Title 235 program enabling low-income people to purchase homes with small down payments and long-term mortgages.

Under the program—which was scrapped when it became public knowledge that unethical real estate speculators were exploiting it to the tune of millions of dollars—poor people purchased homes assuming that, since the government had guaranteed the dwellings, they met FHA standards. But in many cases the homes were riddled with code violations. Furthermore assessors frequently falsified applications of buyers who were financially unable to bear the burden of the purchase. After moving in and finding violations or discovering that they could not afford the house, many buyers defaulted on their mortgages. Although under FHA regulations, no home with code violations was acceptable, fee appraisers, in collusion with the seller, simply ignored them and did not include them in their reports. The multi-racial West Side Real Estate Coalition in Chicago found numerous examples of this practice in a survey they conducted in 1972: Jesse Williams bought a house through FHA on December 28, 1971. After he moved in, he found (1) the furnace was obsolete; (2) carbon monoxide leaked from the chimney flue; (3) the basement had been gutted by fire; and (4) the city later informed him that the house had 15 code violations. Estimated cost of repairs: $8000. The color of the buyer's skin was not the deciding factor in selecting victims. Roman Bryzowski bought a house through FHA in November 1971. After he moved in, the City of Chicago Building Department inspected the house and found nine code violations. Estimated cost: $3000. Newspaper accounts across the United States in 1972 and 1973 provided countless other examples of how the program was being abused before it was discontinued.

The program's goal was commendable but, like numerous other urban programs, it failed because corrupt or indifferent officials permitted fast-buck artists to rip off the poor who desperately need shelter. It contributed to the destruction of many working-class neighborhoods where the homes were purchased because after the buyer defaulted and the inventory of abandoned dwellings mushroomed, long-time residents rushed to sell their homes fearing that the collapse of the housing market was imminent. The taxpayer picked up the tab because the government guaranteed the mortgage on the defaulted homes.

It is not only in places like Chicago, where politicos still quest for boodle with the zest of a Boss Tweed, that government programs are destroying residential communities. The program was abused in New York City too; indeed, reform administrations like those of John Lindsay have been cavalier about the survival of residential neighborhoods in their cities.

In the fall of 1972 commuters on the Brooklyn-Queens Expressway were treated to a horrendous traffic jam when a group of protestors formed a human chain across the busy thoroughfare. Peering through their windshields, those who sat in autos close to the scene of the action noted that the demonstrators were toting signs. One read, "Hell no, we won't go!" The Vietnam war was "settled," so why were peaceniks disrupting traffic? No, they weren't peaceniks—maybe they were women's libbers? But the signs were not helpful on this score because one read, "Mayor Lindsay has a home; what about us?" Another proclaimed, "If you want industrial expansion, take Gracie Mansion." Most of the demonstrators were women, but they did not have that dressed-down chic look which is the uniform many middle-class women's libbers seem to fancy.

Close inspection suggested that they were real honest to God housewives from the Williamsburg section of Brooklyn—the wives and daughters of white blue-collar workers who were employed by the city or by factories in and around the New York Metropolitan area. These women had never before confronted political authority and sitting down blocking traffic was an "illegal act" which caused much guilt and soul-searching on their part. One of the leaders, Mrs. Anastasi Zawakzki McGuinnes, observed, "That was the first time we ever did anything like that in our lives. But it's amazing what you can get yourself to do if it means survival." Survival meant defeating the city's plan to condemn housing which would eventually force some 86 families and several businesses from the predominantly Polish-American "Northside" neighborhood she called home. Frustrated by their powerlessness and angered by the city's refusal to meet with them, the women sought to publicize their plight by sitting down on the Brooklyn-Queens Expressway during rush hour.

City officials claimed it was unfortunate that the homes had to be destroyed but the action was necessary to permit the S&S Corrugated Paper Machinery Company to expand and make several hundred more jobs available. In 1969 the company was offered a low interest Federal loan contingent upon its not relocating in New Jersey (as it had threatened); to sweeten the deal the city Economic Development Administration promised it would make "land available to permit the company to expand its facilities." The City Planning Commission and Board of Estimate held hearings to which community representatives were invited and they attended. But it was apparent that a deal had been made, and the Northsiders did not wield the clout to prompt a serious reassessment of the scheme.

Community spokesmen argued that they certainly were in favor of making jobs available, for they were working people themselves; but they questioned whether the basis for the condemnation was one of providing jobs or whether it was merely a windfall for the company. The city did not give the people proper warning about the condemnation and the hearings were rigged against them; the decision to bulldoze their homes was made final prior to the hearings; the residents were being rewarded below-market prices for their homes; the city never bothered to comply with its own relocation statutes; it was withholding subsidies soon to be put into effect; and it was questionable whether it was legal to condemn property for the sake of a profit-making corporation in the first place. Had the city's planners done their job, they could have taken measures to meet the needs of both the cardboard company and the homeowners.

In the fall of 1973 the Northsiders were evicted; but because of the assistance of an energetic former civil rights worker, Jan Petersen, the help of City Councilman Fred Richmond, and the technical advice of the Pratt Institute's Center for Community and Environmental Development and other outside allies, the people got a better deal than was originally anticipated. Nonetheless, they cannot take much comfort in the measures the city took to soften the blow. Nor can their neighbors who fear that it is only a matter of time before the city decides to remove them as well. This callous use of police power is a poignant example of why Americans are becoming "estranged from government." As one Northsider observed, "The city is showing us and our kids that it doesn't pay to obey the law." She asked, "What do you get for it? My mother always said if you don't make no trouble, you get no trouble. But it's not true. You get it even when you don't make it." A revealing footnote to the Northside episode is that *The New York*

Times reported after the eviction that Paul Levine, an Economic Development Administration official who played "a leading role in the controversy," had resigned his job to join the S&S Corrugated Paper Machinery Company "as a top executive."

The Northsiders' loss, however, is also the city's loss; for while New York spends millions of dollars for "community development" and "crime prevention" on the one hand, it is destroying a stable, crime-free community on the other. Nancy Seifer, a former aide to Mayor Lindsay, claims that this is just the latest of a series of actions which the city has taken at the expense of the Northside neighborhood. The first blow to the integrity of the Northside was delivered in the 1950s when an expressway was built through the community, destroying a hundred homes in the process. In 1961, the area was zoned "manufacturing"; real estate values plunged, homeowner's insurance became more difficult to get, and a commercial street was devastated. Since then the city has closed down the 92nd Precinct which was located in the neighborhood and has rejected the request of Puerto Rican and Polish spokesmen to renovate it as a community center. In spite of numerous requests to get a stop sign for a perilous intersection, the city has refused to comply; and it is anticipated that the local firehouse will soon be relocated elsewhere. The imminent destruction of this white ethnic neighborhood is not an isolated example; several years ago, Italian-American residents of Corona waged a bitter, protracted struggle with the city before they saved their homes from condemnation. Meanwhile, the Chelsea area of Manhattan and Greenpoint in Brooklyn, two of the oldest residential communities in the city, are in danger of being destroyed by industrial development.

These are only a handful of examples detailing how Federal agencies and local governments across the country are destroying stable neighborhoods. Unless this trend is reversed, programs adopted to save our cities, including new schemes to finance them, will represent meaningless gestures providing paychecks for government bureaucrats and urban consultants and enriching contractors, real estate speculators, and the lending institutions which somehow or other always come out on top.

III

The time has now come for responsible policy-makers to acknowledge that destructive business practices are a second source of neighborhood decay; and until the people can hold businessmen accountable for decisions which affect the fate of their neighborhoods, we are not going to check urban blight, much less improve the quality of urban life. The "money people" have a virtual veto over government housing and related urban renewal programs. Herbert Gans, in his highly acclaimed study of a Boston Italian-American community, noted a decade ago that in the initial stages of a West Side redevelopment program, some streets in the target community were excluded because the housing was in good condition. Later the lending institutions involved ordered that they be torn down because it would be difficult to sell cleared land "surrounded by aging if well kept tenements." Harold Kaplan, who has written favorably about Newark's urban renewal program, has illuminated the central role the private sector played in that city's housing programs in the 1950s. "The big question about any redevelopment site was whether a private firm could make a profit on middle-income housing in that area. If the answer was negative, no redeveloper would buy the site, and no FHA official would agree to insure mortgages for construction there." Kaplan's conclusion accurately characterizes joint public-private sector programs today. George Gross, counsel to the House Subcommittee on Housing, in commenting upon the failure of our "low-cost" housing programs, said last summer: ". . . the big decisions are really made by private developers," who ". . . decide where subsidized housing will go, how much each unit will cost within a range set by the Federal government, the size of the unit, and most important, whether there will be any such housing at all."

While the private sector plays a pivotal role in the outcome of governmental programs, independent actions of the business community also have been devastating. The social cost of urban blight is enormous to city dwellers, as the economic cost is troublesome to the taxpayer. But urban malaise has proven to be profitable to unethical businessmen who prey upon the minority poor and their lower-middle-class white neighbors alike. Real estate speculators zero in on inner-city white ethnic communities for the purpose of blockbusting because the residents lack the power to resist. Panic peddlers exploit white fears that the presence of blacks will result in plunging property values and the wholesale exodus of whites from the neighborhood. In some instances, blockbusters set up the neighborhood by inducing one homeowner to sell at an attractive price to a black or Puerto Rican family; and then, citing the presence of that family to his neighbors, they predict a "colored invasion of the neighborhood." An investigative reporter for a Newark paper found, in a probe of blockbusting in the city, that fast-buck artists were manipulating Newark's racial tensions. For example, he spoke to a widow who was told by a real estate agent that she could "not get a nickel more than $7,500" for her home because of the "ethnic situation" in Newark. Eager to relocate her family to South Jersey, she reluctantly sold her home for the quoted price. The reporter, tracing the real estate records, found that the house was sold later that same day for $17,000. Under such circumstances, both the white seller and black buyer are being had. Blockbusting continues to foster wholesale white urban flight, North and South; and to a significant degree, it is responsible for what has now become a truism of many cities: "There are no integrated neighborhoods in our cities, only changing ones."

Blockbusting has received the condemnation it so richly deserves; but an equally destructive practice of the business community, "redlining" by insurance companies and lending institutions, is often ignored. Insurance companies which refuse to provide coverage or charge exorbitant rates to homeowners and small businessmen, and lending institutions which withhold mortgage or rehab money, contribute to neighborhood destabilization. Homeowners in many white ethnic neighborhoods are being told that they live in a "riot," "disaster," "high risk," or "gray" area; hence, they are ineligible for mortgage money or insurance coverage.

Redlining works like a self-fulfilling prophecy. Because rehab money is withheld, small homeowners are unable to take proper care of their dwellings; roofs, sidings, and porches begin to decay, and, as the housing in the community becomes unsightly, homeowners and businessmen fearful that their neighborhood is on the decline are reluctant to "keep up" their property. As the neighbors' dwellings deteriorate and the more mobile residents move, the people largely responsible for the outcome sit back and take pride in their prophetic powers and business acumen. In the Greenpoint section of Brooklyn, banks granting home loans have set a twelve year mortgage limit and a down payment of 50%—which means that the monthly payments of some homeowners are as high as $500.00.

Redlining by insurance companies works in a similar fashion and produces similar results, for residents are apt to panic when they discover that their community has been redlined; it is common knowledge that this almost always results in the gradual deterioration of the neighborhood or a precipitous flight from the community. The inequity here is that individuals pay for the real or alleged reputation of their neighborhood and that landlords are discouraged from making needed repairs. The Chicago organizers cited the example of a Northwestside family that pays $260 annually for $18,000 of insurance on their home while in Lake Forest, a suburb of the windy city, $40,000 of home insurance costs $67 a year. Insurance spokesmen explain this discrepancy by claiming that the Chicago home is located in a high risk area. In another instance a man who had insured his building for 15 years with a large company had his policy cancelled even though he had made no claims and had no code violations because the building was located in a "deteriorating area." Clearly state and Federal authorities who are committed to a viable urban strategy must closely scrutinize business practices which are critical to the survival of residential neighborhoods. Until they do so the private sector will have the option of virtually vetoing the decisions of elected officials who are "guardians" of the public interest.

IV

It is the fate of most white working-class urbanites to stand in mute frustration while the future of their neighborhoods is determined by remote officials or callous businessmen who cannot be held accountable for the destruction of residential communities. The powerlessness of the residents is the third reason why white ethnic neighborhoods are being flattened. This also accounts for their residents being excluded from participation in social service programs which are vital to the welfare of many urban families. This includes individuals who, under law or administrative guidelines, qualify for participation in manpower, housing, drug abuse, crime, and educational programs. Professor S. M. Miller, a forceful advocate of social planning, has observed that this is the basis for much white opposition to public and private urban programs. Because these programs have excluded the white lower-middle-class, they have heightened racial tensions and have fostered the mistaken notion that the problems of minority Americans are "being taken care of." It is a sad fact but among the army of educators, community health specialists, manpower professionals, and other "urban experts," there are few people who are advocates for white working-class urbanites.

Economic deprivation and racial discrimination have prompted urban administrators to respond, though modestly, to the unmet needs of urban minority groups. One can find advocates for their cause in government, the foundations, academia, and the media, as there should be; at the same time, affluent citizens possessing political influence, economic power, and social status make certain that public agencies and private interests play by the rules with them. This accounts for a youngster whose father earns an impressive salary as a corporation executive acquiring a college tuition grant while a truck driver's son who does not know how to "work the system" is denied this assistance. It explains why a pert young coed infected by a venereal disease can receive a free shot at a clinic serving counter-culture youth while the youngster who earns $85 a week pumping gas must pay $20 for similar care. John Fiorillo and Ralph Perrotta of the New York Center for Ethnic Affairs have found, as expected, that poor neighborhoods in New York receive a larger share of city funds than working-class ones—but so do more affluent neighborhoods. Their findings also demonstrated that there was little institutional concern for the "hidden" white poor in the nation's largest city. In the predominantly white neighborhoods they studied, they found anywhere from 25% to 48% of the families could be designated "working poor"—i.e., families earning 2.0 times the Federal poverty figure which, according to family size, meant their annual income was below the Department of Labor's "minimum acceptable income."

In most cities urban administrators and program personnel possess little knowledge about white ethnic communities and lack the proper information or training to work effectively with their residents. The well-meaning radical sociologist from Upper Montclair, who is passionate in his concern for Newark's disadvantaged, often displays frightful ignorance about the city's Italian neighborhoods. He is also inclined to favor stereotypes about Italians and Poles which were first propounded by nineteenth century theorists of Aryan superiority, or blithely dismiss the white worker because "he's part of the problem."

An anomaly of white ethnic neighborhoods is that, while highly organized communities, they normally lack leadership with the experience and skills to effectively articulate community problems, to mobilize available resources, and to use them in a constructive fashion. This condition, in part, is rooted in the notion that family, church, and other private associations can satisfactorily deal with the problems which affect the community and its residents. A contributing factor is the persistence of an immigrant/working-class political legacy (many white ethnics today are second- and third-generation and middle-class, but most of them continue to perceive the world through the prism of that legacy) which treats individual and not community problems. In Chicago and the boroughs of New York, where the old ethnic politicians still enjoy the prerogatives of power, patronage politics may effectively meet the needs of individuals by providing jobs, city contracts, etc.—but ignore community-wide problems. When Washington first began to pump money into a host of poverty and urban programs during the 1960s, many old guard white ethnic politicians viewed them in terms of "black patronage" or as a means to keep the ghettos cool during long hot summers. Others who were worried about the political implications of "organizing the poor" opposed them, and still others ignored social and community programs because the old lucrative sources of patronage kept them busy. The Catholic Church and organized labor, the most powerful institutions in many Catholic urban neighborhoods, have ignored the community problems of their parishioners and rank and file members.

A Corona housewife told Fiorillo and Perrotta that when her neighborhood was threatened by condemnation, she went to the local political club where she had been a block captain for twenty years. She was told there was nothing that could be done. In desperation she tried the largest church in the area and was informed that they could not help her either. "I realized," she said, "that after all those years in the political club, I didn't know anything about politics." The most helpful advice she received was from a black neighbor's son who suggested several community action strategies.

A growing number of white ethnic community leaders and younger politicians have begun to recognize that "voluntarism" and patronage politics cannot treat the awesome urban problems which exist in our post-industrial society. But, given the dependence of our cities upon state and Federal monies and the power of the private sector in implementing urban policies, even the more "community oriented" white ethnic politicians will be unable to plug their constituents into future programs as long as a) Federal policy-makers ignore the critical importance of residential communities and b) the "target population" is excluded from participation in "public decisions" which the private sector makes at their expense.

V

Detroit, Cleveland, Baltimore, St. Louis, Richmond, and New Orleans by the end of this decade will join Newark, Gary, and Atlanta, which already have a black majority population. If this trend is not checked, many, if not most, middle-class blacks and Spanish-speaking Americans will join the white exodus to the suburbs. The outcome will be the appearance of urban reservations housing poor, elderly, and minority Americans without the tax base to meet their varied needs or the leadership to mobilize the slender resources that are available and effectively utilize them. The fate of the urban poor then is inextricably wedded to the stabilization of the residential neighborhoods which still thrive in our urban centers. If we are to escape the imminent scourge of an American version of Apartheid, funds must be provided, policies designed and a political offensive mounted to save residential communities.

Preserving existing urban residential neighborhoods and the housing in them is critical since it is apparent that Congress and the Administration have decided to scrap the commitment Congress made in 1968 to construct 2.6 million housing units annually. Reports from the House Subcommittee on Housing indicate that the yearly target henceforth will amount to one-half that figure. It is imperative, therefore, that we preserve our existing urban housing inventory. Toward this end we must adopt an authentic national urban policy which is adequately funded and properly emphasizes residential neighborhoods, for their survival will contribute to the welfare of all the people who live in our nation's troubled cities.

public lives:
the schools, work
and politics

I would like to touch on the institutional agendas relating to working class ethnic groups: how do we develop them, and how do we engage in intensive discussion within those mainstream structures that seem to have the most impact on our society—government, labor, business, civic groups, women's groups, civil rights groups, public education, the academy, ethnic organizations.

We need to build agendas, and this time I hope with people rather than for people, that will respond to the two major phenomena that are bugging the society economically. On the one hand we have rising expectations on the part of those minority groups that are at the lowest level in the society: Blacks, Chicanos, Puerto Ricans, Mexicans, American Indians, poor Appalachian whites. There is one agenda there. Then there is the lower middle class agenda— for Poles, Italians and other white ethnic groups, and for other lower middle class whites including Jews.

If the most deprived people on the pecking order are moving in response to "rising expectations," those at the next stage are being activated by their own sense of "relative deprivation," a sense that everyone is moving up except them. And when rising expectations meet and have to compete with relative deprivation, you have explosions! We must have an agenda for both economic groups, dealing not only with global long-range ideas of income redistribution but also with more immediate concerns people have about jobs, neighborhoods, health, education, consumer services, and their chances to achieve "the good life."

Conference participant
Consultation on Ethnicity
American Jewish Committee

If white ethnics find some sense of identity and security in their families, parishes and neighborhoods, it is not necessarily so when they enter the secondary institutions of the larger society. Their public lives are at once both more impersonal and less specifically ethnic than those intimate, ethnically rooted aspects of their lives dealt with in the previous section. In schools, work, and politics white ethnics must cope with many groups whose values and beliefs derive from different ethnic and racial backgrounds, as well as with those who describe themselves as "just plain Americans."

There are important reasons for investigating the lives of white ethnics as they are played out in the larger, public world— particularly how they react to schools, work and politics. As we know from Parts I and II, both ethnic background and upbringing permeate the identities of millions of Americans, and each ethnic carries them along in some way into the larger world. This is especially true in school and at work, areas where both white ethnic youths and adults spend most of their day.

The persistence of ethnicity in public life is further indicated by traditional concentrations of specific ethnic groups within each of these three public areas. Jewish school teachers, Italian construction workers, Greek restaurateurs, Irish priests and politicians may now be thought of as stereotypes from the past, but there is evidence that such concentrations are not disappearing as rapidly as is commonly believed.*

The most important reason for looking at the lives of white ethnics within these secondary institutions is to try and understand the complex interrelationships which exist between ethnic identity and socio-economic status. As has been noted before, there is a convergence of statuses for many Americans in the white ethnic and working class populations. This melding of statuses holds several important questions underlying the contributions to this section. When are ethnic identities put aside for alliances on larger socio-economic issues? When is ethnic identity more supportive or divisive in bringing about effective coalitions on working class agendas?

For these and other reasons it is important to provide the reader with some examples of the ways in which white ethnics interact within selected secondary institutions, starting with the efforts of schools to "Americanize" white ethnic children, and

---

* For studies of ethnic concentrations in such occupations see "Characteristics of the Population by Ethnic Origin," U.S. Bureau of the Census, Washington, D.C.: Government Printing Office, 1970.

ending with analyses of the white ethnic factor in contemporary politics.

As Richard Gambino and Paul Wrobel pointed out in the previous section, schooling confronts white ethnic youths with their first conflict of value systems. For most of these students "Americanization" is the most important part of the curriculum; any efforts to identify with a particular set of ethnic values is either ignored or disparaged as having no value in the context of the larger American society.*

Leonard Covello's contribution, "Accommodation and the Elementary School Experience," details the students' situation when there is little fit between the values taught at home and those learned in school. His seminal work chronicles the plight of the first native born generations of Italian-Americans—now largely the older and parental generations—as they experienced sharply discordant conflicts between their family-rooted ethnic values and those proffered by the schools. While the effects of this conflict were more drastic in earlier generations, Covello's study can be applied usefully to the experiences of third and fourth generation youths in school today. Though now the degree of cultural differences is obviously lessened, white ethnic students are still open to the harmful effects which follow when they are compelled to deny their own backgrounds. Witness Paul Wrobel's recent comments on teaching seventh graders in a Polish neighborhood in Detroit:

I asked my students whether they noticed anything about the names of individual characters in their readers. "Sure," one of the girls responded, "none of them are Polish." I asked her why she thought this was the case. "Simple," she said, "if they had Polish names everybody would laugh."

Most text books continue to purvey stereotyped images and life styles of the successful, suburbanized, white middle class family. To date, there have been few attempts to reflect the diverse cultures and values of white ethnic Americans in most school materials.

A white ethnic child entering school quickly becomes aware of the existence of dual value systems—one that is learned within a particular ethnic context and another that holds the larger values of the dominant society. Unfortunately, these dual systems are not interpreted for the child as being of mutual value. On the contrary, the school fulfills its role as an acculturating in-

---

* There are some instances where schools have a closer fit with the white ethnic communities they serve; this usually occurs when they are staffed with personnel of similar ethnic background, or others sensitive to ethnic values.

stitution by denigrating the more conspicuous manifestations of ethnicity in the student population. In Covello's words, ". . . the school instills (in students), not as a complementary, but as an exclusive attribute, the 'broader loyalty' of allegiance to the flag, to the nation."

In "The Schools of Whitetown" Peter Binzen shows that another pervasive source of discontent with schools in many white ethnic communities is the belief that black and spanish speaking minorities receive preferential treatment in the allocation of government funds for educational purposes at all levels. Throughout the 1960's this belief was substantiated by numerous statements from Washington. For example, Harold Howe, a former U.S. Educational Commissioner, said in 1968 that "for the next generation or so I believe we must tip the educational scales in favor of our minority youngsters and commit a major share of our resources to providing superior educational programs for them." Whether or not this belief was actually realized in federal policy is probably less important than the fact that white ethnics think that tax dollars and bureaucratic concern are lavished on black and spanish speaking minorities while their needs are callously ignored.

Likewise, as colleges have vied for student minority enrollments, resentment has increased among white ethnics. No one, it appears, pursues their children so arduously, nor offers them so much financial assistance. The obvious implication is that white ethnics are better off economically, and are better able to pay for their children's college attendance. "Being better off," of course, is relative, for as we will see, most white ethnics have incomes that barely meet basic family needs and leave little room for such extras as college tuition.

The work lives of most white ethnics are also a source of increasing discontent. Statistically, as Perry Weed and Gus Tyler demonstrate, there is a convergence of statuses for many in the white ethnic and working class populations as a whole. Hence, descriptions of the economic situation of the working class in the article by Gus Tyler, while not exclusively about white ethnics, necessarily touch the lives of many white ethnic workers.

Tyler enlarges the commonly used job classification of blue collar worker by including clerical, sales and service personnel, thus arriving at the larger category of working class used throughout this section. A brief look at the data offered by Tyler, Weed and the Bureau of Labor Statistics reveals that affluence is not a condition enjoyed by most working class families. Many of them hover around what the Bureau conveniently describes as a "modest but adequate" income. Not surprisingly, there are times

*when the median family income for this population drops below
even this barely adequate level.*

*Until recently most working class people were content to
work for improved economic status and better job security
through the conventional methods of unionization and strikes.
In recent years, however, many white workers have revealed new
and deeply rooted sources of discontent that are related, Tyler
claims, to the social upheavals of the 1960s. In particular the
acute inflationary pressures generated by the Vietnam War—and
further inflamed by the energy crisis—steadily diminished past
gains in real income. Quite suddenly it became apparent to many
working class families that their living standards were not likely
to increase, that they would actually experience a decline in pur-
chasing power in the coming years.*

*Throughout the late 1960s many white ethnics became in-
creasingly suspect of both the poor of the "welfare culture" and
the affluent middle class youths and their professors of the "counter culture." The former, many of whom are black and Spanish-
speaking, were resented because they supposedly benefited from
such programs as the "war on poverty." White ethnics saw these
programs as an additional tax burden with little direct benefit to
themselves. Likewise, the youth of the "counter culture," with
their outspoken contempt for traditional familial, sexual and religious values, and their scorn for social and economic mobility,
were resented because they rejected practically everything white
ethnics prized. To all of this was added the personal tragedy of
those working class families whose sons were called to serve and
die in Vietnam, while the sons of the more affluent avoided service through educational or occupational deferments.*

*Increasingly, Tyler argues, these open hostilities between
many groups in America encouraged each of them to proclaim
their differences from the dominant culture and express their
willingness to stand alone against all "others." If in the past
ethnicity was muted in public life, now the white worker turned
to his ethnic group for reaffirmation. "Now," Tyler asserts, "in
a retribalized world, he displays his ethnicity—as a pennant to
carry into battle."*

*If the ethnic content of working class populations and
agendas is not always clearly stated, American political behavior,
on the other hand, has always had an unmistakable ethnic component. In the past, as Raymond Wolfinger's essay on "Ethnic
Political Behavior" persuasively argues, the ethnic factor in
American politics has worked against the development of class
consciousness within ethnic groups. He contends that ". . . ethnic salience tended to make economic and social issues less rele-*

vant in party competition by emphasizing nationality group rather than social class."

In American politics ethnic groups have often been satisfied with attaining "divisible rewards"—i.e., the rewarding of coveted political plums and municipal jobs to individuals who would then represent the whole ethnic group. These "divisible rewards," Wolfinger claims are, in the end, of real value only to the individual involved. Against such individual rewards Wolfinger contrasts political tactics which aim at "indivisible rewards," those which can be shared by members of the entire community: parks, schools, hospitals and better municipal services. Such "indivisible rewards" can only be achieved, however, through coalitions built around broad socio-economic agendas rather than through token gestures made toward individual group members.*

Are there any indications that the frustrations of white working class ethnics are beginning to coalesce into a new brand of politics? At present it would be premature to predict the demise of the two party system of national politics in America in favor of class aligned party affiliations. (George Wallace's campaign in the national election of 1968 was such an incipient threat.) As a key to understanding the changing voting patterns of one white ethnic group in America, the slavic voters, we turn to the concluding article by Mark Levy and Michael Kramer.

Picking up on a theme popularized by the Republicans during the 1968 and 1972 national elections—that white ethnics were shifting to Republican candidates—Levy and Kramer demonstrate that the Slavs have not moved away from the Democratic Party in any significant numbers. What the slavic voter and other white ethnics are beginning to do, however, is to vote more selectively on local issues and candidates. Such selective voting patterns, the authors state, means "the slavic voter can no longer be taken for granted" by either party.

Nor can any other white ethnic group, for that matter. What Wolfinger pointed to as the "divisible rewards" given to individual representatives are no longer enough; the hoped for coalitions around major socio-economic issues appear to be slowly forming among both white ethnic and black communities. To Levy and Kramer, these and other developments suggest that a "pattern of ethnic 'community' could be developing" in American politics.

---

* The building of such intergroup coalitions is a central theme of the concluding section of the book.

the schools

accommodation and the elementary
school experience

Leonard Covello

The rigid tradition of Italian family life and the "confinement" of the young child to a rather narrow communal milieu permits little conflict at early age. To be sure, from birth onward, the child is completely subjected to conditions as they exist within an Italo-American community, which to him is neither oppressive nor unusual. He is aware that there are "strangers," other nationalities, Americans, but he is affected scarcely at all by this since his play group consists almost wholly of children of his own kind. All his social contacts are limited to his relatives who frequently live next door or in the same city block. No cultural problem exists for the child of pre-school age. Differences between culture patterns of the child and the patterns of the outer groups do not directly affect him, since all his childhood activities are limited to his own group. It is when the child enters school that this period of more or less satisfactory adjustment is brought abruptly to an end.

There, to his bewilderment, he finds his home and the main aspects of his life under criticism from the teachers in the school, and, even after school hours, from other institutions with which he comes

Covello, Leonard. The Social Background of the Italo-American School Child: A Study of the Southern Italian Family Mores and their Effect on the School Situation in Italy and America. Edited and with an Introduction by Francesco Cordasco. Leiden, Netherlands; E. J. Brill, 1967; Totowa, N.J.: Rowman and Little-field, 1972. Copyright, 1967, 1972, Francesco Cordasco. Reprinted by permission of F. Cordasco.

in contact through his school membership. Whereas before, the child has been involved in disagreements of greater or lesser intensity with members of his family over matters of conduct, he finds that there is a significant difference between the type of criticism which he received at home, and the kind he now receives in the school. At home the criticism which he received was of a personal nature: for those violations of conduct set down for him by his family, i.e., his parents and his relatives, and also by some of the neighbors. At home he is punished for failure to obey definite orders or for his laxity in observing commonly accepted or practiced habits. His offenses at home lie in his own conduct and its failure to conform to standards made clear to him, and which he understands. Whereas at home he is censured, this censure is no greater than a child of any other group receives. And he is censured for very much the same things. He is scolded, for instance, for refusing to eat what is distasteful to him, not because he protests against the "foreignness" of the food but for the same reason that another child will refuse to eat oatmeal or spinach. He may be scolded for his failure to go to bed on time; but not because his bed-time is later than that of children of a different environment.

Although his specific problems at home may be different from those of a child of another nationality, they are distinctly in the nature of universal childhood problems, and involve nothing but his adjustment and his adherence to the requirements of a home. His home life, however, is based upon a concept of conduct and customs which paves the way for difficulties which the child will experience at school. For in the school the child is frequently subjected to criticism not for his misdemeanors but because he acts as he has been taught to act at home. The social world in which he has been trained is condemned by the new world into which he has moved.

In the school the child finds, *with practically no warning and no preparation,* that many things which are taken for granted as the proper procedure in his home and in the immediate environment of his home are undesirable in the school or even forbidden. He becomes acquainted with ideas that are strange and incomprehensible to him. The world to which he renders sincere allegiance—his family—is shown to him to be a source of grossly improper conduct. The methods of keeping house, feeding of children, clothing that the parents provide are pointed out unfavorably. The teacher makes it clear to the child that it is not sufficient for him to "take a bath twice a month, whether he needs it or not"; the mother comes in for a great deal of criticism for allowing as a lunch meal a sandwich of gargantuan proportions, instead of a "balanced repast."

In the school he is made to feel that his family is discouragingly ignorant and is, because of its mode of life, actually unpatriotic. The child is not merely told that the ways of the school are highly prefer-

able, but he is censured if he fails to follow the suggestions, regardless
of whether they conflict with the patterns at home. Without being
aware of the fundamental significance of the child's intense loyalty to
his family, the school instills in him, not as a complementary, but as an
exclusive attribute, the "broader loyalty" of allegiance to the flag, to
the nation. He is pressed with reiterations of his obligations to the
society at large, not necessarily in terms of army service alone.

The co-existence of two worlds requires for the child some adjustment. On the one hand, the world represented by the school has an
appeal for him because it invites him to identify himself with America.
As the school reflects the American feeling of superiority, he is assured
that no greater fortune could befall him than that of becoming an
American,[1] for otherwise one is ridiculed, even excluded from the
highly desirable service to one's country. And is he not born in America and therefore entitled to the prestige of being an American? He
speaks English, a language which sounds much more authoritative
than Italian which is useful only while talking to parents and relatives
or to purchase food from the Italian store-keeper around the corner.
On the other hand, there is the family in which everything is in its
proper place. No confusion, no misunderstanding, there. And the food
is not at all as bad as the teacher says. And it is quite all right to hit a
girl because boys are better than girls, anyway.

Thus the child finds himself in two cultural worlds, and friction
is unavoidable if he is compelled to participate in both cultures. He is
not happy in either of them; for at home he is constantly reprimanded
for adopting American manners, tastes, and conduct unbecoming a
buon educato Italian child. Parents and relatives begin to call him
Americano, giving the word a coloring of reproach which does not
escape the child's perception. The child senses the parental hostility
toward almost all categories of knowledge that the child acquires at
school, and feels keenly the difference between the two worlds. Pro-
nouncements by the teacher, severe as they may be, find a fertile field,
for the child begins to realize the impediment of adhering to parental
customs if one wishes to become American. Conflict is rife, and the psychological makeup of the child leads to the necessity to make adjustments. But whereas the older members of the family may find solace in
the Italian community or in the old-world tradition, the child is compelled to make the adjustment within himself.

The cultural duality in which the child lives has a definite effect
upon his personality makeup, much more so since it applies also to the
immigrant parents who, needless to say, are also living in two worlds.
The difference is, of course, a marked one, since the child, as has been
said before, reacts to two cultures while his parent reacts to only one.

1. Ida L. Hull, Report of the *National Conference of Social Work,* 1924, pp.
288–289.

The immigrant parent has, at all times, the possibility of finding adjustment within a familiar tradition. Lyons states, "The immigrant may become disgusted with conditions and withdraw into his own colony and remain essentially unchanged, but a deeper, more harrowing struggle awaits the child of alien parents born into an alien home in America." [2] Whether it is a harrowing struggle or not, no objective information is available to demonstrate the truth of this statement for the child of Italian parentage.

There is no doubt, however, that in the presence of two cultural backgrounds the children of Italian parents are beset by the experience of having to "oscillate between two worlds, concealing many things from their parents by using one set of behavior patterns in their home and another outside. . . . They are in two culture worlds and conflicts inevitably arise." [3] Indeed, the fact of their having been born in America, their indoctrination at school with the inferiority of the parental culture, their lesser loyalty to the old Italian customs and traditions than is held by their parents, their greater contact with things American—all these make it difficult for them to repeat the way in which their parents once sought solace by taking refuge in their Italian community. At school, at play, on the streets, in the movies, or through reading the newspapers and magazines, they are forced to witness and experience a way of life which is different from that of their parents. Oscillating between the parental demands for loyalty to the old-world traditions and his own desire to enter more fully into associations and practices of the larger American community, the child of Italian parents, and particularly the elementary school child, is without doubt adversely affected in his cultural orientation, in his social development, and therefore in his personality.

SENSE OF INFERIORITY DERIVED FROM THE ELEMENTARY SCHOOL EXPERIENCE

An outstanding trait of the Italo-American school child is the feeling of inferiority which he experiences in his dealing and contacts with the American world. The comparative ease and frequency with which this sense of inferiority is observable among elementary school children supports the belief that though the school may not necessarily provide the inception of this feeling, it (i.e., the school), greatly stimulates its growth and the quest on the part of children for overcompensation. This investigator has collected a substantial volume of documentary evidence to this effect. For instance, the following statements made by college students:

2. Eugene Lyons, "Second Generation Aliens," *The Nation*, Volume 16, 1923, pp. 400–401.

3. Hannibal C. Duncan, *Immigration and Assimilation*, p. 645.

The area in which I lived was an Italian community known as "Goat Hill" for the many goats that could be seen grazing. In elementary school I distinctly felt the dislike of the teachers and other pupils of any student who lived on "Goat Hill". . .

And I remember my embarrassment at the need to admit that I was one of them. All non-Italian boys appeared to me as superior creatures. And though I was born in America and spoke English as any normal American boy, I was greatly thrilled when a non-Italian boy would invite me to play . . . When other boys once treated me to a piece of candy my happiness lasted for several days.

(J.G.-NYU-1940)

Others state:

Our school, as I recall it, "solved" the problem of the Italian group which characterized our neighborhood by ignoring the subject. To be Italian was virtually a *faux pas* and the genteel American ladies who were our teachers were tactful enough to overlook our error. As a result, I can remember a feeling of shame; the same which the neighborhood children felt toward their parents and their ways of life.

(B.F.-NYU-1941)

The school . . . never suggested respect for my parents and for the cultural tradition which they unconsciously would use to guide themselves in bringing me up. In fact, it did just the opposite. It made me hesitate to mention my parents' fatherland, as though it were a most unfavorable characteristic about my family history.

(C.L.T.-NYU-1941)

The time that I felt miserable in school was during my elementary period. In elementary school I was often ridiculed for the clothes I wore till I began to believe myself that the dresses of other girls in school were by all means more proper than mine . . . The difficult thing was to convince my mother and since I knew there would be no way to make a change I suffered quietly and envied those boys and girls who were fortunate in not having Italian parents.

(A.V.-NYU-1941)

A social worker's report reads:

B.C. told me that he was never happy in public school because he felt inferior to non-Italian boys. Other Italian boys in his class felt the same way. Though most of the Italian boys, B.C. told me, were husky fellows and could fight anyone, they meekly submitted themselves to pummeling by non-Italian kids . . . B.C. told me that they were awed by anything that was American.

(D.M.-NYU-1940)

Shame of parents' background, superiority of American habits, an aura of "goodness" of everything American are disclosed in a long series of documents. The existence of this trait has been recently verified also by Tait[4] who utilized a questionnaire technique with Italian school children between the ages of eleven to fifteen. A sense of inferiority appears to coincide also with an awareness on the part of Italian school children of being rejected by the American children.[5] Thus the sense of inferiority seems to be nurtured by the high prestige of American norms (as a result of school influence), and also by awareness of the disrepute into which the non-Italian group places the parental background of the Italian children.

REJECTION OF THE FAMILIAL CULTURE
AT ELEMENTARY SCHOOL AGE LEVEL

The conflict in which the Italian child finds himself demands an adjustment, an accommodation which, because of the subordinate social position of the school child within the parental home, must be essentially a vicarious process; that is, to live in a make-believe world. The boy who suffers because of being a resident of the "Goat Hill" community cannot change his domicile; the girl who is ashamed of her clothes cannot easily induce the mother to substitute the apparel for a proper dress. Inflections of speech, the name, and so forth, cannot be removed. The only way to resolve the conflict is for the Italian child to develop a negative attitude toward the parental culture and, vicariously at least, cease to identify himself with it. Thus rejection of the parental culture at elementary school age level is a common phenomenon, attested also by Tait.[6]

Sensing the low prestige of his culture group and the weakening of his personal prestige by identification with his group, the Italian child suppresses all overt manifestation of his identification with the Italian community, the cultural background of his parents, and so on. He professes not to understand Italian, although he speaks it at home; in his play group he conceals certain disciplinary patterns of the home. He conceals his name, his home address, and almost anything that may be associated with his Italian origin. For example:

> Lunch at elementary school was a difficult problem for me. To have a bite I either stole some money from home or took it from my shoe shining on Saturdays and Sundays. With this money I would buy the same stuff that non-Italian boys were eating. To be sure, my mother gave me each day an Italian sandwich, that is half a loaf of French bread filled with fried peppers and onions, or with one half dipped into oil and some minced garlic on it. Such a sandwich would certainly

4. Joseph Wilfred Tait, *Some Aspects of the Effect of the Dominant American Culture upon Children of Italian Parentage,* Bureau of Publications, Teachers College, Columbia University, 1942.

5. *Ibid.,* p. 33.

6. *Ibid.,* p. 34.

ruin my reputation; I could not take it to school . . . My God, what a problem it was to dispose of it, for I was taught never to throw away bread, which I still think is a very nice custom.

(B.V.-H.S.-124)

The rejection of the parental culture becomes operative wherever the child's identification with his group causes him discomfort and stigmatizes his semblance of prestige within the American milieu. It is practiced primarily in school since this is the child's main area of contact with the American world. This rejection of his traditional culture is carried to the threshold of the parental home.

In my early years . . . we were highly critical if not disrespectful of the many traditions that the old folks wanted us to live up to and conform to. We were tired of hearing about how good the old town in Italy was. Many of my Italian friends would say, "They have lived their own lives in their own way. We want to live our lives in our own way and not be tied down to fantastic customs that appear ridiculous not only to us but particularly to our 'American' friends." And I can assure you we were particularly keen about that ridicule. In fact so much so that we never invited our "American" friends to our home. And while "American" boys took their parents to some of the school functions, we not only did not take our parents but never even told them they were taking place. That was *our* life—exclusively ours and that of the other boys. The deadline was the threshold of the door of the house or the tenement in which we lived. Beyond that the older folks went their way and we went ours.

(L.C.-E.H.)

The forms which this rejection take on within the parental home are less drastic or violent, however, than is commonly assumed to be the case. Of course, there are many families where the children have openly rebelled and broken away from the rigid traditional patterns, and even at elementary school age have chosen to "live their own lives." Such rebellions are primarily manifestations of a process of individualization; and since they involve personal relationships within the family, the conflicts within the home become acute, and the emotional disturbances both on the part of the parents and the child are accompanied by the inability of the parent to keep the child within the tradition of the home, and, so to speak, lead to the decline of parental control.

In general, however, the rebellious attitudes of the children do not seem to be observable. Of course, it may be argued that the very inclusive character of family life among the former *contadini* permits little opportunity for the actual conflicts to become known to outsiders; that the family tradition is rigid in keeping all family tribulations a concern only of the family members—a characteristic which has been accepted even by the American-born children. Therefore, one may argue that the conflicts are merely suppressed and are unknown to the investigator. But even so, such reasoning postulates a definite adherence of the children to the parental patterns of family life. If this investigator, therefore, was unable to observe acute conflicts within the home as a common phenomena, it was not because of his inability to penetrate the sphere of intimacy of Italian family life, but because they are, at least as is relevant to the large Italo-American communities, not as frequent as one would expect them to be.

The possibility that under the impact of two cultures the Italian child does not experience greater conflicts than do actually occur is due to the strong allegiance of the child to the familial tradition. His adaptability to two sets of cultural patterns—if his present-day normal behavior at elementary school is a criterion—derives from his basic gravitation toward the familial patterns. In the first place, the structural relationships of the Italian family do not emphasize the position of the father, or the mother, or any other authoritative member of the family as personalities but as persons who merely play a certain role, exercising certain power, certain privileges. So in the matter of parental control, it is actually not the parents *per se* who control the children but that abstract force which is known as the familial tradition. The inculcation of the children with such a concept of the tradition brings about a situation where the child may "reject" the "parental culture" without, however, impairing the relationships between the parents and himself. As an illustration of this can be cited a typical statement by a college student:

> At elementary school I was thrilled with everything that was taught about America; its history, geography, and what it stands for. It was very pleasant to hear about it. But when I came home in the afternoon, I felt a painful contrast between what I saw at home and what had been taught during the day. The teacher had said, for instance, that clean hands, clean clothing, and a toothbrush are essentials. And that plenty of milk should be taken in the morning. I felt so ashamed, so inferior, when I realized that my parents do not exemplify such things at home . . . My mother showed even opposition to the teacher's recommendation about food. She began ridiculing all my teachers for their ideas, and this made me very sad, for she ruined my dreams of becoming a real American.
>
> I felt that I needed milk in the morning more than anything else. But my mother, and so my father, insisted that this was not according to the good customs; that American milk was poison. "These teachers of yours are driving us crazy," they told me. I realized that everything I learned at school was met by my parents with disapproval. So I did not bring up such things any more for I did not wish to be accused of being a disobedient son and cause trouble between myself and my other relatives. The family came first, and, besides, I knew that my parents were not the only ones who had a say in these matters . . .

I loathed the Italian customs with all my heart but I would never let anything stand between me and our family . . . I managed to become American without upsetting the peace of the family. Even the lack of milk at breakfast was taken by me as a sacrifice to the good relationships between me and the family.

(D. diB.-By.-114)

Doubt as to the validity of the above statement may arise because of its retrospective character. However, the statement contains a significant indication as to the distinction between "Italian customs" and the integrity of one's own family. Indeed, there is a great deal of evidence to the fact that a child may loathe Italian customs while at the same time preserving his allegiance to the familial patterns and thus remaining under the control of the parents.

Another element which permits a "rejection" of the parental background without defiance against parents and the family tradition —except in isolated cases—is the particular area of cultural values within which rejection of Italian and the acceptance of American patterns occur. The impact of the American culture complex upon the Italian child in the elementary school—and also through the movies, through newspapers or the radio—involves only its most overt manifestations. The greatness of America, in terms of space and wealth, American architecture, housing, business, sports, compulsory education, American food, political system, slang, inventions, sanitation, etc., is within the comprehension of the school child. These are what sociologists have denoted as elements of *public culture,* as distinct from *private culture* which embraces the sentiments of the American tradition as, for example, the American family pattern which is not accessible to the Italian children of the big cities. As the school, and other educational sources, provide no contact with the latter aspect of the American culture, the stimulation toward rejecting the parental background is based mainly upon the perception of elements of the American *public culture* against which the corresponding values within the Italian milieu are appraised and subsequently debased. Italian children therefore reject the primitive tools within the household, the illiteracy of their parents, un-American dress, Italian food, the Italian language, probably even parental antagonism toward the school, without involving the moral aspects of their Italian tradition. Because of this it is possible for the child to "loathe Italian customs" and at the same time to practice the custom of strict obedience to parents and those acting in *loco parentis.*

Whereas the conflict between the parental home and the child involves primarily the rejection of the material and the open manifestation of the parental culture, while at the same time there is, relatively speaking, harmony in relation to the moral concepts of family life, the conflict necessarily leads to an adjustment in the form of an accommodation. That is, the relationships between the child and the American world are so organized that, in spite of a continuous conflict, a measure of prestige or recognition amidst the American milieu can be achieved. Thus the child accommodates by rejecting the parental background in any situation in which he otherwise would feel unhappy, inferior, unaccepted. In the home there is no need for accommodation; he therefore can behave in the traditional manner. So a boy who is ashamed of eating an Italian sandwich at school will delight in any Italian food his mother offers him. A girl who at school denies her ability to speak Italian finds no difficulty and uneasiness in doing so at home. Of course, it must be realized that within the home or within the Italian community the child does not sense the same degree of inferiority that he does on the outside. In school, however, rejection seems imperative.

> . . . our teachers made us feel that we came from a different world. We felt the same toward them. We watched them as they came to school in the morning from "somewhere" outside, from what was to us a different world—the women teachers surely from a different world . . . We never got close to our teachers. We felt that they were perfect and come from a perfect world . . .
>
> Boys would change their first names invariably and sometimes would attempt even to "Americanize" their last names. They would be tickled at the opportunity to make friends with "American" boys . . . To us all those who were not Italian were Americans. Boys denied their ability to speak Italian or the dialect . . . They usually said that their parents came from Rome . . .
>
> Consistent attempts to hide our identity were made when we were in the school or out of the immediate Italian community. It was usually in the school that we were trying to hide our real identity. We seldom took our home prepared lunch to school, although we much prefered Italian bread and Italian food. We were ever on the alert not to do the wrong thing—which meant doing things the Italian way. By the time I got to high school much of the glamour of the teachers had disappeared.
>
> (L.C.-E.H.)

The degree of rejection of parental culture, as the means of accommodation, and the conflict which accompanies it within the home is determined largely by the ethnic components of the school population and also by the homogeneity of the Italian community in which the child spends most of his time. For obviously as the sense of inferiority so the rejection is stimulated where the contrasts between the Italian child and the other groups are brought into sharpest focus. That is, a single Italian child in a classroom composed of non-Italians must inevitably experience a greater sense of inferiority and an urge to deny his cultural patrimony than if, say, 50 per cent of the children are of Italian origin. A common statement regarding this type of experience is taken from a life history.[7]

> My carefree days vanished when I entered another school. As soon as I entered this school where there were few Italian kids, I got the idea that I was not as good as other people. I felt very inferior to the other fellows—I was afraid to get up and speak in class and consequently it showed its effect on my work, and I was on the verge of quitting school.
> (L.H. 32-A39)

Another statement describes an experience in an opposite situation:

> When my parents moved to East Harlem and I was transferred to public school, I sighed with relief. I don't think there were any other kids but Italians. It made me feel at home. What a difference! In the old school I was nervous from nine o'clock in the morning until three or so in the afternoon. I never spoke right, I did not walk correctly; my tie was atrocious; my mother did not take good care of me. And so it went.
> In this school even the teachers were nicer; at least they didn't pester us with obeying traffic rules and what not. Even the cop in front of the school was an Italian . . .
> Though I must admit that here in East Harlem I lost interest in school. Everybody around me (I was thirteen then) spoke of nothing but making dough. Well I think I did more work for money than school work.
> (Excerpt from L.H. 32-A39)

The determining factor in this situation is whether or not the school population is representative of the physical and geographical environment of the child. For in a large, homogeneous Italo-American community in New York City, an elementary or junior high school population composed of over 90 per cent of Italian children is a normal occurrence. In such a situation the child's need for accommodation must obviously be at a minimum for neither the sense of inferiority nor the urge to reject the parental folkways are greatly stimulated. Tait supports this observation, suggesting "that the more Italian children come into contact with native American children[8] the more they experience a feeling of inferiority." [9] The feeling of inferiority seems to coincide with a strong showing of disfavor by American school children toward the Italian foreign background. And the unfavorable attitude toward their own background appears to make for a higher degree of inferiority feeling when there are increased contacts with native American

---

7. The writer is indebted for the availability of several life histories from a Motion Picture Study of New York University by Dr. Frederic M. Thrasher and Dr. Paul G. Cressey.

8. Defined by Tait as those whose parents and grand-parents were born in the United States.

9. Tait, *op. cit.*, p. 31.

children.[10] Of course, no community is fully isolated from contact with the American world. A certain degree of inferiority feeling and rejection are always present. Yet the fact remains that the probability of a cultural conflict within the home is least when the child attends a school with a high percentage of Italian pupils and comes home to a community composed of Italo-Americans. Whereas increasing contacts of Italian children with American children make for a greater degree of emotional instability, they become somewhat more stable emotionally the less they associate with native American children.[11]

EDUCATIONAL IMPLICATIONS OF CULTURE REJECTION

The difference between a child from a homogeneous Italian community attending a preponderantly "Italian" school and a child from a less "Italian" environment attending a school with an "American" school population must therefore produce a difference in school behavior and attitude toward schooling. In the latter situation, the tendency to reject the parental tradition is greater and the urge to identify himself with the American world is stronger than would be expected in the former situation. And this undoubtedly gives impetus to more normal school attendance, greater desire to participate in various extracurricular activities. The "leniency" of the Italian parent toward the elementary school, because of his having accepted a longer childhood span, is being augmented by the child's urge to imitate the behavior of American children. Although a greater degree of rejection is followed by greater probability of a conflict within the home, it does not follow that this conflict impairs the child's attitude toward the school. Rather the contrary, for the school appeals to him as an escape medium from the conflict at home. For example, the school has great appeal because of the recreational opportunities it offers Italian children. Italian boys and girls of the lower elementary school age are eager for school because it offers them a release from repressions within the parental home. The school provides the girl with the only chance to indulge in locomotory play which is denied her at home. Likewise, a boy can play at school more than is permitted by the parents.

Though the appeal of the school does not necessarily imply the child's liking for schooling, it makes it possible for him to undergo a greater degree of acculturation than would be the case of a child whose environment and school milieu induce little rejection of the parental background. The effect of the former situation upon the child is that he has the opportunity to observe how non-Italian adults and children talk and act, whereas he may not have had this opportunity except at a distance. The effect of the school is to induce him

10. Tait, *op. cit.*, p. 32.
11. *Ibid.*, p. 51.

to take part in many social situations where rewards and punishments are administered by persons who are American in background and whose behavior is frequently determined by a deliberate policy of encouraging him to act like an American. At the same time, adoption of American traits and expression of allegiance to American ideals are rewarded by approval on the part of the teachers and by specific acts of friendship on the part of the (non-Italian) classmates and are thus reinforced.[12]

The possibility of the child's becoming alienated from his parental home is, under such conditions, of course, present. But the rigidity of the Italian family life and the child's acceptance of the moral elements of the home tradition counteract this influence and prevent conflict between the child and the parent from becoming acute.

Different is the situation in an Italian community like East Harlem. Here the child's attitude toward the school is determined almost exclusively by the attitudes of the parents. The parental "tolerance" of elementary school education is augmented but very little by the appeal that the school makes to the child. A minimum of a sense of inferiority—at least at this age level—leads to no appreciable rejection of the parental tradition, and the process of schooling is, in the main, what the parents and the community wish it to be. The allegiance to the family tradition is the primary interest of the parent, and all schooling is considered by both parents and children in the light of this tradition. Whatever appeal the school may have to the child is negated by the force of this tradition.

12. Child, *op. cit.*, p. 40.

the schools of whitetown

Peter Binzen

Any attempt to help the "stepchildren" of Whitetown should start
with their schools. For in our increasingly complex and technological
society education is the passport to progress. As the Transit Ads say:
HA-HA (*Think school is a laugh? See how funny it is when you can't
get a good-paying job.*)

To be sure, the implications of this nation-wide, hell-for-leather
obsession are frightening. There's no blinking the fact, however, that
to get ahead these days young people must put in the requisite years
in school and college. In other words, one advances by degrees—bache-
lor's degrees, master's degrees, doctor's degrees. Black America generally understands this. In most of the big cities, black communities now
are pressing hard to improve ghetto schools and to gain a greater voice
—a controlling voice, if possible—over school supervision and management. In this effort, they often are receiving strong support from white-
liberal intellectuals.

White towners see what is happening. To them it is nothing less
than a conspiracy to rob them of the schools they have always known
and still want. In changing times, the White towners oppose change. In
their thinking about education, they tend to reflect what Margaret
Mead, in *The School in American Culture*, termed the "Little Red
Schoolhouse Ideal." Theirs is a "beloved image" of "the school in a
world which did not change." They look back to a "past golden age
which has been lost" (and which was never really golden but only
seems so now with the passage of time). Embedded in the "Ideal,"
wrote Miss Mead, is the notion: "What was good enough for me is
good enough for my children." And at a school meeting in Philadel-

"The Schools of Whitetown." From Peter Binzen. "The Schools of Whitetown
Then and Now;" *Whitetown, USA* (New York: Random House, Inc.). Reprinted
by permission of Random House, Inc.

phia one night I heard a hard-core Whitetowner utter those very words.

The Whitetowners' suspicions about present-day school policies are understandable if not justifiable. In fact, public schools have become instruments of social change, levers to help bring black America into the "mainstream." The role of schools as agents of change is new —and it is threatening to ethnic groups still struggling to "make it" in America. When the Whitetowners' immigrant forebears were flocking to this country, the schools served as social controls. Certainly there was no thought of turning the schools over to the immigrants.

Their children entered classrooms in strange clothes, with alien interests and foreign tongues, and came out speaking English, playing baseball, wearing knickers, eating ice cream—and often detesting their parents' peculiar ways of speaking and living. The schools thus transmitted the values and styles of older Americans (Protestants) and made the new arrivals (largely Catholics and Jews) conform. Sociologically, the schools' job was to perpetuate the *status quo* and to keep peace in the urban ghettos, which were then predominantly white.

In the process, the middle-class white school systems often were just about as callous and cruel to lower-class white children as these same systems are accused of being to black children today. . . .

Having survived discrimination themselves, today's Whiteowners can't understand what all the current shouting is about. They are appalled that black students wear dashikis, calls themselves Afro-Americans, and insist on attending courses in black-African history. They forget that the Irish, who once considered themselves a mystical breed apart, held "race conventions" of their own and in this century (1903) petitioned for the teaching of Irish history in New York schools. More important, though, has been the failure of Whitetowners, indeed of most white Americans, to see that black Americans are not just another ethnic group. Like the Jews, Poles, and Italians, the Negroes have had to confront the disadvantages of underclass immigrants on the urban frontier. But the problem of pigmentation has been paramount. In white America their blackness has made all the difference. On the one hand, they've been taught in school that they've got to conform to get ahead, and on the other hand, they've learned the cruel lesson that because they're black they can't conform. Hence the excruciating dilemma that whites often fail to recognize.

Beyond the fact that many Whitetowners are totally unsympathetic to Negro aims and efforts in education, there are three reasons why the school situation in Whitetown and Blacktown today is so explosive. First, education is vastly more important in this age of electronics, moonshots, instant communications, computerized everything, than at any previous time in history. When the immigrants were tipped out of school at eighth grade in 1910 or 1920, it didn't matter very much because America's relatively crude, unsophisticated economy had jobs for unskilled, undereducated workers. Less so today.

Second, the Negro thrust in education has come at the time of the first really substantial Federal spending on schools. For about a century and a quarter after the schools were started, Washington treated public education as almost exclusively a state and local responsibility. Its only aid went for vocational training. Important Federal assistance began with the National Defense Education Act of 1958 and was greatly expanded with the Elementary and Secondary Education Act of 1965. Through ESEA's Title I alone, a billion dollars a year now goes to schools with concentrations of pupils from low-income families.

The third point is that the Federal government, seeing greater educational needs and deficiencies in Negro areas, wants to put most of its emphasis—and money—there. To the extent that this is being done, it is being done at the expense of Whitetowners whose educational shortcomings are often almost as serious as those of the Blacktowners.

"For the next generation or so," Harold Howe II, then United States Education Commissioner, wrote in the *Harvard Educational Review* in the winter of 1968,

> I believe we must tip the educational scales in favor of our minority youngsters and commit a major share of our resources to providing superior educational programs for them.
>
> In a sense, this is inequality in reverse—an extra loading of the balance in favor of those who for generations have seen the weights on the other end.

One of the difficulties with Howe's "extra loading of the balance" is that the scales, as the examination of nineteenth-century and early twentieth-century schools indicates, have never been heavily tipped in favor of working-class white children. Not historically and not now. In his mammoth, Federally financed study in 1966, *The Equality of Educational Opportunity,* James S. Coleman of Johns Hopkins University found no significant difference in the school facilities currently provided white and nonwhite children in this country. His surprising discovery is often overlooked.

"The [Coleman] study set out to document the fact that for children of minority groups school facilities are sharply unequal and that this inequality is related to student achievement," reported Harvard researchers Susan S. Stodolsky and Gerald Lesser in the *Harvard Educational Review* in the fall of 1967. "The data did not support either conclusion. What small differences in school facilities did exist had little or no discernible relationship to the level of student achievement." *

Coleman decided that schools' physical facilities weren't of major importance in determining school "output"—despite what everybody had thought. The job ahead, as he saw it, was to "overcome the difficulties in starting point of children from different social groups."

But the children of Whitetown haven't been getting much of a head start. Since Sputnik, says Mario Fantini, of the Ford Foundation, improvements in American education have merely "strengthened the *status quo*, enabling the system to serve better those it has always served best." And those it has always served best are the white middle class, now largely in the suburbs.

Certainly, one finds little to cheer about in the schools of Whitetown, U.S.A. Philadelphia's Kensington section is an example. Its schools are old, its classes large. Its dropout rate is very high and its college-going rate is very low. Kensington has more cases of pediculosis —nits and lice—in pupils' hair than any other section of Philadelphia, and a greater proportion of underweight children and children with cavities.

Most significantly, the administrative district comprising Kensington and adjoining black North Philadelphia regularly ranks last among the city's eight districts on all measures of academic promise and achievement, from the Iowa Test of Basic Skills to the California Test of Mental Maturity. Some inner-city districts that are ninety per cent or more Negro produce slightly higher test scores than does Kensington's district. Despite its glaringly obvious deficiencies, Kensington is excluded from such Federal programs as Model Cities. Many of its schools fail to qualify for aid under ESEA. The neighborhoods, though poor, are not quite poor enough.

The Whitetowns of other cities evidence similar inequities. "Boston's poor whites," says Assistant Superintendent of Schools William L. Cannon, "face the same educational deficiencies as the 'soul brothers.' " He sees a "very high correlation" in the test scores of black and white pupils in low-income sections. Says George Thomas, assistant dean of Harvard's Graduate School of Education, "The poor whites in Boston are less well served than the poor blacks. Less money goes into their areas—partly because of Federal directive. The whites are prouder and more quiescent, the blacks more concentrated. Only in rare cases have the whites learned a lesson from the hustling black community. There's more action in [black] Roxbury than in the white areas. In general, Roxbury is much more together."

* Daniel P. Moynihan, President Nixon's Special Assistant for Urban Affairs, thinks Washington sought to conceal this crucial fact from the press and public. Its fifty-two-page summary of the Coleman Report dealt mostly with school segrega-

Charlestown's Harvard School is testimony to what has been permitted to happen in that old section of working-class Caucasians. The school was built in 1871, its outside fire escapes are rusty and its wooden doors creak, it is a certified firetrap. (In an interview, its principal defended the school's continued use on grounds that "schools almost never burn on school time.")

The Harvard School is dimly illuminated. In one room, when I was there, a lone light bulb (it appeared to be sixty watts) dangled from an eight-foot cord that ran from the high ceiling to a point just above the teacher's desk. The building is a rabbit warren of little closets and rooms tucked planlessly here and there off corridors. You encounter the dusty auditorium by surprise on the third story. There is one toilet seat per floor. There is no play yard.

An elevated line linking Charlestown to downtown Boston, five minutes away, rattles nearby. The school sits back from a busy commercial street and heavy trucks trundle past all day long. (The trucks run within six feet of the living room of a Charlestown resident who has an important job in the Boston city government. Like so many Whitetowners, he's proud of the old place and is damned if he will move.)

The principal of Harvard School is responsible also for two other Charlestown elementary schools, one built in 1866 and the other in 1893. All three schools are small, enrolling a total of only about eight hundred children, mostly of French-Canadian, Polish, and Italian descent. In the next few years they are to be replaced by a single new building. The point is, though, that the "morbid, desolate crumbling" school of "rank smells" and pervasive gloom that Jonathan Kozol, in *Death at an Early Age,* found destroying the hearts and minds of Negro children in Boston's Roxbury section, exists in white Charlestown, too.

Some of the oldest schools in Cleveland serve its polyglot West Side. This is a section in advanced stages of decay. It lost four thousand people between 1960 and 1965, now counts twenty-seven thousand, 96.9 per cent of them white. You still see Polish delicatessens, Ukrainian social clubs, and Russian Orthodox churches there. In the last fifteen years, however, many of these ethnic groups have moved to suburbs like Parma (using freeways that slice through their old neighborhoods to get back and forth). In schooling, employment, and family income, the West Side rates under Cleveland city averages.

---

tion and "withheld from all but the *cognoscenti*," says Moynihan, "any suggestions that major and, in effect, heretical findings had appeared." His article appeared in *Harvard Educational Review*'s Winter 1968 issue.

Especially hard hit is the so-called Near West Side, across a smoky, industrial valley from central Cleveland. In this dingy, trash-strewn neighborhood many of Cleveland's estimated fifty thousand Appalachian whites live in urban hillbilly squalor. Despite their poverty, these people, like all Whitetowners, have pride. To them, the public-welfare program is nothing more than a huge black boondoggle. Staying off relief, therefore, becomes a badge of distinction. Stay off they do—and their schools suffer.

"We measure poverty by welfare cases," explains Mrs. Rose Cira, research associate in the Cleveland Board of Education's division of educational research. "Because they lack welfare cases, the Near West Side schools often fail to qualify for Federally financed programs. They are not considered target schools. They don't get the concentration of moneys and services that the [predominantly black] East Side does. There is a discrepancy that we're constantly trying to eliminate."

Another reason why Appalachian whites don't sign up for welfare is that they're often on the move—down to West Virginia and Kentucky, and then back again. They don't stay put long enough to qualify. The result is that their schools have the highest pupil-transiency rates in the entire city. When I visited the Kentucky Elementary School on the Near West Side in June 1968, its pupil turnover stood at 130 per cent—and climbing. The school enrollment was nine hundred but twelve hundred boys and girls had been admitted or transferred out since the previous September.

"No sooner do we get children working to an acceptable pace," complained Mrs. Mary B. Diggs, the principal, "than they're gone. Many of the families still own farms back in the hills or have relatives there. They go 'home' for the spring plowing and we don't see them for six weeks."

Principals and teachers report the Appalachian white youngsters now are falling behind Negro pupils not only in attendance but in effort and achievement. "Negro parents," said Miss Mary Gulmi, principal of the Tremont School, which dates from 1875, "are aware of the importance of education. They take advantage of the opportunities offered them. The poor whites are satisfied with truck-driver jobs paying ninety to a hundred dollars a week. They don't stress education, they don't push, they're not too concerned that their kids aren't doing well. We've made the Negroes conscious of the need for education but not the poor whites. One of these days they're going to be outstripped."

At the one-hundred-fifteen-year-old Hicks Elementary School, teachers said the twenty-five per cent Negro enrollment was, on the whole, more interested, curious and aware than the fifty percent Appalachian-white enrollment. "The Southern whites are ignorant of the help available to them," said one teacher, "or else they refuse it. They want to go back to the hills. They don't talk to teachers as Negroes do —that is, as equals. There is less parental participation among the whites."

"Motivation of family is greater among Negroes," agreed Mrs. Marian B. Harty, a principal who has served in poor-white and poor-black schools. A veteran teacher saw a psychological difference: "When I first came here thirteen years ago," she said, "the Negro was hangdog. Now he'll fight, push, he's very aggressive. It's the Appalachian whites who are insecure. It's hard to motivate them. The best readers are the Negro children. Not that they're brighter; they've just got more drive."

Detroit's Ruddiman Junior High School serves a predominantly Polish neighborhood in the northwestern part of the city near the militantly all-white suburb of Dearborn, where police teach housewives how to shoot guns. Many of Ruddiman's families would like to move to Dearborn but can't afford to. A large public-housing project gives the school its only Negro pupils—about ten percent of the enrollment of almost eleven hundred.

Ruddiman dates from a one-room school built in 1861 that is still standing and is still used. Four additions have been tacked onto it and all are under one roof. The inevitable freeway carries motorists within fifteen yards of Ruddiman's front entrance. For two-thirds of Ruddiman's families incomes range from six to nine thousand dollars a year. The other third are in the three-to-four-thousand-dollar poverty range. Since the school neighborhood ranks just above Detroit's poverty level, Ruddiman doesn't get a dime under Title I of ESEA.

When I visited Ruddiman, its principal, Mrs. Dorothy P. Cooper, a peppery little woman with glasses, an upswept hairdo, and a sense of outrage, was scrounging around for half a dozen spotlights for the school's upcoming fine-arts festival. "If this were a Title I school," she said bitterly, "I could order these lights and have them in a week. But as it is, we'll just have to go without."

Even among Ruddiman whites with the highest family incomes cultural deprivation is acute, although not always obvious, according to the principal. Of the Polish parents, she said:

> Many have enough money but lack the cultural background of selectivity. They are permissive, indulgent, well meaning but poorly advised. They let their children make course decisions, and it's the children themselves in many cases, not their parents, who elect not to take college preparation.
>
> Social life is limited. Many of our children have never been downtown [six miles away]. Shopping centers are their social gathering

places. When they take a summer vacation trip they come back talking about how many miles they covered, how many states they passed through, not what they saw. This is the way people out here think. They visit Disneyland but not the Grand Canyon.

Mrs. Cooper's indictment extends across the board of American society generally. Her point was, however, that although most Ruddiman children aren't poverty-stricken, they still need special programs to lift their sights and their values. The school offers none. There is much racial prejudice in the neighborhood (and one suspects it might exist within the school faculty and administration), but there are no special intergroup education efforts aimed at improving the racial climate at Ruddiman.

Ruddiman is a typical Whitetown case: its constituency is poor but not poor enough. Its problems, while genuine, are hidden. Its people are, in the main, uncomplaining. "They don't ask for anything," said Mrs. Cooper, who seemed both admiring and vexed. "They have pride. This is the one thing these people have. They plug along as best they can. They don't expect help and they don't get any."

At Detroit's school-administration building, Assistant Superintendent Louis D. Monacel recognized the problem. Dr. Monacel directs state-Federal projects for the Detroit schools. "We're not programming Federally for these [white] people," he said. "The criteria are tightly woven to the ghetto."

What this means, he suggested, is that the sons and daughters of white factory workers are probably getting shortchanged. "We assume too much," he said. "We assume that we don't have to counsel them, push them, make sure they take advantage of every opportunity. But without that counseling they drift out of school. I've kind of ignored these people and assumed they were doing fine. They aren't. We've got to take some of the responsibility."

Monacel contrasted the expectations of a young, bright, ambitious black student today with those of a white trade-unionist. "If the Negro has anything he can make it," said Monacel:

Colleges and universities all over America are running for Negroes. They've got to have them. In a way, this is shabby. Where were the colleges ten years ago? But it's also good because Negroes who want to and have ability can get into the best universities.

Meanwhile, the white unionist feels the ground being cut from beneath him, or thinks he does. The one thing he has is job security and the new rules are changing that, too. Detroit is a union town and Detroit schools deliberately close apprentice training classes if they're not racially integrated. It is only right and just that we do this. But think how it affects the white unionist.*

After my visits to the Whitetowns of American big cities, I paid a call on Harold Howe II in his Washington office. It was a hot day in August 1968. The United States Education Commissioner's tie was loose and his half-smoked cigar was unlit. His feet were up on a coffee table, where they remained as we talked.*

About the school concerns of Whitetown, U.S.A., Howe professed to be stumped. "It's a hell of a perplexing thing," he said, "using Federal dollars to bring about social change. This process is bound to cause abrasions. We're living in a very abrasive time and I see no likelihood of a letup."

Howe said there was no question but that the working white American identified by Robert Wood needed help. "But if you have to make a hard choice in deciding who will get Federal education aid," he added, "you're forced back to the zero-to-three-thousand-dollars-level group."

Under Title I of ESEA, the biggest and most comprehensive Federal school-assistance program ever devised, about nine million students in 16,400 school districts have been served. Howe's office had no racial breakdown. He thought that, including all programs in suburban and rural as well as urban areas, more white than nonwhite children were aided but that the proportion of black children served was much higher.

"In any program," Howe said, "you have the problem of the cutting point. It's pretty clear to us that if you disperse funds among a very large number of youngsters, much of the money will just be frittered away without doing much good. We have pressed for concentration. Without much success, I might add. The natural tendency is to give everybody a little, and that's what the school districts have done."

Commissioner Howe favored reducing sharply the number of children served so that more money could be spent—a critical mass, he

* In a letter to the *New York Times*, August 3, 1963, a white unionist offered a classic defense of the apprenticeship system. "Some men," he wrote, "leave their sons money, some large investments, some business connections, and some a profession. I have only one worthwhile thing to give: my trade. I hope to follow a centuries-old tradition and sponsor my sons for an apprenticeship. For this simple father's wish it is said that I discriminate against Negroes. Don't all of us discriminate? Which of us when it comes to a choice will not choose a son over all others? I believe that an apprenticeship in my union is no more a public trust, to be shared by all, than a millionaire's money is a public trust." (Quoted by Robert Wood and others.)

* Howe resigned as Education Commissioner on Dec. 31, 1968.

called it—on fewer pupils. In 1968–1969, the districts averaged $110 per pupil in Title I programs. Howe wanted this raised to maybe $250 per pupil, with no increase in Washington's outlay. "We want to move from our present position of serving nine million children under Title I to a point where we will be serving only six or seven million," he said. "We will deny help to some youngsters but more will get solutions to their problems. The trouble is that at present Title I's billion dollars are spread too thin."

In Howe's view, working-class whites were "really hurting, particularly in terms of expectation. What they tend to do," he said, repeating a point I had heard in several cities, "is deny themselves necessities in order to respond to what they see in magazines and on television. There's an element of tragedy about this."

Black people, said Howe, have historically been denied mobility in American society. The doors now are opening, but Howe did not fear "overcompensation." He considered it inevitable and probably necessary that city school systems should favor black administrators over white ones of comparable training and experience. "Since central-city school systems are full of black children," he said, "there is some sort of vague rationality in having black administrations. If in doing that you awaken feelings of resentment among those who haven't been able to use the mobility always available to whites, I guess what you have to say is, 'That's too bad.'

"That's where the element of tragedy comes in. I don't know what you can do about it."

Reflecting later on what Howe had said and what I had seen and heard in the big-city school systems, I concluded that the failures of urban education—and suburban and rural education, too—can't be blamed on money alone. Perhaps they can't be blamed on money at all. Lack of money didn't cause the basic problem today and a surfeit of funds won't solve it. It's much more complex and more difficult to deal with. Historically, the job of the schools has been to transmit the American culture as a coherent and credible system of values and ideas from generation to generation. As long as the national life style, with all its imperfections, proved generally acceptable to most Americans the schools seemed to do an adequate transmission job.

But what we appear to be witnessing now is a mass rejection of this culture by Americans of all ages. The schools, and especially the colleges, are thus caught in a bind. They can no longer be mere transmission belts because the things they've been transmitting are now widely discredited as shoddy and second-rate. They must therefore seek to improve the culture by reforming the society. Hence their role as social-change agents. But in seeking to perform this function, the schools have managed to alienate everybody. Those favoring social change are convinced the schools, as currently constituted, are doomed to failure if, in fact, they ever really make the effort. These critics point to self-serving educational bureaucrats of narrow vision and social and racial biases—I saw many who fit this general description—as Exhibit A. Such limited people, they say, simply could not effect social change even if they wanted to. And there's some doubt that they want to.

Yet the schools are also distrusted by those opposed to change. They see school reformers seeking, however clumsily, to effect change. And they don't like it. These are the Whitetowners. They are ubiquitous and their number is legion.

work

white workers: blue mood

Gus Tyler

> *"It's us they is always chokin' so that the rich folks can stay fat."*
>
> —*A twenty-eight-year-old Kentucky miner on the "freeze."*
> New York Times, *September 24, 1971*

What are the facts about the American workers—especially white workers? Of the 77.902 million gainfully employed in 1969, 28.237 million wore blue collars; that is, 36 percent. But others might as well have worn that collar. Of the 36.844 million "white-collar" workers, about 18 million were in clerical and sales—an added 22 percent of the employed. In addition, there were another 9.528 million engaged in service trades—a category that earned less than the blue-collar, clerical, or sales people. The total in all these blue and bluish jobs comes to 69 percent of the employed.

Who, besides farm workers, is not included? There is the class listed as professional, technical, managerial, as officials and proprietors, who make up about a quarter of the employed. Despite their lofty titles, millions of these are just plain, worried workers. Consider that Italian "professional" who teaches in Franklin K. Lane High School or that Jewish "proprietor" who owns a candy store in Harlem.

The white worker is currently called "middle American," a description that evokes the image of a man and his family at the center of American affluence. But what is the reality?

The white worker is not affluent—not even near-affluent. The median *family* income in 1968 (pre-Nixon) was $8,632, about $1,000 short of what the Bureau of Labor Statistics calls a "modest but adequate" income. That this median family cannot meet the American standard of living refutes the mischievous myth that poor means black, and white means affluent. The myth is mischievous because it turns an ethnic difference into a class struggle and implies—and sometimes states—that the way to end poverty is simply to end racism. This myth, as that of "the vanishing American worker," is based upon a truth that when exaggerated becomes an untruth.

While it is true that a much higher percentage of nonwhites than whites is officially poor, it is equally true that in 1968 two-thirds of the poor were white. Nor is this white poverty limited to Appalachia.

Our latest report on who is poor (March 1970) reveals that of the 5.047 million U.S. families listed as living in poverty, 1.363 million or 25 percent are black: only one out of four poor families is black. In the

TABLE 1 BREAKDOWN OF EMPLOYED PERSONS AGE 16 AND OVER BY OCCUPATION AND COLOR

(in thousands)	White	Nonwhite
Blue Collar	24,647	3,591
Service	7,289	2,239
Clerical	12,314	1,083
Sales	4,527	166
Professional-Technical	10,074	695
Manager, Officials	7,733	254
Proprietors, Farmers	2,935	356
Total	69,519	8,384

TABLE 2 PERCENTAGE OF THE TOTAL EMPLOYED IN VARIOUS CATEGORIES OF WHITE LABOR

(percent)	White Percentage of Total Employed of All Races
Blue Collar	32
Service	9.3
Clerical	16
Sales	6
Professional-Technical	13
Managers, Officials	10
Proprietors, Farmers	1.7
Total	88

Whites, then, make up 88 percent of the employed; nonwhites 12 percent. Of the whites, the categories that compose the blue-mooded (exclude farmers and include about half of those in the professional, proprietor, etc., category) make up about 75 percent of the employed.

metropolitan areas of America in 1968, there were 2.477 million poor families of which 777,000 were black: less than one-third. In the central cities of these metropoles, there were 748,000 poor families, of which 358,000 were black: less than half.

The poor are not mainly the unemployed. One-third of the family heads listed as officially poor work full weeks at least fifty weeks a year. Others work part years. Most of the poor have jobs—and are white.

While families with incomes under $3,000 are officially poor, those with incomes above $3,000 are not all rich. Twelve percent of the families in America have an income between $3,000 and $5,000. (A recent Labor Department study found that an urban family of four needed at least $5,895 a year to meet its basic needs. If $6,000 a year were used as a cut-off poverty line, then 29.3 percent of the families in America are living in poverty.) A high 52 percent of the families had an income of less than $9,000 a year—a figure still below the official "modest but adequate" income. Seventy-two percent of the families have an income below $12,000 a year—a sum just above what the BLS considers adequate for a family of four in New York City. In round figures, about three out of four families struggle along.

If so many Americans are nonaffluent, who gets the money in this affluent society? Here are some facts on income distribution.

In 1968, the bottom fifth of the nation's families received 5.7 percent of the country's income; the top fifth received 40.6 percent. The middle three-fifths were bunched between 12 and 23 percent. These figures, from the U.S. Department of Commerce publication *Consumer Income* (December 1969), actually understate the great gap between top and bottom. In calculating income the Department of Commerce excludes "money received from the sale of property, such as stocks, bonds, a house, or a car . . . gifts . . . and lump sum inheritances or insurance payments." If these items were included, the income of the top fifth would be appreciably increased—and, by the inclusion of these receipts in the total calculation of income, the percentage of income of the other fifths would be automatically decreased.

Between 1947 and 1968, income shares did not change. The bottom moved from 5 percent to 5.4 percent; the top from 43 percent to 41.2 percent. The change is negligible—and, after allowance for other receipts not counted as income, we find that there has been no meaningful redistribution of income in the quarter-century since the end of World War II.

This iron law of maldistribution applies not only to the nation as a whole but also to the nonwhite families of America, which darkly mirror the class structure of the mother culture. Among nonwhite families in 1968, the lowest fifth got 4.8 percent of the income and the top fifth 43.6 percent; in 1947, the lowest fifth got 4.3 percent and the highest 45.7 percent. In sum, whether we look at white or dark America, in 1947 or 1968, the maldistribution remains almost constant—an economic fact regardless of race, creed, etc.

If, however, the maldistribution of income is an inequity of ancient origin, whose persistence we have noted for this whole century, why is the white worker turning restless at this particular moment? The reasons: (1) a quantitative erosion of income; (2) a qualitative erosion of living; (3) a frightening erosion of social order.

Although not living in affluence, the white worker was better off in the '60s than at any other time of this century. In the recovery years following the Great Depression of the early 1930s, he and his family were enjoying an ever-rising standard of living. In 1947, the median family income (in constant 1968 dollars) was $4,716; by 1967, it rose to $8,318, an increase of about $4,000—after allowing for inflation.

During the same period, the percentage of families making under $7,000 a year decreased and the percentage making more increased sharply—again in constant dollars. In 1947, 75 percent of the families had an income of less than $7,000, and 25 percent had an income above that figure. In 1967, on the contrary, 63 percent of the families had an income above $7,000 and only 36 percent had an income below that figure.

All this was happening, however, without any basic redistribution of income in America. Per capita income was growing because the total national income was growing at a rate faster than that of the population. There was more available for everybody.

The rise in income was reflected in a life-style based on rising expectations. You mortgaged your life for a home, because you expected to earn more in the days to come. You bought on the installment plan, everything from baby carriage to auto. You planned a future for your kids: a nice neighborhood, a good school, a savings plan to put the kids through one of the better colleges—maybe even Harvard or Vassar. You were out to "make it," no matter how hard you worked, how much you scrimped, how often you borrowed, how late you moonlighted. You had hope!

You didn't even mind paying ever-higher taxes, so long as your take-home pay was bigger. The tax was an investment in the future— a town or a country where things would be better. You would enjoy it tomorrow, and the kids would enjoy it for generations. You were future-minded.

As a result, this numerous class became the mass base of social stability in America. It was not status quo-ish in the sense that it would be happy to have its present frozen forever; it was constantly pushing for change. But it sought change within a system that it felt was yielding more and could continue to yield more. And to keep moving, this class joined unions for economic advance and voted Democratic for socio-economic legislation.

Sometime in the mid-60s, however, this social structure began to fall apart. Almost unnoticed by the media was the decline in the real income of the nonsupervisory employee. Between 1965 and 1969, the buying power of the worker was in steady decline—despite sizable wage increases. The pay envelope was being chewed up by inflation and taxation.

The year 1965 was the first of the escalated involvement in Vietnam, and this imposed a triple burden on the American worker. First, he had to pay a greater tax to help finance the war. Second, he had to pay more for consumer goods because this war, like any other, automatically increased demand without increasing supply. Third, he supplied his sons for the military; the affluent found ways to escape in schools and special occupations, the poor were often too ill or illiterate.

The year 1965 is also the mid-point of a decade in which America began to respond to poverty and discrimination. The Johnson years produced a spate of national legislation to provide income and opportunities for the poor, especially the blacks. Local governments were trying to cope with their crises. At all levels, America began to spend public money to resolve pressing problems.

The American worker supported these social measures through the unions and the Democratic party. He saw these bits and pieces of socio-economic legislation as a spur and parallel to his upward effort.

It was not apparent to this same worker that the upside-down system of taxation in the United States placed the cost of these measures on the shoulders of the huge "middle" sector—the sector neither poor nor rich enough to escape taxes. Although the federal income tax supposedly is graduated so as to make the wealthy pay at a higher rate, this expressed intent is annulled by the many loopholes for those who derive income from sources other than wages or salaries. At the local level, it is the small homeowner who pays the tariff through *ad valorem* property taxes and the small consumer who pays through the nose for city, county, and state sales taxes.

The worker feels that he is paying triple: he pays for his own way; he pays for the poor; he pays for the rich. He is ready to do the first; he resists the others.

Finally, this same worker has been squeezed by a system of private taxation, operated through monopoly pricing. Everything from electricity to eggs is manipulated in closed and increasingly enclosed markets. As buying power goes up (current dollars in income), the response of dominant sectors of the economy is not to *increase* supply but to *limit* production (or distribution) to keep the consumer on the same level while increasing profits for the seller.

To add insult to injury, the worker is advised by the media and, more recently, by the administration, that if prices are going up, it is his own fault: high wages make high prices. If he wants to buy for less, he must work for less. This logic boggles the worker who cannot understand how he can live better by earning less. Once more, he is the victim of a myth. The truth was stated in an editorial by the sober *Wall Street Journal* on August 5, 1968:

> In the past 20 years, there have been three distinct periods in which factory prices climbed substantially over a prolonged interval. In each instance, labor costs per unit of factory output were *declining* when the price climb began—and these costs continued to decline for a considerable period after the price rise was underway. In each case, corporate profits began to increase sharply well before the price climb started.

To keep up with rising prices, workers demand higher wages and salaries—through unions and as individuals. But they never catch up, for in a monopoly-oligopoly conglomerate economy, the man who can fix the prices must always end up winning the game.

The result is that millions of workers feel they are paying more and more for less and less. They are paying for a war—with their sons, their taxes, and their overcharged purchases—only to feel they are losing the war. They are paying more for what they buy—and get more cars doomed to early obsolescence, phones that ring wrong numbers, houses that are jerry-built, doctors who make no home visits. They pay more and more in local taxes—and feel they are subsidizing crime and riot.

Hard work seems to have brought nothing but hard times. After federal taxes are taken out of the pay, after local taxes are paid, and then the rest is used to buy debased goods and services at inflated prices, the worker knows—and his wife knows still better—that he is no longer moving up.

The worker in urban America, however, is the victim not only of income maldistribution but also of population maldistribution, a catastrophe whose impact he cannot stand and whose origin he does not understand. Few city dwellers even suspect that much of their urban crisis started down on the farm.

Since World War II, about a million Americans a year have moved from a rural to an urban culture. This massive shift of about twenty million people in one generation has been described as the most gigantic migration in the history of man. Such a collision of cultures has always meant crowding, crime, and conflict. In the 1960s, history repeated itself—except that the immigrant was invisible because he was an in-migrant.

What set this wave in motion? Two contradictory national policies: to increase agricultural productivity and to restrict its production. Subsidized science found ways to make four stalks grow where one grew before. Subsidies to farmers, then, reversed the process by rewarding growers for nonproduction. The result was less and less need for labor on the soil. Farm workers went jobless; small farm owners went bankrupt or were bought out. Rural Americans were driven from their familiar farms into the unfamiliar cities, from warm earth to cold concrete.

This rural-push–urban-pull has been in motion ever since the turn of the century. But what was once a drift became a flood in the 1960s. The discomfort and disorder that followed set another dynamic in motion: the urban-push–suburban-pull.

If the worker can afford it, he generally flees—to outskirts and suburbs. He does so whether he is black or white. (Between 1964 and 1969, 600,000 blacks fled the central cities for other parts of the metropolitan areas.) Those who cannot flee, stay and get ready for the fight.

A current notion holds that the central cities are black and the suburbs white, dividing metros into separate but unequal societies in geographic separation. Again this is a half-truth which, if it were totally true, might well lessen social conflict. But the truth is that many whites cannot move because they cannot afford to. Typically they are white workers of more recent stock: economically unmonied and geographically immobile. Often their neighborhoods abut black ghettos where—after the flight of the more affluent blacks—there are left, according to James Q. Wilson, "only the most deprived, the least mobile, and the most pathological."

Through the '60s, the crush became a crunch—not simply because there were more bodies in the central cities but also because there were fewer places to put them. By public action, we have torn down about twice as many housing units as we have put up. Private builders have bulldozed slums to erect luxury highrises. Hundreds of thousands of units are abandoned annually by their landlords because the rotting property is all pain and no profit. As decay sets in at the ghetto core, rats and rain and fleas and fire take over to deprive the most deprived of their turf. So these newly dispossessed become the latest in-migrants, driven from their holes into the surrounding neighborhoods, spreading panic in their path.

Under these pressures, the ethnics—white and black—move from economic frustration and personal fear to political fury. The physical stage on which this tragedy is unfolding is a tiny piece of turf. Now 70 percent of the people—our urban population—live on 1.6 percent of the total land area. The American worker—white or black—is the victim of maldistribution—of people as well as income and wealth.

In the 1970s, fury comes easily to the white worker. It's stylish. He sees it everywhere. In the form of common crime—in the subway, on the street, at his doorstep; in the form of riots in the ghettos or the campus or the prison. The present generation of workers has grown up in an age of war: World War II, Korea, Vietnam. For three decades, they have lived with mass violence, directly and vicariously.

Retribalization reawakens ancient feelings. The white worker has always had the sense of belonging to some special group. There were constant reminders of ethnicity in neighborhood names, groceries, bars, funeral parlors, holidays, papers, ward politics, gang leaders, subtle prides and prejudices. But in an America that was devoted to the mythos of the melting pot and in a period dedicated to the ethos of one world, the white worker tucked his ethnicity up his sleeve. Now, in a retribalized world, he displays his ethnicity—as a pennant to carry into battle.

The young among the white workers, like the young everywhere, add their special stridency to the clamor. They are high on expectations and low on boiling point. To a civilizational distemper, they add their hot tempers, turning ethnic salvation into a moral justification for violence.

Our white worker is ready for battle. But he does not quite know against whom to declare war.

As a child of toilers he holds the traditional view of those who labor about those who don't. He feels that those inflated prices, those high taxes, those inadequate wages are all part of a schema for fattening up the fat. While he rarely, if ever, uses the words "establishment" or "system," he instinctively assumes there's an establishment that exploits him through a devilishly devised system.

Part of the system, his experience teaches, is for the rich to use the poorest to keep the once-poor and the possibly-poor as poor as possible. For generations, employers who demanded protection against foreign imports were importing foreigners to depress wages and break strikes. Out of this arose the Know-Nothing party that threatened, within a couple of years, to become a major national movement. In the mid-nineteenth century, Irish workers (themselves recent immigrants) feared that the Emancipation Proclamation, ending chattel slavery for the blacks, would intensify wage slavery for the whites. Out of this fear rose the sadistic Draft Riot of 1863 with its lynching and burning of blacks. In the 1920s, the white worker opted for immigration legislation to stem the flow of cheap hands.

As we move into the '70s, many workers fear that the Brass is using Underclass to undermine the Working Class. They seldom use this language but often feel these sentiments. As they hear it, this is what the rich are saying: "We must fight poverty and discrimination to the last drop of *your* blood. Share *your* job; share *your* neighborhood; pay *your* taxes." These moral exhortations come from the high and mighty, economically ensconced in tax havens far from the madding crowd.

In protest against this establishment, the worker turns to strikes for higher wages and revolt against taxes. But neither remedy works. Wage gains are offset by higher prices. Lower taxes mean lower services —schools, streets, travel, sanitation, police, medical care. What looked like a direct way out turns out to be a maze.

Since our worker does not know how to deal with the system, he tries to do the next best thing: to act within the system to protect his own skin. And in our torn and turbulent cities, it is too often his "skin" that determines his mood.

This mood is generally called "backlash," a reawakening of ancient prejudice directed against blacks because they have dared to raise their heads and voices. But to explain the growing tension simply as "backlash" is once more to create a mischievous myth out of partial truth. To deny that prejudice exists is naive; to ascribe rising racial clash to a simple proliferation of prejudice, equally naive. The white worker feels economically threatened, personally imperiled, politically suckered. His anxieties make him meaner than he means to be. Racial suspicion turns into tribal war when people—no matter their color— are oppressed by their circumstances. Maldistribution of income and people must multiply strife. This strife, ironically, tends not to change but to continue the system that produced the conflict. So long as black battles white and poor battle not-so-poor, the establishment can continue to "divide and rule."

The further irony is the innocence of those on top who are, in a depersonalized way, responsible for the turmoil on the shrinking turf. The upper 1 percent rarely suspects that its incredible wealth is the prime reason the lesser people, without urging, are at one another's throats. As the wealthiest see their role, they are the great creators: investing, employing, making. They are the great givers, turning tax exempt funds to do God's work.

In short, there is no devil: those at the top merely move their money around in a depersonalized way through impersonal channels (corporations) to multiply their money so they may do man's and God's work better; those in the middle merely try to lift their real incomes so they and their family can live—better; those at the bottom merely want what man needs to stay alive and kicking. Yet somehow they all end up in a fight, with the top acting genteelly through finances, and the lesser people resorting intemperately to fists.

If there is a devil, he is—as he always is—invisible, ubiquitous, and working his evil will through the way of all flesh. In our case, he is the inherent imperative in a culture that has badly distributed its wealth and people: the devil still is the system.

politics

13

ethnic political behavior

Raymond Wolfinger

The non-British immigrants who began to come to this country's growing cities in the 1840's were largely poor, ignorant of American customs
and language, and non-Protestant. They were exploited by Yankee[1]
businessmen and scorned by old settlers of all classes. They lived in
miserable surroundings and also were handicapped by their lack of
education. The cultural traditions, patterns of authority, forms of social organization, and personal habits formed in centuries of European
peasant life were incompatible with those of industrial America; the
immigrants were discouraged from identifying with American society
and did not share equally in American prosperity. Such deprivation
and alienation are supposed to be fertile soil for radical political appeals. But the immigrants and their descendants have been largely un-
responsive to ideologies of protest and unreceptive to class-conscious
political organizations.

Lack of interest in radical politics has characterized almost all

"Some Consequences of Ethnic Politics" by Raymond Wolfinger. From M. K.
Jennings and L. H. Zeigler, *The Electoral Process* (Englewood Cliffs, N.J.: Prentice-
Hall, 1966). Reprinted by permission of the editors.

1. *Yankee* is used in its New England sense to refer to more or less old
settlers of Anglo-Saxon stock. I will use the terms *ethnic group* and *nationality group*
interchangeably to refer to people whose national origins set them apart from the
predominantly Protestant majority. This usage includes Jews and excludes racial
minorities.

elements in American society.[2] Many of the familiar explanations of this disinterest were least relevant to urban immigrants. The prospect of homesteading on the frontier was never important to them. Given their intrinsic handicaps and the prevailing prejudices, they did not have the same chances of attaining prosperity as did other groups in the population. Even the myth of social mobility must have been attenuated for many of them. Such explanations do not go to the heart of the matter. The immigrants not only eschewed radical politics, but —prior to the New Deal—they were not notably strong supporters of milder forms of social protest. Their votes were often cast predominantly against Populist and Progressive candidates. Neither of these movements had much specific appeal to urban workers, who were unmoved by Populist demands for cheap money, easy credit, low tariffs, and railroad regulation, or by the Progressives' enthusiasm for trust-busting, civil service reform, and more efficiency in government. These two movements were the main expressions of moderate social protest between the Civil War and the New Deal. The ethnics in their tenements had more tangible and symbolic grievances than either the agrarian Populists or the genteel, middle-class Progressives, yet the ethnics did not consistently generate any reformist demands of their own. They supported the New Deal but their political leaders were by no means the most progressive element in that coalition, and since then the ethnics have not lived up to their reputation as "radical urban masses." [3]

Democratic politicians from ethnic milieux have been conservative more often than not. The Irish, being the first to take over from the Yankees, were the first to show how mild their substantive demands were. As Glazer and Moynihan put it, "The Irish did not know what to do with power once they got it. . . . The main thrust of Irish political activity has always been moderate or conservative in New York.[4] Other ethnic politicians have followed the precedent set by the Irish. The classic urban political machines are almost all run by ethnic politicians supported by ethnic constituencies. These organizations are not

2. The chief exceptions to this statement were the support given the Industrial Workers of the World and other radical movements by Western loggers and miners, and the interest in various Leftist parties prior to the mid-1940's by some residents of New York and other large cities. The immigrant proportion of radical party membership varied enormously from one decade to the next, but at no time was it more than a tiny fraction of any nationality group, with the possible exception of the Finns. See Nathan Glazer, *The Social Basis of American Communism* (New York: Harcourt, Brace & World, Inc., 1961), Chaps. 1–3.

3. One very important factor in the ethnics' pro-Democratic swing was Al Smith's candidacy in 1928, with its virulent anti-Catholic aspects. See V. O. Key, Jr., "A Theory of Critical Elections," *Journal of Politics,* XVII (February 1955); and Samuel J. Eldersveld, "The Influence of Metropolitan Party Pluralities in Presidential Elections since 1920: A Study of Twelve Cities," *American Political Science Review,* XLIII (December 1949), 1196.

4. Glazer and Moynihan, *Beyond the Melting Pot,* pp. 229, 264.

noted for their progressive policies.[5] Friction between "the organization" and middle-class, liberal party elements has become characteristic of the Democratic party in recent years.[6]

Oscar Handlin has suggested that the source of the ethnics' conservatism is their largely Catholic peasant origins.[7] This argument is given added plausibility by the fact that Jews, of all the major immigrant groups, were the most attracted to radical politics. But Handlin's argument is less persuasive when one remembers that millions of these same peasants also migrated to European industrial cities, where their Catholic heritage has not kept them from enthusiastic support of Communist and socialist parties.

A more tenable proposition is that ethnic politics tended to make economic and social issues less relevant in party competition by emphasizing nationality group rather than social class.[8] Regardless of the effect of politics, ethnic salience inhibited the development of class consciousness. Initially the immigrants must have associated their hardships with their ethnicity. But, in addition to being the source of their miseries, ethnicity also became an important comfort to them. As some immigrants made good, their success gave vicarious pleasure and self-respect to their fellows, by showing that Irishmen (or Italians or Poles), given half a chance, could do as well as Yankees. These achievements also made class-based political appeals more difficult. Even at the outset working-class solidarity was impeded by the existence of a Yankee proletariat,[9] as well as by the inevitable hostilities among different nationality groups.[10] But once some immigrant social

5. See, e.g., Martin Meyerson and Edward C. Banfield, *Politics, Planning, and the Public Interest* (New York: The Free Press of Glencoe, Inc., 1955); Harold Gosnell, *Machine Politics: Chicago Model* (Chicago: The University of Chicago Press, 1937); and Raymond E. Wolfinger, *The Politics of Progress* (New Haven: Yale University Press, forthcoming). Since some people, including some politicians, are Democrats "because of" their ethnic backgrounds, the influence of ideology as a factor in party identification is reduced even below the rather low level found in the United States as a whole. Thus such comments as "If X weren't an Irishman, he would be a Republican."

6. See Lockard, *New England State Politics*, pp. 231n, 268–69; and James Q. Wilson, *The Amateur Democrat* (Chicago: The University of Chicago Press, 1962).

7. Oscar Handlin, *The Uprooted* (Boston: Little, Brown & Co., 1952), pp. 217–18.

8. Dahl has developed this point at some length; see *Who Governs?* Chaps. 4, 5.

9. Because the immigrants often competed with working-class Yankees, the latter had additional reasons for nativism. Until the present generation, American labor unions generally were opposed to unrestricted immigration because of its depressive influence on wages.

10. See W. Lloyd Warner and J. O. Low, *The Social System of the Modern Factory* (New Haven: Yale University Press, 1947). Employers sometimes fomented such ethnic conflict as a way of avoiding organization of their workers. See, e.g., James B. McKee, "Status and Power in the Industrial Community: A Comment on Drucker's Thesis," *American Journal of Sociology*, LVIII (January 1953), 364–70.

mobility occurred, solidarity also meant turning one's back on fellow ethnics who had made good. To put it more formally, class consciousness and ethnic salience posed the problem of conflicting reference groups. It appears that the ethnic group was a more satisfying and tolerable reference group than the proletariat. Even class-conscious political movements were split by ethnic separatism. As late as the 1920's, Communist and other radical parties often had separate organizations for different nationality groups, even at the local level.[11]

SYMBOLIC AND TANGIBLE REWARDS IN ETHNIC POLITICS

The salience of ethnic identifications led politicians to classify the electorate in terms of national origins and to develop strategies based on this classification. This practice was also fostered by limitations in the kinds of political intelligence available to politicians. Prior to the development of survey research, the easiest way to analyze voting behavior was to study returns from voting units with particular characteristics. Because of the tendency for immigrants and their descendants to cluster together in ghettos, such voting units were more homogeneous in ethnicity than in any other characteristic. Thus the use of aggregate data involves an implicit bias for ethnic explanations of election outcomes, a bias from which politicians have been freed by the techniques of survey research.[12]

The ways in which the ethnics participated in politics, and the tactics used by politicians to win their support, reinforced—and continue to reinforce—the diversion of class-based political demands in favor of tangible rewards for a few ethnics and consequent symbolic gratifications for many of the rest. Politicians tried to win votes from members of ethnic groups by making alliances with their leaders. In most cases these leaders either owed their positions to "outside" business or political interests (e.g., as foremen of labor gangs) or were prosperous men whose economic interests were not shared by most of their fellow ethnics.[13] Such leaders, with one foot in the outer world, rarely

11. Theodore Draper, *The Roots of American Communism* (New York: The Viking Press, Inc., 1957.)

12. For this reason, Glazer and Moynihan's contention that survey research has stimulated the use of ethnic political appeals (evidently because the politicians who commission such research categorize the respondents ethnically rather than by income or education) seems to reverse the causal relationship. Furthermore, there is no intrinsic reason why survey data must be analyzed by ethnicity; the decision to do so would seem to depend on assumptions about what independent variables are important in the respondents' voting behavior. Glazer and Moynihan note this point, but are unmoved by it (*Beyond the Melting Pot,* pp. 301–2, 305).

13. For a discussion of these social patterns, see Handlin, *The Uprooted,* Chaps. 7, 8.

led their deprived followers in demands for social justice. William F. Whyte described this double allegiance in his famous study of the Italian community in the North End of Boston:

> He [the candidate] tries to convince his listeners that he is so well qualified by education and experience that he will be able to meet the "big-shots" of politics on an even footing, but at the same time he points out that he is still of the common people and will be loyal to them no matter how far he advances. The most important qualification a politician can claim is that he has been and will always be loyal to his old friends, to his class, and to his race. . . . They seek to show people that they have such good connections that they will be able to do favors, win or lose.[14]

Outside politicians sometimes gained the support of such leaders by simple bribery. The more common (and contemporary) method, however, was to show, by judicious distribution of public jobs and nominations, that one party or the other "recognized" the merits of a particular ethnic group. "Recognition" is the prize in ethnic politics. When the first Irishman was nominated for alderman in the mid-nineteenth century, this implied a recognition of the statesmanlike qualities of all Irishmen. The same process works in the mid-twentieth century. It is an economical strategy, for the benefits given to a few ethnics are appreciated by many others.

The political process is often described as one in which politicians offer inducements to interest groups in hopes of winning their votes. The nature of the inducements varies with the reference-group memberships of the voters. In ethnic politics, politicians compete for votes by giving jobs, contracts, and more symbolic gratifications to individuals on the basis of ethnicity. In class politics they compete by offering substantive programs to satisfy policy demands. Success in ethnic politics means recognition. Success in class politics means expanded educational, welfare and recreation programs, progressive taxation, liberalized labor laws, and so on. Recognition is an inappropriate strategy in class politics. No one thinks of appointees in terms of their social status, and this is seldom an important dimension in the evaluation of candidates.[15] Appointees and candidates symbolize ethnic groups, not social classes. Furthermore, most public positions—whether elective or appointive—require qualifications that eliminate most proletarians from consideration. By structuring politics so that expectations are for recognition rather than substantive policies, ethnic strategies divert working-class energies away from substantive policy demands. If the

14. William F. Whyte, *Street-Corner Society*, enlarged edition (Chicago: The University of Chicago Press, 1955), p. 232. Here *race* means *nationality group*.
15. Cf. Lowi, "Economic class origin is not taken into account by appointing authorities unless that origin is extreme wealth or high status, in which case it tends to work negatively" (*At the Pleasure of the Mayor*, p. 51).

vote of a worker who happens to be of Italian descent can be won by putting an Italian on the ticket, why should the party promise him better schools?

Glazer and Moynihan offer a different interpretation of the relationship between ethnic politics and substantive class interests. They say that, because any ethnic group has distinctive economic characteristics, *ethnicity* is a way of referring to *social classes* without incurring the traditional American distaste for class distinctions. Thus ethnic politics is a way of having class politics without offending egalitarian myths.[16] Glazer and Moynihan do not explain why the myth of classlessness is more sacrosanct than the myth of the melting pot, nor do they explain why different ethnic groups with similar economic characteristics often cast their votes in very different ways. Furthermore, any single ethnic group is now differentiated enough in occupation so that its members have diverse economic interests. Although different groups may predominate in some occupations, all groups are represented throughout the economic spectrum. For example, many small shopkeepers may be Jews, but most Jews are not small shopkeepers.[17]

The most important flaw in this argument is that ethnic groups are rarely interest groups as far as substantive policies are concerned. They seldom make policy demands on the basis of their ethnicity. There are a few policy questions in which tangible or symbolic ethnic interests are at stake, but usually the ethnic involvement is somewhat extraneous to the substance of the issue. Nationality groups used to lobby on various foreign issues involving their particular homelands. Central European immigrants played a role in the creation of the Succession States at the end of World War I. For generations Boston's representatives in Congress took the lead in the passage of congressional resolutions deploring the partition of Ireland. It is said that German, Italian, and Irish voters registered their disapproval of Franklin D. Roosevelt's foreign policies by voting Republican, and that their fathers had done the same in response to Woodrow Wilson's diplomacy. This sort of foreign-policy interest seems to have declined. The major remaining example is Jewish interest in Israel's fate, which is reflected in recurring attempts by Congressmen with Jewish constituencies to limit American aid to the United Arab Republic. Appeals to Jewish voters often take the form of expressions of concern for Israel. Senator Robert Kennedy, for instance, liked to remind Jewish audiences that he had been present in Palestine as a newspaper correspondent when the state of Israel was founded.

In some issues, ethnicity is not explicitly involved, but the com-

16. Glazer and Moynihan, *Beyond the Melting Pot*, pp. 17, 301–2.
17. See Glazer and Moynihan, *Beyond the Melting Pot*, pp. 317–24 for tables showing the representation of various ethnic groups in occupations in New York City.

position of at least one set of participants gives the controversy some ethnic coloring. One common example involves issues in which the Catholic Church has an interest, such as birth control, education, and censorship. Disputes in these areas often find Protestants and Jews pitted against Irishmen and Italians. The other major issue of this type has to do with land use: where to locate a freeway or housing project, where new schools should be built, and so on. Such issues, which are among the most important and common in local politics, generally define interest geographically. Because of the ethnic homogeneity of many neighborhoods, land-use issues often take on ethnic overtones. The increasing importance of urban renewal is likely to mean a new area of ethnic political involvement.

Dahl has suggested that the ways in which individuals benefit from politics can be classified according to their generality:

> Certain benefits are *divisible* in such a way that they can be allocated to specific individuals, . . . Other benefits are more nearly *indivisible;* parks, playgrounds, schools, national defense and foreign policies, for example, either cannot be or ordinarily are not allocated by dividing the benefits piecemeal and allocating various pieces to specific individuals.[18]

The tangible benefits of ethnic politics are largely divisible. Demands typically have been for jobs and favoritism—for a bigger share of the rewards that the system already distributes, not for a different method of distribution. Ethnic politics weaken demands for indivisible welfare policies. This political style has advantages for politicians and for the rich. Recognition of minority groups might affront Yankee businessmen, but it was cheaper than socioeconomic reform. The public jobs that are the essence of ethnic strategies were not coveted by the wealthy. Thus, so long as no new jobs were created, the only losers were the former jobholders. Although the eventual political ascendance of the ethnics deprived Yankees of one arena of power and status, this loss was made easier to bear by the restrained behavior of the new rulers, who were respectful of both status and wealth. Politicians found ethnic strategies convenient because they evoked less opposition from conservative elements than would have ensued if reformist tactics had been widely employed. To the extent that they could exclude substantive issues from partisan competition, there was less pressure on politicians to make policy commitments to win votes.[19]

It has been argued that recognition provides tangible benefits to members of ethnic groups because their economic interests are looked

18. Dahl, *Who Governs?* p. 52. Italics in original.
19. V. O. Key argued that racist appeals had the same result in the South. See his *Southern Politics* (New York: Alfred A. Knopf, Inc., 1949), Chap. 7 and *passim*.

after by ethnic officials. It does not appear that ethnic ties are much of a guarantee in this respect. Such appointments are often made because it is expected that voters will be happy with the recognition and will not make substantive demands as well. The appointees owe their positions to outside selection, often with the implicit understanding that they will dissuade their fellow ethnics from making policy demands.[20] The more liberal municipal administrations in New York City have had more Protestant and Jewish high officials than the status-quo, less progressive regimes, which make more upper-level appointments from Catholic ethnic groups.[21]

Although ethnic politics have generally constituted a conservative force in the United States, there is one important sense in which this political style has been used for liberal ends. The ability to appeal to ethnic loyalties is a political resource, similar to such other resources as money, social status, and legal skill. Ethnic-oriented political systems have sometimes produced politicians who have made use of nationality-group solidarity as a means of building support for innovative policies. Such men (e.g., Al Smith, Fiorello La Guardia, or Richard C. Lee, the energetic Mayor of New Haven) usually have tried to build reputations for achievement as a means of proceeding to a higher political level.[22]

The tangible benefits of ethnic politics have been concentrated largely in the governmental sector. In those regions where ethnic politics flourish, most government and party leaders are members of ethnic groups.[23] Data from New Haven make this clear. In 1959 members of the three major ethnic groups—Italians, Irish, and Jews—comprised 57 per cent of the city's population, but accounted for 82 per cent of all elected municipal officials (see Table 1).[24] Similar patterns are found in most of the Northeast and the industrial areas of the Midwest. This

20. The same tactic is used with Negroes, whose "representatives" in public jobs not only refrain from pressing for action on civil rights, but also try to persuade civil rights groups to moderate and delay their demands. This has been true at the national level as well as in local politics. For a description of this phenomenon in Chicago, see James Q. Wilson, *Negro Politics* (New York: The Free Press of Glencoe, Inc., 1961), pp. 70, 131, 162.

21. Lowi, *At the Pleasure of the Mayor*, pp. 197–98. On this same theme see also Wilson, *The Amateur Democrat*.

22. Lee is described at length in Dahl, *Who Governs?* and in Raymond E. Wolfinger, *The Politics of Progress* (New Haven: Yale University Press, 1966).

23. This is truer for the Democrats, but the Republican party is by no means a Yankee monopoly. See, e.g., Elmer E. Cornwell, Jr., "Party Absorption of Ethnic Groups: The Case of Providence, Rhode Island," *Social Forces*, XXXVIII (March 1960), 205–10.

24. A "fair share" for Italians is a fairly recent development. See Jerome K. Myers, "Assimilation in the Political Community," *Sociology and Social Research*, XXXV (1951), 175–82.

TABLE 1 REPRESENTATION OF ETHNIC GROUPS AMONG REGISTERED
VOTERS, MAJOR ELECTED OFFICIALS, ECONOMIC ELITE, AND
SOCIAL ELITE IN NEW HAVEN IN 1959

Ethnic Group	Registered Voters (N = 525)	Major Elected Officials* (N = 41)	Economic Elite (N = 123)	Social Elite (N = 198)
Italian	31%	34%	4%	1%
Irish	11	29	4	2
Jewish	15	19	20	1
Other	43	17	72	96
Total	100%	99%**	100%	100%

* Includes aldermen and citywide officials.
** Does not sum to 100% because of rounding.
Sources: Data on registered voters are from a survey (conducted under William Flanigan's direction in 1959) of respondents randomly chosen from voting lists. Respondents were identified as Italian or Irish only if a parent or grandparent was born in the corresponding country, with father's birthplace taking precedence. Because most Irish immigrants came to this country before 1900, this probably underrepresents the number of Irish in New Haven. Ethnic affiliations in the other groups were determined by names and direct information. Almost all the officials were Democrats. Because most defeated Republican candidates were of the same ethnic group as the respective victors, a change in regime would not greatly change the ethnic proportions among officials. For a description of the procedures for identifying the social and economic elites, see Raymond E. Wolfinger, *The Politics of Progress* (New Haven: Yale University Press, forthcoming), Chap. 2. A similar but not identical method was used by Robert A. Dahl, *Who Governs?* (New Haven: Yale University Press, 1961), pp. 63–68; and by Nelson W. Polsby, *Community Power and Political Theory* (New Haven: Yale University Press), Chap. 4. Briefly, the economic elite consists of the men who control the city's economic resources. The social elite are the Cotillion's guest list.

has led many observers to say that ethnic politics have provided a channel of occupational mobility for the immigrants. This is true, but in the case of elite positions only with respect to the sphere of government; political success has not been accompanied by parallel achievements in other areas. Politics has not been a pathway enabling ethnics to attain equality in social and economic life.[25] This is illustrated by Table 1, which shows the proportions of various ethnic groups serving as elected government officials and the proportions that have entered the highest levels of New Haven's business and social worlds. With the exception of Jewish success in business, these groups have failed almost totally to match their political attainments.

The major tangible benefit of ethnic politics, then, has been the divisible one of public office. Some writers have said that ethnic politics

25. Cf. Glazer and Moynihan, "Instead of profiting by their success in the all-but-despised roles of ward heeler and policeman, the Irish seem to have been trapped by it" (*Beyond The Melting Pot,* p. 256).

also has aided the immigrants' assimilation into American society.[26] It it difficult to support this proposition, if by *assimilation* one means that a group's differentiating characteristics become less important to it and to the society as a whole. Just as the feasibility of class-based political appeals depends on class consciousness, so ethnic politics depends on ethnic salience. The proposition that ethnic politics hastens assimilation is analogous to saying that class consciousness would be minimized if politicians treated class distinctions as fundamental, if individuals made their voting decisions by calculating class advantage, and if public jobs were filled on the basis of class origins. It does not seem likely that political strategies that emphasize ethnic identity will hasten the eclipse of that identity. The opposite conclusion is more tenable. Because continued enjoyment of the benefits of ethnic politics depends on the maintenance of ethnic consciousness, it would seem likely that politicians would continue to employ strategies that reinforce this consciousness among their constituents. It seems to be the case that where political appeals to ethnic differences are most uncommon, assimilation is most advanced—i.e., on the Pacific Coast rather than in the Northeast.

CONCLUSION

Competition between the two major American political parties is thought to foster consensus and social unity because each party must win support from uncommitted middle-ground elements and because party loyalties moderate class conflict.[27] This model assumes that parties compete by offering substantive policies to uncommitted voters. Ethnic politics conforms to this model so far as class conflict is concerned, but not with respect to ethnic conflict. In the latter area, parties compete for votes by offers of recognition, a tactic which heightens separate identification and structures politics as ethnic conflict. It was Henry James, I believe, who called campaigning in Massachusetts "exploitation of racial hatred." [28]

I think it likely, however, that in some ways ethnic politics did help to integrate the immigrants into American society. This integration has not brought with it an end to a sense of separate ethnic identity, but it has given the immigrants a stake in society.[29] This integra-

26. See, e.g., Dahl, *Who Governs?* pp. 33, 59; Elmer E. Cornwell, Jr., "Bosses, Machines, and Ethnic Groups," *The Annals*, CCCLIII (May 1964), pp. 31–34. Dahl also alludes to the divisive effects of ethnic politics; see *Who Governs?* pp. 33, 54.

27. For an extensive and explicit analysis of data on this subject see Heinz Eulau, *Class and Party in the Eisenhower Years* (New York: The Free Press of Glencoe, Inc., 1962).

28. The parallel to Negro-baiting in the South is obvious.

29. I should make it clear that I do not assert that assimilation has not occurred, and is not well advanced in many places and for many groups. My point here is that ethnic politics have hindered, not helped, this process.

tion-without-assimilation came about in two ways. First, the strategy of recognition brought ethnic leaders into the system and rewarded them for going along with the status quo and not making reform demands.[30] Second, the fact that some ethnics attained public office showed their fellows that it was possible for some Irish, Jews, Italians, or whatever, to succeed in the United States. From all accounts, this is a powerfully persuasive symbol to members of any minority group.

Dahl's categories of indivisible and divisible benefits are a useful way to summarize this article. The characteristic recognition strategy employed in ethnic politics has provided symbolic indivisible benefits to those ethnic voters who were gratified by the recognition. In a sense, these voters accepted recognition rather than substantive policies that would have satisfied more tangible needs. By thus moderating class-based demands ethnic politics muted class conflict. At the same time, by accentuating ethnic salience, it hindered the assimilation of the ethnics, while giving them a stake in society based on a sense of their own separateness.

30. It has been suggested that Southern leaders would have been wiser to appease Negro leaders by selective concessions—e.g., letting a Negro elite register to vote, instead of blindly oppressing all Negroes. Such a policy, although it would require more political discipline, would reduce the stake that well-to-do and educated Negroes have in the civil rights movement. This is the course followed in many Northern cities; see, e.g., Wilson, *Negro Politics, passim.*

the slavs: not at all republican

Mark Levy & Michael Kramer

Vice-President Agnew and Senator John L. McClellan call them "Po-lacks." Senator McClellan apologizes. The media think of them as hard-hats. Supposedly enlightened people tell tiresome and derogatory jokes about them, and others taunt them with cries of "Hunkie." Both socially and politically, Americans of Slavic descent face ethnic barriers.[1] And until recently Slavic-Americans seemed unwilling or unable to do very much about it. They were "represented" by mild-mannered umbrella organizations like the Polish-American Congress, and although politicians always attended Pulaski Day parades, most never seemed to be around when important issues like housing, schools and civil rights were being discussed.

But all that is changing. Slavs are taking positions in the ethnic-power movement. In Baltimore, for example, Barbara Mikulski of the Southeast Community Organization says Slavs are tired of "phony white liberals, pseudo black militants and patronizing bureaucrats" who make things difficult for the Slavic community. And in Indiana's Lake County, a thousand delegates from church, civic and fraternal organizations met recently to found the Calumet Community Congress with the goal of helping the Slavs living in the industrial towns of Gary, Hammond and South Bend to achieve a better life. In Detroit, black Congressman John Conyers and a Polish priest named Daniel Bogus have started the Black-Polish Conference to help "depolarize" the community. If such efforts are successful, perhaps these natural allies will awaken to their community of ethnic interest. (One is re-

Reprinted from M. Levy and M. Kramer, *The Ethnic Factor* by permission of Simon and Schuster, Inc., New York.

1. Throughout this chapter we will use the generic term "Slav" instead of naming a specific nationality group. Poles are the most numerous of all the Slavic-American groups, but there are also Czechs, Slovaks, Ruthenians, Slovenians, Russians, Ukrainians, etc. Hungarians, who are not really Slavs, are included in this grouping; interestingly, the slang term Hunkie, which is used to denigrate all East Europeans, is derived from *Bohunk,* a corruption of *Hungarian.*

minded of the recent summit conference of Jewish Defense League and Italian-American Civil Rights League officials; a pattern of ethnic "community" could be emerging.)

Slavic-Americans have much to complain about. For years the power structure ignored them, and now they are blamed for institutional racism. For the distraught Slavic-American one way to do something about all of this is to utilize the political process. Slavs have traditionally voted for Democratic candidates, and they continue to do so. But increasingly, Slavic Democrats are thinking about their vote.

THE POLITICAL DEMOGRAPHY OF SLAVIC AMERICA

In electoral politics, numbers are everything. Politicians pay attention to voters in direct proportion to their real or presumed strength in the electorate. It is not surprising, therefore, to find that spokesmen for ethnic groups often overestimate their group's numerical strength. A check of several different sources disclosed a wide variance of thought regarding Slavic-American numbers. Congressman Dan Rostenkowski of Chicago, a leading Polish-American politician, said there are fifteen million Americans of Polish descent. Professor Joseph Wytrwal estimates the number at ten million. The *Polish-American Journal* put the figure at seven million, and a recent account in *The New York Times* reported that there are six million Polish-Americans. A much lower figure, but one which is at least free from ethnic exaggeration, comes from the U.S. Census Bureau. In its special 1969 survey the Bureau found four million Americans whose families came from Poland. Not all of these four million are Catholic. About one quarter of America's Poles are Jewish. So at most, there are 3.2 million Catholic Poles. Added to this 3.2-million figure are some 1.5 million Czechs, Slovaks, Slovenians, Lithuanians, Bohemians, et cetera. In all, then, a fair but conservative estimate would place the total Slavic population of the United States at around five million, or 2.5 percent of the total.

About half of Slavic America lives in the urban centers of the Northeast. New York, Philadelphia, Buffalo, Bridgeport and Pittsburgh, all have sizable Slavic minorities. Most of the rest live in the Midwest. The largest single grouping of Slavs is said to be in Chicago, where there may be as many as 800,000, and there are also substantial Slavic communities in Detroit, Milwaukee and Cleveland.

Of all the white ethnic groups, Slavs are the least assimilated. They tend to live together in "Little Polands," read Polish newspapers —of which there are five dailies—and celebrate Slavic holidays together. They maintain many of the "old ways" long after arriving in the United States. A survey reports that in two thirds of Polish families, the Polish language is spoken by the children, and other studies have found substantial numbers of third-generation Slavs still fluent in their grandparents' language. A Catholic education, and particularly a Catholic ethnic education, is also important to Slavic-Americans. There are, for instance, more than six hundred Polish parochial schools, and nearly ten thousand fraternal, social and athletic clubs based on ties to the old country. One organization alone, the Polish National Alliance, has more than 300,000 members.

Poles are second only to Italians in the percentage who own their own homes, and those homes are likely to be neat, spotlessly kept small houses found in areas like Cleveland's "Buckeye Road" and Southside Milwaukee. As with Italians, Slavs normally live close to friends and relatives, are extremely conscious of property values, and outsiders, be they white or black, are generally not welcome on the block.

By most measures, Slavs are at the bottom of white urban society. Father Greeley reports that only one out of six Poles holds a "prestige" job, and a survey of Slavs in Connecticut found three quarters were blue-collar workers. Approximately 40 percent belong to labor unions. Nationally, less than one out of every five Poles earned more than $14,000 a year in 1963, and in Connecticut only one out of five earned more than $10,000 a year in 1968; one reason for these low income figures is that less than half of Slavic America has graduated from high school.

The relatively low social status indicated by these statistical measures yields powerful political and sociological implications. Slavs are strongly attached to the Democratic party for economic reasons; but, being only one rung ahead of blacks on the economic ladder, they often find themselves competing with blacks for jobs and housing. The politicians say this leads to the Republican party. But apparently no one has told the Slavs that their "numbers" mandate a political switch. They remain Democrats.

SLAVIC VOTERS: THE "TWO THIRDS" DEMOCRATS

Of all the white ethnics, Slavs are most likely to consider themselves Democrats. According to Father Greeley, 77 percent of all Poles say they belong to the Democratic party; and the figure is even higher in the Midwest, where eight out of ten Poles identified with the Democrats. This high level of Democratic party identification is reflected at the polls.

Slavs showed a remarkably consistent record of support for the Democrats through the 1964 election. In 54 of 57 elections for senator, governor and President from 1958 through 1964, the Democratic percentage was at least 65 percent of the vote. In 19 of these elections (one third of the total), the Slavs' Democratic vote exceeded 80 percent.

Since 1964, Democratic candidates have consistently carried the Slavic vote, but have been unable to maintain the extraordinary pre-

1964 pluralities. In 37 of 40 races for senator, governor and President since 1964, Democratic candidates won a clear majority. The Democratic vote was greater than 65 percent in 29 of 40 elections, or nearly three quarters, yet surpassed 80 percent only twice.

The post-1964 returns certainly represent a plurality decline for the Democrats among Slavs. However, there is no pattern in the 1966, 1968 and 1970 election returns to suggest a steadily eroding Democratic base, nor is there any suggestion other than that the average Democratic candidate should expect two thirds of the Slavic vote. Republicans who win more than one third of the Slavic vote are exceptions to the rule.

What is happening to the Slavic vote? In places like Gary, Indiana, and Cicero, Illinois, there are Slavic voters so beset by racial worries that they do vote a backlash ticket for Republican candidates. But Slavs in cities like Buffalo, Youngstown, Hartford and South Bend remain staunchly Democratic. These working-class Slavs may be troubled by racial problems, but they seem to vote their class interests; and they perceive those interests as dictating a vote for the Democrat. At the same time, Slavic voters in other cities, like Chicago, Milwaukee and Hamtramck, Michigan, continue to vote Democratic, but in slowly declining numbers.

SLAVIC VOTERS AND LIBERAL DEMOCRATS

Ask the average politician, and he will probably tell you that Slavic voters are tending to become conservative and Republican. It's a foregone conclusion in some circles that liberal Democrats don't stand a chance with Slavs. This simply is not true. When Robert Kennedy ran for the Senate from New York in 1964, he swamped moderate Republican Kenneth Keating by nearly three quarters of a million votes. Certainly Kennedy had a liberal image, he was closely associated with the New Frontier social programs of his brother. But Kennedy also had two other things going for him: he was Catholic and he had a reputation for being a tough Attorney General. Both of these factors helped him with New York's Slavic voters, and Kennedy won nearly eight out of ten Slavic votes against Keating, or more Slavic votes than any Democratic candidate for statewide office won during the sixties in New York.[2]

In 1968, Indiana's Slavic voters helped reelect liberal Birch Bayh to the United States Senate. Bayh was opposed by William Ruckels-

2. Kennedy's hold on the Slavs was not quite so strong outside New York, however. In the 1968 Presidential primary in Indiana, Kennedy won only 44 percent of the vote in Slavic precincts along Lake Michigan, while Eugene McCarthy, the Left Democratic candidate, won 30 percent. Indiana's Governor Roger D. Branigin took the rest. What is interesting about the Indiana Slavic vote is that three quarters of it went to two very liberal Democrats.

haus, who claimed that the Senator was not conservative enough for most Hoosiers. These charges failed to persuade many of Indiana's Slavic voters, and they gave 71 percent of their votes to Bayh, 20,000 votes of his statewide margin of 70,000.

The 1970 Senate contest in Illinois was a classic confrontation between a liberal Democrat and a conservative Republican. Democrat Adlai Stevenson III opposed the A.B.M. and called for federal programs to help the cities. His opponent, Ralph Smith, who had been appointed to fill the vacancy caused by the death of Everett McKinley Dirksen, attacked Stevenson as an ultraliberal who was "soft" on dissident students and hippies. Stevenson stuck an American flag in his lapel and hired the prosecutor of the Chicago Seven to run his campaign. Probably what helped Stevenson the most though, were his family name and his liberal credentials. In Chicago, the Daley machine cranked out better than 70 percent of the Slavic vote for Stevenson. He did almost as well statewide, winning more than 60 percent of the Slavic vote, a showing that was better than the Democratic polling of either Governor Otto Kerner in 1964 or Senator Paul Douglas in 1966.

Another Midwestern Senator, Philip A. Hart of Michigan, ran even better with the Slavic voters of his state than did Adlai III in Illinois. In 1970, Senator Hart was opposed by Mrs. Lenore Romney, wife of George Romney, a former Michigan governor and now Nixon's Secretary of Housing and Urban Development. Mrs. Romney attacked Hart for failing to support the Nixon administration's legislative program, while Hart traded on his long-time interest in programs for Michigan's large blue-collar population. The state's G.O.P. failed to unite behind Mrs. Romney, and she lost some support, particularly among white Catholics, when H.U.D. pushed its plans to integrate the Detroit suburb of Warren. Hart won an easy victory of more than 66 percent. A survey taken in mid-September showed that among Slavic voters, Hart was running 10 percentage points ahead of his statewide average. Assuming that the vote on election day reflected the earlier poll—and it most likely did—Hart received nearly three quarters of the Slavic vote.

The preceding elections clearly demonstrate that Slavic voters are not turned off by liberal Democrats. Some liberals like Robert Kennedy won Slavic votes through a unique combination of issues and political "magic," but others without the Kennedy mystique, like Stevenson, Bayh and Hart, win Slavic votes because Slavs believe these liberal Democrats represent their best interests.

SLAVIC VOTERS AND JEWISH CANDIDATES

A Polish-American businessman ran an advertisement in two Detroit newspapers in the fall of 1970, trying to drum up trade with Poland.

Part of the advertisement read, "Seven centuries ago, a Polish king knew that men could differ and yet live productively and did something about it." The ad cited the Edict of Kalisz, signed in 1264, and continued, "For the first time in Christian civilization, a Government granted equal protection under the law to Jews." The advertisement was particularly interesting because it chose to deal directly with a controversial subject, Polish anti-Semitism. Despite the Edict of Kalisz, Jews in Poland historically have had a very difficult time with the Polish people. The list of pogroms and injustices is a long one. What is pertinent today, however, are the attitudes of American Slavs toward American Jews; research indicates that the carry-over from the old country is startling.

Father Greeley found that of all the white Catholics, Poles are most likely to be highly anti-Semitic. The data shows that 53 percent of first- and second-generation Poles score high on sociological tests of prejudice against Jews. Most significantly, this anti-Semitism is not limited to the immigrant generation or its children; just as many third-generation Poles held strongly anti-Semitic views, according to the survey.

All of this does not usually result in anti-Semitic voting. In 1962, Abraham Ribicoff, a liberal Jew, who had been Kennedy's Secretary of Health, Education and Welfare, and Connecticut's governor before that, barely defeated veteran Republican Congressman Horace Seely Brown for a seat in the United States Senate. Ribicoff ran on a very liberal platform and stressed his ties to the Kennedy administration, while Brown strove to be considered as a militant anti-Communist who wanted to temper the social legislation of the New Frontier. Slavic voters were distinctly pro-Ribicoff, with two thirds voting for the Democrat in Hartford and Bridgeport. His margin over Brown was 20,000 votes in Slavic precincts, and he won statewide by only 26,000.

Ribicoff ran again, in 1968, this time against Edwin May, Jr., a moderate Republican and former Congressman. The Senator was a controversial figure in 1968 following his shouting match at the Democratic national convention with Mayor Daley. May attacked Ribicoff for his dovelike stance on the Indochina war and for siding with "ultraliberal dissent groups." Remarkably, Ribicoff won an easy victory, with 54 percent of the vote. Ribicoff's Slavic vote actually increased slightly from six years before to nearly 70 percent.

In the 1968 Illinois gubernatorial election, Democrat Samuel Shapiro, a liberal and a Jew, lost by 127,000 votes to Republican Richard Ogilvie, a law-and-order Republican from Cook County. But the Slavic vote held for Shapiro. Slavic voters in some "machine" precincts of Chicago voted better than two to one for Shapiro, and overall the Democrat won 57 percent of the Slavic vote. That was just about as well as Otto Kerner did in 1964 and as Paul Douglas did in 1966.

And in Pennsylvania Slavic voters had little difficulty voting for liberal, Jewish Democrat Milton Shapp. In 1966, when Shapp lost to moderate Republican Raymond P. Shafer, he nevertheless won 64 percent of the Slavic vote or just about what senatorial and gubernatorial Democrats were accustomed to winning in Pennsylvania. In 1970, Shapp defeated Republican Raymond J. Broderick by a half million votes. According to a survey taken in early fall, in Slavic precincts Shapp was running ten to fifteen points ahead of his statewide percentage. Assuming that there was no fall-off in Shapp's Slavic support as the campaign progressed, he probably captured at least two thirds of the Slavic vote in 1970 as well.

The pattern does break down, but only slightly, and the Democrat still receives a substantial majority of the Slavic vote. In the Michigan gubernatorial election of 1970, liberal Democrat Sander Levin, a young Jewish state senator, lost to Republican incumbent William Milliken, one of the nation's most progressive Republican governors. Milliken had proposed a sweeping program of state aid to parochial schools, a measure which was warmly received in the Slavic community. Levin opposed the Parochiaid plan. Milliken started far ahead of Levin, but the Democrat fought hard and lost by only 44,000 votes. One of the reasons Milliken won was Slavic defections from Levin to the G.O.P. Levin did win a majority of the Slavic vote, about 58 percent, but that was the lowest Slavic tabulation any Michigan Democrat had received in years. Had Levin run as well with Slavs as liberal Neil Staebler did in 1964 against George Romney, or Zoltan Ferency did against Romney in 1966, he would have wiped out Milliken's lead and won. Slavic voters did not vote against Levin because he was Jewish, but Levin's social philosophy led him to oppose Parochiaid—and that cost him Slavic votes.

In Ohio too, the Slavic vote cut against another liberal Jewish Democrat, Howard Metzenbaum, and he lost to Robert A. Taft, Jr., by 70,000 votes. Metzenbaum's share of the Slavic vote was a reasonably good 66 percent. But in some Slavic precincts of Cleveland, Taft won clear majorities. And while Metzenbaum was getting about two thirds of the Slavic vote, the liberal Democratic candidate for governor, John J. Gilligan, was runing ten to twenty points better with the same voters.[3] At least 25,000 Slavic voters who cast ballots for Gilligan did not vote for Metzenbaum. It is not clear whether it was Metzenbaum *qua* Jew who lost votes with Cleveland's Slavs, or whether it was more directly Metzenbaum's liberal style. Whatever the reason, Metzenbaum did not get his full share of the white Catholic vote and it hurt him.

In New York Arthur Goldberg failed to run as well as he might have with Slavic voters. No survey taken during the campaign found

3. In 1968, too, when he lost to William Saxbe, Gilligan won 76 percent of the Slavic vote.

anti-Semitic feelings toward Goldberg on the part of Slavic voters, but still the former United States Supreme Court Justice won only 58 per-cent of the Slavic vote. In Buffalo, where the political machine of "Boss" Joe Crangle was in good working order, Goldberg beat Rocke-feller by two to one in some Slavic precincts. Outside of Buffalo, how-ever, Goldberg and Rockefeller ran neck and neck with Slavs. Overall, Rockefeller won 36 percent of the Slavic vote and the Conservative gubernatorial candidate Paul Adams, who really wasn't a factor in the race, won only 6 percent. Slavic voters were not impressed with either Goldberg's credentials or his liberal political philosophy. Rockefeller courted the Slavic vote. He ran full-page advertisements in the Slavic-language press for weeks before the election, and his aid-for-parochial-schools plan was welcomed in the Slavic community. In all, Rockefeller simply outperformed Goldberg, and it was therefore not surprising that the Democratic share of the New York Slavic vote was so low.

Even though many Slavic voters hold highly unfavorable atti-tudes toward Jews in general, they appear quite willing to leave their prejudices outside the voting booth. When the Slavic vote declines from its normal Democratic percentages because a Jew is running, other factors—the social issues, a strong G.O.P. candidate, and paro-chial-school aid—seem at least partially to explain the fall-off. As we have seen, liberal Democrats and even *Jewish* liberal Democrats often run quite well with Slavic voters.

SLAVIC VOTERS AND THE G.O.P.

If Slavic voters are to be considered part of any emerging Republican majority, they should be giving a substantial portion of their votes to Republican candidates for statewide office. They don't.

First, the rule: Republican candidates do not win a sizable Slavic vote. Thus, George Romney, in three winning races for governor of Michigan, never received as much as 30 percent of the Slavic ballots. Nelson Rockefeller won less than a quarter of the Slavic vote in 1962 and 1966, and barely more than one third in Slavic precincts in his 1970 landslide victory over Arthur Goldberg. William Saxbe took only a quarter of the Slavic vote in Ohio in 1968 while defeating John Gilli-gan for the Senate, and Warren Knowles never carried more than 25 percent of the Slavic vote in his three successful Wisconsin guberna-torial campaigns. Even Jacob Javits failed to crack the Slavic vote in 1962 when he beat James Donovan by more than 980,000 votes, losing the Slavic vote to Donovan by two to one. Against ultraliberal Paul O'Dwyer six years later the Senator improved his Slavic vote—but in-significantly.

The worst Slavic-Republican showing in any statewide election since 1964 was recorded by Spiro Agnew. In the 1966 Maryland gubernatorial election, the then Vice-President of the United States beat Democrat George Mahoney and Independent Hyman Pressman, but lost the Slavic vote. For the Slavic voters of east Baltimore, there could not have been a more crucial issue than open housing (opposed by Mahoney and favored by Agnew). They feared the encroaching black ghetto, and they voted their fears. It would have been hard for them to vote Republican under any circumstances, but the coincidence of Democratic party loyalty and the race issue made it an easy choice. Mahoney won nearly five out of every six votes in Slavic precincts, or twice his statewide percentage. Agnew, the liberal in the race, took only about 10 percent of the Slavic vote, and Pressman won what was left. It was not a very impressive start for "Agnew the ethnic-vote-getter."

In view of this performance it should not be surprising that Agnew's endorsement was of little help to the successful Conservative senatorial candidacy of James L. Buckley in New York in 1970. Prior to that election, Buckley had taken only 7 percent of the Slavic vote in 1968, when he pulled a million votes against Jacob Javits and Paul O'Dwyer. In 1970 Buckley captured only 22 percent of the Slavic vote, an improvement over 1968, but considerably lower than his statewide portion of 37 percent, and hardly a very conservative showing by the ethnic group widely thought to be a mainstay of independent conservative movements.

And the exception: The most successful Republican candidates among Slavs are either moderate or liberal Republicans.

In New Jersey, liberal Republican Senator Clifford Case did very well with Slavic voters when he last ran for office in 1966, winning 49 percent of the Slavic vote against Democratic liberal Warren Wilentz, the son of the Middlesex County Democratic boss. (Interestingly, Case won better than 60 percent of the vote in the Slavic precincts of Middlesex County.) The Senator's low-key Republicanism, his support for the Johnson administration war policies, and his higher public recognition factor, all added to an easy statewide Case victory.

Another liberal Republican who runs well with Slavic voters is Charles Percy of Illinois. When Percy lost to incumbent Otto Kerner for governor in 1964, he won three out of seven Slavic votes. Although not a majority, it was the best that any G.O.P. candidate for governor would do in the sixties. And in 1966, when Percy beat liberal hawk Senator Paul Douglas, he carried nearly a majority of the Slavic vote. Overall he captured 49 percent and in some sections of Southside Chicago, Percy took almost 60 percent of the Slavic vote.

The first and so far the only Republican to win a clear majority of the Slavic vote statewide is William T. Cahill of New Jersey. In the gubernatorial election of 1969 Cahill ran against former Governor Robert B. Meyner.[4] Both Cahill and Meyner spoke out against rising crime and student unrest, but apparently New Jersey's Slavs were not moved by Meyner's tired campaign rhetoric, and they found former F.B.I. agent Cahill's straight talk appealing; he won 54 percent of the vote in Slavic precincts and in some Slavic areas of Middlesex County captured more than 60 percent.

The New Jersey Slavic Republican majority did not last long, however. In the senatorial election of 1970, Republican candidate Nelson G. Gross ran against incumbent liberal Democrat Harrison A. Williams, Jr. Gross tried to convince New Jersey's voters that he could do more for them in Washington and President Nixon went out of his way to stump for Gross. Williams countered by stressing his seniority on the important Senate Labor Committee, and apparently New Jersey's voters in general, and Slavic voters in particular, were more impressed with Williams' actual power than Gross's potential clout. Gross lost by 250,000 votes statewide, and he won only one third of the Slavic vote.

With the exception of one candidate, moderate Governor Cahill of New Jersey, none of the Republican office seekers whose races we've outlined won a Slavic majority. The most conservative candidate, James Buckley, managed a dismal 22 percent, while the two Republicans who came closest to winning Slavic majorities were liberals Case and Percy. The Republicans still have a long way to go in turning Slavic voters into members of the G.O.P., and those Republicans who stand the best chance of doing it are moderates or liberals.

Whatever the intelligence both major parties may glean from present-day Slavic voting, one conclusion is readily apparent: the Slavic voter can no longer be taken for granted by the Democrats or ignored by the Republicans as unimportant to their coalition. The Slavic voter is more discriminating than ever, and the politician who forgets this political axiom does so at his peril.

4. Meyner had beaten five other candidates including Bergen County Congressman Henry Helstoski to win the nomination. However, Slavic voters showed their loyalty to a fellow ethnic (and a Kennedy-McCarthy-type Democrat) and in the primary Helstoski won 45 percent of the Slavic vote, compared to 32 percent for Meyner, with the rest scattered.

a resurgence
of white ethnicity

BILL OF FRUSTRATIONS

America is not a melting pot. It is a sizzling cauldron for the ethnic American who feels that he has been politically courted and legally extorted by both government and private enterprise.

The ethnic American is sick of being stereotyped as a racist and dullard by phony white liberals, pseudo black militants and patronizing bureaucrats. He pays the bill for every major government program and gets nothing or little in the way of return. Tricked by the political rhetoric of the illusionary funding for black-oriented social programs, he turns his anger to race—when he himself is the victim of class prejudice.

He has worked hard all his life to become a "good American"; he and his sons have fought on every battlefield—then he is made fun of because he likes the flag.

The ethnic American is overtaxed and underserved at every level of government. He does not have fancy lawyers or expensive lobbyists getting him tax breaks on his income. Being a home owner, he shoulders the rising property taxes—the major revenue source for the municipalities in which he lives. Yet he enjoys very little from these unfair and burdensome levies.

Because of restrictive eligibility requirements linked either to income or "target areas," he gets no help from federal programs. If he wants to buy in "the old neighborhood," he cannot get an F.H.A. loan. One major illness in his family will wipe him out. When he needs a nursing home for an elderly parent, he finds that there are none that he can afford, nor is he eligible for any financial assistance.

His children tend to go to parochial schools, which receive little in the way of government aid and for which he carries an extra burden. There is a general decline of community services for his neighborhood, e.g., zoning, libraries, recreation programs, sanitation, etc.

His income of $5,000 to $10,000 per year makes him "near poor." He is the victim of both inflation and anti-inflationary measures. He is the guy that is hurt by layoffs, by tight money that chokes him with high interest rates for installment buying and home improvements.

Manufacturers, with their price fixing, shoddy merchandise and exorbitant repair bills, are gouging him to death. When he complains about costs, he is told that it is the "high cost of labor" that is to blame. Yet he knows he is the "labor" and that in terms of real dollars he is going backwards.

The ethnic American also feels unappreciated for the contribution he makes to society. He resents the way the working class is looked down upon. In many instances he is treated like the machine he operates or the pencil he pushes. He is tired of being treated like an object of production. The public and private institutions have made him frustrated by their lack of response to his needs. At present he feels powerless in his daily dealings with them and with his efforts to change them.

Unfortunately, because of old prejudices and new fears, anger is generated against other minority groups rather than those who have power. What is needed is an alliance of white and black, white collar, blue collar and no collar, based on mutual need, interdependence and respect, an alliance to develop the strategy for new kinds of community organization and political participation.

> *Barbara Mikulski*
> America,
> *December 26, 1970*

What are the main reasons behind the reawakening of white ethnic identity in America? The contributors to this final section of the book probe some conventional answers to this question and offer some of their own clarifications. While each of their answers reveals some of the complexities involved within the new ethnic consciousness, no one has all of the answers to explain this new and potent social phenomenon for it is still developing.

William Newman argues that what we are witnessing is not so much a renewal of ethnicity itself, since that would require a closeness to the original ethnic cultures now lost. Rather, we are experiencing a renewed ethnic consciousness, an awareness on the part of many ethnic Americans of their distinctive ethnic cultures, partly as consciously remembered from the past, partly as inherited customs and beliefs. One aspect of this consciousness is the exploration by many racial and cultural minorities of their own uniqueness. This, claims Newman, ". . . allowed the white ethnics to endorse a theme in which they believed all along, but which was never socially fashionable: the right to be different." *

Another condition related to this "right to be different" was the multi-faceted attack on "the system." One aspect of this included the push for civil rights by black and Spanish-speaking Americans. Another was the often violent cry for American disengagement from the Vietnam War, and the "youth culture's" diffuse attack on American culture in general. Here, then, were a host of Americans tearing apart the very system which the white ethnics were finally becoming a part of. Having been taught to cherish America over their own ethnicity, many wondered how something as valued as the American way of life could now be so insistently maligned by others? What, they asked themselves, could they hope for when so many other Americans were challenging its very system and traditions?

Part of these attacks on the American system were also for a part of that system. Demands for better housing, schools and jobs on the part of urban minorities threatened the white ethnics' newly gained status into the system. White ethnics were angered, in addition, by what America's leaders seemed to be saying: "Share what little gains you have recently made with blacks and hispanic minorities for there are no new resources to be allocated among you." The middle of the socio-economic pie in America appeared fixed; if the new urban minorities were to gain, it would come about only at the expense of the white ethnics. It was predictable, then, that this renewed ethnic interest on the part of many groups, coupled with their manifold demands, would lead to heightened intergroup conflict and competition for limited resources. **

Michael Novak's essay leads off this probe of the new ethnicity by redefining it and disputing the conventional wisdom popularly associated with white ethnics. By exposing this "wisdom" for what it is, he demonstrates how blacks and white ethnics have more interests in common than society is willing to admit. In an age obsessed with questions of individual identity, Novak encourages us all to ask larger questions about our cultural origins. In so doing, Novak offers a personal vision of the new ethnicity as a "conscious self-appropriation of one's own cultural history."

---

* For a fuller description of these aspects of intergroup life see William M. Newman's *American Pluralism: A Study of Minority Groups and Social Theory.* New York: Harper & Row, 1973.

** This intergroup conflict need not be a disorganizing factor in American life for it can serve as a necessary "balancing mechanism" whereby groups continually redefine their own positions and relationships to one another in a pluralistic society.

Nathan Glazer, in the concluding essay asks several hard questions which all who are genuinely interested in the new ethnicity must face: first, ". . . is it honest, or is it a cover for racism?" and, secondly, ". . . what does it mean for a decent and harmonious relationship between ethnic and racial groups in America?" Part of our society's struggle to come up with real answers here, Glazer claims, is due to our confused usage of the word culture. Neither the general population nor social scientists have developed an adequate language for dealing with the cultural diversity present in our American society.

Glazer sees our society as going through two phases in its efforts to come to grips with cultural diversity in America. These include both the phase of asking what groups owe each other, particularly to the more deprived minorities, and the phase of searching for what groups owe themselves. Glazer argues that diverse groups in America are presently in this second phase, searching within themselves for their own identities and needs. While both phases are necessary, he points out the dangers of overreacting to either of these positions.

His selection concludes by offering a framework which encompasses both phases of the problem and takes in the larger needs of the whole American society. All Americans face the difficult tasks of balancing intergroup needs and demands against those of the larger society, of taking cultural pluralism seriously in America. If we are to do so, Glazer concludes, ". . . we all have to change a lot of rhetoric, judge the weight of interests, and decide whether there is indeed a decent American pattern for a multi-group society."

probing the new ethnicity

Michael Novak

I

Since 1967, when the American Jewish Committee held its first national conference on "the white ethnic" at Fordham, the word "ethnic" has been gradually moving back toward its broader usage. Most British-Americans, I believe it will be found, have hardly ever thought of themselves as "ethnic." But that is perhaps true of many Southern and Eastern Europeans, too. The pressure was almost entirely to think of oneself as "American." "We're all Americans!" That is, "We're all equal; I'm just as good as you are." Whatever the sufferings of the past, they are better forgotten. Concentrate on the future.

On the other hand, many can't forget. In Newark, in Canarsie, in Forest Hills, in Cicero, in Cleveland Heights, in Warren and in a hundred other places yet unknown to the media there are large concentrations of "white ethnics" who have normally been the vanguard of the only progressive political party we've got, the Democratic Party. In the last few years they have become the fall guy, the villain, in the eyes of many who wish to bring about a greater measure of justice in American society. Richard Daley, George Meany, labor union "bosses," political "machines," cops with little American flags on their uniforms, beer truck drivers, angry crowds . . .

Well, suppose you want to understand what makes people feel the way they do, think as they do—particularly if you notice odd discrepancies in the usual intellectual descriptions of their behavior. For example, construction workers are pictured as pro-war—but according to a Stony Brook study, no profession in New York City in 1970 was more *opposed* to the war than construction workers. Books of political intelligence sometimes call a Slavic district near Pittsburgh "Wallace country"—but Humphrey took 60% of the vote there in 1968, Wallace 14%. 60% is a landslide. Where, actually, did F.D.R., Truman, Ken-

Reprinted from Michael Novak, "How American Are You . . ." by permission of *Soundings*, New Haven (Spring 1973 edition).

nedy, or Johnson (notably on civil rights) get their majorities? Questions like these raise warning signals about one's own prejudices. What actually is going on among such people? What has their history been like? What in their lives is admirable and beautiful? What are the evils that prey on them? Since all people are evil as well as good, what are their evil tendencies?

Such questions are one part of what is now called "the new ethnicity." For reasons suggested above, the initial focus has been on descendants of immigrants from Southern and Eastern Europe. But if such persons reclaim their own ethnicity, why not others? "Black history" and "Indian history" reopened the study of American history; so did "cold war revisionism." All of a sudden, almost everyone was discovering that the questions "Who am I?" and "Who are we?" led to a much deeper cultural pluralism than we had long been accustomed to imagine. In each of our traditions, good and evil are mixed. Self-discovery does not entail either ethnocentrism or self-glorification. An awakened consciousness of one's social past requires neither chest-thumping nor breast-beating.

II

There are several theses about white ethnics that are conventional but wrong. Let me state them and argue against them.

1. Ethnic Consciousness Is Regressive

In every generation, ethnic consciousness is different. The second generation after immigration is not like the first, the third is not like the second. The native language begins to disappear; family and residential patterns alter; prosperity and education create new possibilities. The new ethnicity does not try to hold back the clock. There is no possibility of returning to the stage of our grandparents.

Nevertheless, emotional patterns that have been operative for a thousand years do not, for all that, cease to function. Those of white ethnic background do not usually react to persons, issues, or events like Blacks, or like Jews, or like Unitarians. In a host of different ways, their instincts, judgments, and sense of reality are heirs to cultural experiences that are now largely unconscious. These intuitive leads, these echoes of yet another language, yet another rhythm, yet another vision of reality, are resources which they are able to recover, if they should so choose.

Jimmy Breslin, for example, has lamented the loss of language suffered by the American Irish. He urges Irish Americans to read Brendan Behan: "For a style is there to examine, and here and there you get these wonderful displays of the complete lock the Irish have on the art of using words to make people smile." Breslin loves "the motion and lilt that goes into words when they are written on paper by somebody who is Irish." He compares Behan's tongue to the language of the 100,000 Irishmen marching down Fifth Avenue on March 17: "You can take all of them and stand them on their heads to get some blood into the skull for thinking, and when you put them back on their feet you will not be able to get an original phrase out of the lot of them. They are Irish and they get the use of words while they take milk from their mothers, and they are residing in the word capital of the world and we find that listed below are the two fine passages representing some of the most important Irish writing being done in the City of New York to-day." He then lists business notices from Brady the Lawyer and Walsh the Insurance Man.

Jewish writers are strong by virtue of their closeness to the Jewish experience in America—e.g., their sense of story, and irony, and dissent. Mike Royko writes with a hard realism and a blend of humor that is distinctively Slavic; like *Good Soldier Schweik*. Phil Berrigan refers to Liz MacAlister as "Irish," and shares a traditionally tough Irish priest's suspicion of liberal intellectuals.

Authenticity requires that one write and act out of one's own experience, images, subconscious. Such materials are not merely personal (although they *are* personal) but also social. We did not choose our grandfathers.

2. Ethnic consciousness is only for the old; it is not shared by the young

It is true that hardly anyone in America encourages ethnic consciousness. The church, the schools, the government, the media encourage "Americanization." So it is true that the young are less "conscious" of their ethnicity. This does not mean that they do not have it. It does not mean that they do not feel joy and release upon discovering it. Often, all one has to do is begin to speak of it and shortly they begin recollecting, begin raising questions, begin exploring—and begin recovering.

Consider the enormous psychic repression accepted by countless families—the repression required for learning a new language, a new style of life, new values and new emotional patterns, during a scant three or four generations of Americanization. Many descendants of the immigrants who do not think of themselves as "ethnic" experience a certain alienation from public discourse in America, from the schools, from literature, from the media, and even from themselves. Nowhere do they see representations of their precise feelings about sex, authority, realism, anger, irony, family, integrity, and the like. They try to follow traditional American models, of course: the classic Protestant idealism of George McGovern, for example. They see a touch of their experience in *Portnoy's Complaint*. But nowhere at all, perhaps, will they see artistic or political models expressing exactly their state of soul. Nowhere do they find artists or political leaders putting into words what remains hidden in their hearts.

The young are more ripe for the new ethnicity than the old, for the new ethnicity is an attempt to express the experience of *their* generation, not of an earlier generation. It treats past history only as a means of illuminating the present, not as an ideal to which they must return. The new ethnicity is oriented toward the future, not the past.

3. Ethnic consciousness is illiberal and divisive, and breeds hostility

The truth is the reverse. What is illiberal is homogenization enforced in the name of liberalism. What is divisive is an enforced and premature unity, especially a unity in which some groups are granted cultural superiority as models for the others. What breeds hostility is the quiet repression of diversity, the refusal to allow others to be culturally different, the enforcement of a single style of Americanism. Our nation suffers from enormous emotional repression. Our failure to legitimate a genuine cultural pluralism is one of the roots of this repression. Our rationalization is fear of disunity; and in the name of unity, uniformity is benignly enforced. (The weapon of enforcement is ordinarily shame and contempt.)

Countless young Italians were given lessons in school on how *not* to talk with their hands; Latin girls were induced to shave their lips and legs; Irish girls to hide their freckles; Poles to feel apologetic about their difficult names; Italians to dread association with criminal activity; Scandinavians and Poles to hate misinterpretations of their taciturnity and impassive facial expression; Catholics to harden themselves against the anti-Catholicism both of intellectual culture and nativist America.

The assumption that ethnic consciousness breeds prejudice and hostility suggests that Americanization frees one from them. The truth is that *every* ethnic culture—including mainstream America, and, yes, even intellectual America—has within it resources of compassion and vision as well as capacities for evil. Homogenized America is built on a foundation of psychic repression; it has not shown itself to be exempt from bitter prejudices and awful hostilities.

America announces itself as a nation of cultural pluralism. Let it become so, openly and with mutual trust.

4. Ethnic consciousness will disappear

The world will end, too. The question is how to make the most fruitful, humanistic progress in the meantime. The preservation of ethnicity is a barrier against alienation and anomie, a resource of compassion and creativity and intergroup learning. If it *might* disappear in the future, it has *not* disappeared in the present. And there are reasons to work so that it never does. Who would want to live on a thoroughly homogenized planet?

5. Intermarriage hopelessly confuses ethnicity

Intermarriage gives children multiple ethnic models. The transmission of a cultural heritage is not a process clearly understood. But for any child a "significant other" on one side of the family or another may unlock secrets of the psyche as no other does. The rhythm and intensity of emotional patterns in families are various, but significant links to particular cultural traditions almost always occur. One discovers these links best by full contact with ethnic materials. It is amazing how persons who claim themselves to have a "very mixed" ethnic background, and "no particular" ethnic consciousness, exhibit patterns of taste and appreciation that are very ethnic indeed: a delight in the self-restraint of Scotsmen, discomfort with the effusiveness of Sicilians—or, by contrast, a sense of release in encountering Sicilian emotions, a constriction of nervousness faced with the puzzling cues of the culture of the Scots.

Cues for interpreting emotion and meaning are subtly learned, in almost wholly unconscious, informal ways. These cues persist through intermarriage for an indeterminate period. Cues to pain, anger, intimacy and humor are involved. (Many of the passages of *The Rise of the Unmeltable Ethnics* were intended ironically and written in laughter; many reviewers, almost exclusively British-American ones, took them seriously, incredulously.)

6. Intelligent, sensitive ethnics, proud of their heritage, do not go around thumping their chests in ethnic chauvinism

Who would want chest-thumping or chauvinism? But be careful of the definition of "good" ethnics, "well-behaved" ethnics. Many successful businessmen, artists, and scholars of white ethnic background carry two sets of scars. On the one hand, they had to break from their families, neighborhoods, perhaps ghettoes, and they became painfully aware of the lack of education and experience among those less fortunate than they. On the other hand, they had to learn the new styles, new images, new values of the larger culture of "enlightenment." The most talented succeed rather easily; those of lesser rank have quietly repressed many all-too-painful memories of the period of their transition. As surely as their grandparents emigrated from the homeland, each generation has had to carry the emigration farther. Americanization is a process of bittersweet memory, and it lasts longer than a hundred years.

7. The new ethnicity will divide group against group

The most remarkable fact about the new ethnic consciousness is that it is cross-cultural. We do not speak only of "Polish" consciousness or "Italian" consciousness, but of "white ethnic" consciousness. The new ethnicity is not particularistic. It stresses the general contours of *all* ethnicity and notes analogies between the cultural history of the many groups. The stress is not only on what differentiates each group but also upon the similarities of *structure* and *process* in which all are involved. In coming to recognize the contours of his or her own unique cultural history, a person is better able to understand and to sympathize with the uniqueness of others'.

8. Emphasis on white ethnics detracts from the first priority to be given Blacks

On the contrary, blindness to white ethnics is an almost guaranteed way of boxing Blacks into a hopeless corner. A group lowest on the ladder cannot advance *solely* at the expense of the next group. Any skillful statesman could discern that in an instant. The classic device of the affluent and the privileged is to pretend to a higher morality, while setting the lower classes in conflict with one another.

The most divisive force in America today is, ironically, precisely the "new class" of liberal and radical academics, media personnel, and social service professionals that thinks itself so moral. Perhaps out of guilt feelings—or for whatever reason—they have projected all guilt for "white racism" onto others. And, without undergoing any of the costs themselves, they take sides or plainly appear to take sides in the very sharp competition between lower-class people, white and black, for scarce jobs, scarce housing, scarce openings in colleges, scarce scholarship funds. They take sides not only with Blacks against whites but also with militant Blacks against other Blacks. For almost a decade they have made "white racism" the central motif of social analysis, and have clearly given the impression that vast resources were going for Blacks, nothing for others. The "Open Admissions" program in New York City schools, e.g., was trumpeted as a program for Blacks and Puerto Ricans. Not much realism would have been required to predict, as turned out to be the case, that 75% of the students taking advantage of the program were white ethnics previously unable to enter colleges.

It is easy for Blacks, at least militant Blacks, to voice their grievances on television and in the papers. It is extremely difficult to get coverage of white ethnic grievances. They are not supposed to *have* grievances, it seems, only prejudices. All problems are defined as black-white problems, even when there are obviously real economic issues for real families in straitened circumstances. With all good intentions, therefore, the desire of liberals to give Blacks highest priority has become exclusionary and divisive.

One can still give Blacks highest priority, but in an inclusionary way that aims at coalitions of whites and Blacks on the grievances they have in common. Newark is divided almost wholly between Blacks and Italians; Detroit between Poles and Blacks. Inadequate schools, the dangers of drugs, insufficient housing, the lack of support for families and neighborhoods—these grievances afflict white ethnics and Blacks alike. If these problems are, by definition, problems of race, what sort of practical coalition can possibly grow? If they are perceived as problems of *class* (with ethnic variables) there is at least a practical ground for effective coalition.

In order for a political coalition to work well, people do not have to love one another; they do not have to share the same life style or cherish the same values. They have to be realistic enough to pursue limited goals in line with their own self-interest. Lower-middle-class Blacks and white ethnics share more self-interests in common than either group does with any other. It is on the basis of shared self-interests that lasting political coalitions are built, and on no other.

9. Ethnicity is all right for minorities, but not for the mainstream

In America, every group is a minority. Even among white Anglo-Saxon Protestants there are many traditions. What is often called "mainline Protestantism," centered in the Northeast: Episcopal, Congregational, Presbyterian, is only one tradition within a far larger and more complex Protestant reality. The father of Senator George McGovern experienced prejudice in South Dakota because the kind of Methodist fundamentalism he represented was closer in style to the lower classes, not fashionable either among "mainline" Methodists nor among Germans and Scandinavians, who were mostly Lutheran. Each of these traditions affects the imagination in a different way. British-Americans from small towns in New England live and work in quite different emotional and imaginative worlds from British-Americans who are Brahmins in Boston and New York. Anglo-Saxon Protestants who are dirt-farmers in Georgia, Alabama, or East Tennessee feel just as much prejudice from Northeastern-style settlers as Polish or Italian

Catholics: stereotypes of the Southern sheriff and the redneck function like those of the Irish cop and the dumb hard-hat. The Scotch-Irish and the Scots have a vivid ethnic consciousness, as a conversation with John Kenneth Galbraith and Carey McWilliams, Jr., would make plain.

There is no good reason why we do not all drop our pretensions of being *like* everyone else, and attempt instead to enlarge the range of our sympathies, so as to delight in every observed cultural difference and to understand each cultural cue correctly and in its own historical context. Styles of wit and understatement vary. Each culture has its own traditions of emotional repression and expressiveness. Our major politicians are often misunderstood, systematically, by one cultural group or another; the cues they depend on are absent, or mean something else.

III

"The new ethnicity" has at least three components. First, there is a new interest in cultural pluralism in our midst. It calls for a new sensitivity toward others in their differences. It means looking at America alert to nuances of difference, more cautious about generalizations about "Americans." Second, there is the personal, conscious self-appropriation of *one's own* cultural history—a making conscious of what perhaps one before had not even noticed about oneself. This component is a form of "consciousness raising." It is useful because ways of perceiving are usually transmitted informally, without conscious design or articulation. As one makes progress in appropriating one's own complexity, one finds it necessary to give others, too, more attentive regard. Thirdly, there is a willingness to share in the social and political needs and struggles of groups to which one is culturally tied, as a way of bringing about a greater harmony, justice and unity in American (and world) society. Rather than pretend to speak for all, or to understand all, we can each make a contribution toward what we can do best.

Each of these components requires further comment.

1. Many liberal persons seem to imagine that social progress demands greater unity, and melting away of social differences. The new ethnicity suggests a form of liberalism based on cultural diversity rather than on cultural unity. It argues that diversity is a better model for America, for the self, and indeed for the human race upon this planet. Is the most pressing danger today homogenization or divisiveness? Does the fear of divisiveness breed conformity, fear of difference, repression of genuine feelings? When ethnic cultures and family values are weakened in the pressures of the melting pot, is anything substituted except the bitch goddess success and the pursuit of loneliness? What else might be proposed? How *are* values taught? These questions prompt the new ethnicity.

2. Some persons are expressly aware of their own ethnic background and interpret the signals from divergent backgrounds successfully. They ask, "What's all this fuss about the new ethnicity?" Well, even their awareness may be first awareness rather than second: accurate enough but not very articulate. It is always a delight to see someone in whom a tradition is alive, even if they *show* better than they *tell.* But in America some of our cultural traditions have been brought to a high degree of articulation and others lie virtually dormant. The Slavs, for example, boast no novel like *Studs Lonigan,* or Mario Puzo's *The Fortunate Pilgrim,* or the whole shelf of American Jewish novels, or even the burgeoning Black literature. How nourishing for the imagination and the sensibility to grow up Jewish, with all that intelligence and energy against which to measure one's own experience, rather than Slavic and virtually solitary. Much remains to be done within many traditions: among Appalachians, Missouri Lutherans, Slovaks, Greeks, etc. And even those which seem to be in stronger shape have strange gaps and self-blindnesses.

3. The political aims of the new ethnicity are not ethnocentrism, nor group struggle; they are, rather, a greater degree of justice, equality, opportunity, and unity in American society. But the *strategy* of the new ethnicity is somewhat different from that of, say, George McGovern or the "new politics" generally. From the point of view of conceptualizers of the new ethnicity like Monsignor Geno Baroni, who worked for many years among Blacks in Washington, D.C., the root flaw in the strategy of "the new politics" is that it is unconsciously divisive and self-defeating. It pictures the white ethnic as the enemy. It drives a wedge between the white ethnic and the Black and/or Latino. It fails to extend friendship or insight. It fails to share the daily burdens of the actual struggle for justice in jobs, housing, and schools. *Both* the Black and the white ethnic are defrauded in this society. No doubt the Black suffers more; no one denies that. The question is, how can one most practically *help* him? The response of the new ethnicity is: By helping *both* the lower-middle-class white ethnic *and* the Black together. Otherwise no coalition is possible. Without that coalition, no one advances.

The alternative is that the Republican Party will, as President Nixon has done, reap the benefits of the breakdown of the alliance between the intellectuals and the white ethnics. A drop in the Slavic Democratic vote from 82% to 60% is a catastrophe for Democrats; and it does not have to happen. If the university wing of the Democratic Party sides with the Blacks *against* white ethnics, and sets up a social pattern whereby gains for Blacks are possible only as losses for white ethnics (or vice versa), the outcome is plain—and deplorable. The social pattern must be fair to *all* groups. Divisive tactics are fatal.

It is not necessary to idealize white ethnics in order to construct a social scheme within which it would be to their advantage to work for equality for Blacks in jobs, housing, and good schools. It is not even necessary to *like* white ethnics. But it does help to understand their history in various parts of America, their spiritual resources, and their chronic weaknesses. Fear of the new ethnicity is very like the early fear of "Black power." Even some Blacks sound, with regard to the new ethnicity, like some whites with regard to Black pride. Such fears must be proven groundless.

If we knew all we had to know about Poles, Italians, Greeks, and others in America, there would perhaps be no need for the almost desperate tones with which the new ethnicity is sometimes announced. But the fact is, we know very little about them. Our anthropologists know more about some tribes in New Guinea than about the Poles in Warren or Lackawanna. We have encouraged too few of the talented white ethnics to stay with their people and to give voice to their experience. Local political leadership is often at a very low level. Community organizers who spring from the community are all too few. Uncle Toms are many. If there is anomie, fear, or rage in such communities (often there is a great deal of bottled-up political energy and great good will), it is to no one's advantage.

The new ethnicity gives promise of *doing* something creative in such places. The new ethnicity is the best hope of all who live in our major urban centers. What we have without it is not promising at all.

the issue of cultural pluralism in america today

Nathan Glazer

Two questions are paramount, I believe, in talking about the current wave of ethnic feeling in America. One is, is it honest? And by that, people mean, is it a cover for racism? Is it a way of justifying anti-Negro prejudice? Is it simply a defensive reaction to black pride? All these are important questions.

And the second is, what does it mean for a decent and harmonious relationship between ethnic and racial groups in America? Does it mean a better America or a worse one? Does it mean more emphasis on group differences, on conflict, on prejudice? And if it does, how are we to avoid these consequences?

I recall when Martin Luther King marched in Chicago and Groppi marched in Milwaukee, both in largely working class, low-income, ethnic areas, and were met with screams and posters and hatred, "We want to save our homes," or "Get out of our neighborhoods." It was very difficult to make the case that there was any motivation for such action but a simple racial hatred. No blacks allowed; they will reduce the value of the property, bring in crime, ruin the schools.

These incidents—and many like them—raise the question, is ethnic feeling honest, in the sharpest form possible. What was there to the Polish or Lithuanian or Italian group and its "culture" that could justify such behavior?

Liberals answered, nothing. The South said it was protecting white culture and white womanhood, something else was said in the North, but it was all the same—racism.

I thought at the time this was an inadequate analysis of what was going on. Let me say at the outset that I do not deny there was some admixture of simple racial prejudice. I won't say how much, and would accept any estimate from 10 to 90 percent. But there was something else. There was a sense that a valued way of life was being threatened. And that kind of motivation for that kind of behavior was different

"The Issue of Cultural Pluralism in America Today." From Nathan Glazer, *Pluralism Beyond the Frontier.* National Project on Ethnic America of the American Jewish Committee, San Francisco.

from racism and different from racial prejudice. It had to be understood—conceivably it had to be protected.

One argument of those who insisted it was only racism went; after all, how much of Polish or Lithuanian or Italian culture actually existed in these areas? Who read Mickiewicz, or Dante, in such areas? If there was no real commitment to the heights of culture, how could one claim that a positive motivation in favor of maintaining a community and its culture dominated, as against a negative hatred of outsiders? The fact is, however, we confuse the meanings of the word culture.

It has always meant, on the one hand, the high culture. But it also means, as anthropologists use it, simply the way of life—the customs: the language, or if the language goes, the accent, the food, the stores, the weddings, the street life, the comfortable expectation that you know what will happen next in your own group, that you know how to approach a person on the street or how to address someone. All this is culture too.

I think it reflects snobbery to take the position that some communities have a right to protect their culture because it is high and others do not because we refuse to accept it as valuable. A known and experienced way of life is always of value to those who have been raised in it, and a reflexive effort to defend it demands at the least sympathy and understanding, if not acquiescence. Because every value may be inferior to a superior value, the Lithuanian neighborhood may have to go to give justice to another group. But we don't know that in advance and it is worth taking the initial claim seriously and sympathetically.

> One problem in this effort to defend certain values is that we do not have a language that justifies this kind of action in America. We do not have a rhetoric that justifies it. The very people who are acting obscurely to positively defend something they conceive of as valuable do not have a ready-made ideology and rhetoric to lean on. Denounced as racists, and incapable of giving sophisticated voice to their own feelings, they may well say, "very well, we are racists," and in effect do themselves an injustice.

We do have a language that justifies losing one's distinctive cultural traits, and becoming as fully as one can an American. The whole ideology of the melting pot justified it. And don't forget that the immigrants and their theorists were as much in favor of the melting pot as native American nationalists, indeed more so, because they thought the melting pot, if they really succeeded in dissolving into some American mass, would give them access to every position in society; while native American chauvinists, trying to monopolize these positions, were not nearly so much in favor of so complete a disappearance of the immigrant groups.

The ideology of the melting pot was fought by the ideology of cultural pluralism, but this was never a widespread and accepted ideology. The biggest moment in the history of cultural pluralism came in World War II, when it seemed that we could strengthen America most not by insisting that everyone forget his national origins, but rather that everyone remember it, because so many nations had been overrun by Hitler. So we encouraged everyone to remember his national origins—everyone but the Germans, of course.

But this was not a great success. After World War II we had a religious revival and Will Herberg developed the ingenious thesis that this was the only legitimate way in which the real ethnic attachments of people—their desire to associate with people of their own group, to have their children marry within their own group, to maintain some associations of their group—could be maintained. To remain ethnic in the 1950's still had a faint color of being insufficiently American. While not actively suppressed, it was not actively encouraged. The war after all was over. It also had a color of lower social status—it meant being working class, immigrant, European.

But if one could do this through one's religion, then it was perfectly legitimate. Religion was not only fully American—any religion, as Eisenhower put it—but it was also indubitably middle class. The Jews were the luckiest in this respect. Whatever it was they were up to in raising money for Israel, conducting a huge afternoon school system, setting up all day schools, maintaining a host of distinctive ethnic institutions, they could say it was religion, and indeed it was. The Jews are a religion. But they are also a people, and they were able to maintain both sets of interests—the religious and the national—through one set of institutions.

Other groups were not so fortunate. Their ethnic reality was one thing, their religion another. Sometimes they worked together, but rarely as completely as did Jewish religion and ethnicity in the postwar years. (There were conflicts between religion and ethnicity even among Jews—some extreme Orthodox and extreme liberal religious groups were anti-national, and some extreme secularist national groups insisted on remaining anti-religious.)

But my main point is—whatever was happening to ethnic groups in the United States, we didn't have a language, a rhetoric, an ideology, that explained it. And we need language even to explain ourselves to ourselves. If not, we borrow the language of the others who have named us. So the blacks, in the old days, borrowed the description of themselves as shiftless and lazy and childlike, and many became that; and the ethnics who resisted the effort to change their neighborhoods borrowed the description of themselves as racist—and many became that. But I insist that was not the whole story. And now we are engaged in an effort to forge a language, rhetoric, and ideology that justifies some line of decent group maintaining behavior by ethnic groups.

One ideology for a multi-group society we have already abandoned, and it is clear it will not play a major role in American life for some years to come. This is the position that insisted on "Americanization," assimilation to a common culture, and that denied dignity, support, role, to the efforts to maintain the culture, religion, loyalty of ethnic groups.

There are many evidences of the crumbling of this position. It was for a long time axiomatic that American culture and society and polity required knowledge of the English language. A knowledge of English is still required for citizenship. But in New York State at any rate it is now possible to vote without demonstrating capacity in English. Bilingual education now receives federal support. It is hard to believe that Spanish will not play an important role in California and other states in the future.

Another aspect of this process of "Americanization" was the insistence that foreign loyalties must be subordinated to American loyalties, or rooted out. This demand rings very hollow at a time when no one is very clear what American loyalties are any more. Certainly we are used to our best educated youth parading with Cuban, or North Vietnamese flags. After what has happened to American patriotism in the last six years, it is hardly likely that anyone can be upset if Jews demand support for Israel, Irish for Ireland, Greeks for Greece—or if anyone *is* seriously upset, it is more because of the political implications of such demands (imperialism, the fascist colonels) than because it is a demand in favor of a foreign country.

But we are still not at all clear as to what will take its place. We have proceeded through two phases in the effort to cope positively with a multi-ethnic America.

In the first phase, inspired by the black revolution, our chief concern was to solve the problem of what groups owed to each other. Except we did not see it quite that way. We thought of it in terms of what "whites" owed to "blacks." The agenda was long, created by 300 years of oppression. As the more outrageous inequalities were overcome—those dealing with access to public facilities, with the right to vote, with inequality in the courts, with direct discrimination by major institutions, public and private—the problem of what the races owed to one another became ever more complicated. Did whites owe blacks, for example, precedence in civil service appointments, and how much? Did they owe sending their children to black schools for certain benefits to be achieved by the mixture? Did they owe silence when black leaders denounced them as racists and called for violence? These were all painful and difficult decisions.

They became more complex when we began to see the issue not in terms of what whites owed to blacks, but as one of what groups of many kinds owed to one another. Black militancy inspired Chicanos, American Indians, others. Whites, on the other hand, began to openly recognize, despite the black-white rhetoric, that there was really no one "white" group. It was one thing for whites to say they owed Negroes more places with support in institutions of higher education. It was another thing for Poles and Italians or the white working classes—who also had few supported places in higher education—to say that they owed blacks more places with support in institutions of higher education. As Leonard Fein has pointed out, "white" made up a single average—of rich groups and poor, and of richer parts of groups and poorer parts of groups. Wealthy Jews who lived in the East Side of New York and sent their children to private schools and never dreamed of having their children become school teachers were quite happy to give up the positions of teachers in the public schools to blacks. Poor working-class Jews in Brooklyn who hoped their children would become teachers were by no means so happy to graciously surrender these posts.

The period in which groups thought of what they owed each other has been replaced by one in which groups considered what they owed themselves. The black experience, and black behavior, convinced many groups they owed more to themselves than they originally thought they did. The black demand for black studies convinced Chicanos they should have Chicano studies. Even rather modest and self-effacing Japanese and Chinese students became convinced that they should have Asian studies. Black assertion convinced many groups that they too had been robbed of their heritage by American society. Many argued the demand for English, for public school attendance, for conformity to middle class standards, had effectively destroyed their culture.

Now the blacks undoubtedly had a much better basis to this claim than any other group. They had been brought unwillingly as slaves. But the Chicanos pointed out that they had been conquered, the Native Americans and Puerto Ricans likewise, the Chinese and Japanese pointed out that poverty had forced them to come as indentured servants, and even the free white immigrants from Europe could point to religious, political, and economic deprivation and insist that they too had been forced into an unfair bargain, the bargain of Anglo-conformity. They now wanted their heritage back, along with full rights in the American society, economy, and polity. They too insisted that they had sold themselves too cheaply and now demanded what the larger society owed them.

Some of the demands on the face of it appear comical. Some of the protestors are not clear just what the culture was that they gave up, and wouldn't want it if it were given back to them. The immigrants also fled from their cultures—it was not only a matter of being forced into conformity. But the black rhetoric is overwhelming. Young Jews now attack their "Uncle Jakes" as blacks attack their "Uncle Toms."

> I think it is that phase we now find ourselves in, the phase in which everyone asks, what do we owe ourselves as a group, while we are still trying to remember, what do we owe the more deprived groups?

Both of these phases have some validity, but both also have their pathology.

Let me describe some of the problems that arise when we focus only on the question of what one group owes to another. One reads in *The New York Times* a story about a woman who has to walk one block in Harlem, from a meeting to a subway station. She is robbed of her pocketbook in the course of her one block walk by black children. The purpose of her article is not to decry crime. If it were, of course, *The New York Times* would hardly find it worth publishing. It is to explain that the proper response, in place of her initial anger and distress at the loss of her money, papers and keys, is sympathy—sympathy with young boys who unfortunately will lead, even with her pocketbook, a worse life than she will.

Clearly in focussing on the question of what one group owes to another, this woman's perceptions have become distorted. Presumably the mothers and fathers of these children are trying to teach them not to rob the pocketbooks of women, even of white women, their ministers and teachers are doing the same. Her understanding—which might be suitable in some analytical framework—can only serve to undermine the behavior—the minimal behavior—that underlies any civilized society, and any multi-group society.

There is also a pathology to the position which emphasizes what we owe to ourselves and our own group. We have all become students of the blacks, and the unashamed insistence on self-interest has legitimated the same kind of behavior in many of us—not that we have needed one group to teach us selfishness. It is a natural human failing. A few days ago, a black student who was a candidate for chairman of the Stanford Student Senate was being questioned by the Senators. In answer to the question would he be impartial, he said, no, he would be partial to blacks. He was elected to the position.

At what point does the perfectly legitimate interest in one's self and one's group become illegitimate? I think we have become very confused about this point. I believe that when all the positions of power or high income or influence are withheld from members of a substantial and numerous group, it is unjust and it is also unstable.

We have long lived with such a society. I believe—more than others—
that we have made impressive efforts in the past half dozen years to
change this unjust and dangerous situation, efforts revealed when we
look at the enormous increase in the numbers of blacks—and to some
lesser extent of other deprived groups—in college, in high civil service
positions, in white collar and professional positions, in elected and
appointed political posts, and the like. But I also believe that in this
phase we have not come up with any sound standard which both de-
fends the interests of all groups and advances the interests of deprived
groups. Rather we have a naive and childish ideology which insists
there are no standards, there is no justice, there is only brute power.
I do not believe this was the case in the United States in the past—
otherwise it is hardly to be explained how some groups, white and nonwhite, achieved income, property, influence and respect, when they
clearly lacked brute power. It is not true now. The fostering of this
dangerous and delusive ideology is one of the serious challenges to a
decent society in this country that we now face. I have given one
example of this dangerous and delusive ideology in the case of the
black Stanford student. Maybe only college students are still so guilt
ridden that they are willing to accept as their chairman someone who
openly confesses that he will not be impartial. Adult voters will not be
so silly.

   We have been strong in insisting to many groups that they could
not defend their interests as they conceived them to the exclusion of
the rights of others. They could not band together to deny Negroes
homes. They could not keep them out of schools. They could not keep
them out of jobs. This battle is scarcely won—I imagine it will never
be in any simple sense "won." But thousands of people are engaged in
the battle to defend these rights, and powerful legislation exists to
defend them. But in all honesty I believe the greater danger to this
country today is not in the denial of the rights of the minority groups
with an officially recognized status of deprivation, but in ignoring the
rights of groups without such a recognized status.

   San Francisco offers now one of the major cases we have of such
a reverse denial of rights. It is well known that a very substantial part
of the Chinese population of this city did not want its children bussed
to other schools. It is well known that many of the Spanish surname
community of the Mission district did not want its children bussed to
other sections. A good part of the black community felt the same way.
Parents in all groups found some virtue in having their children near
them. These virtues were not only those that any parent might see in
having children attend school nearby. They also had a community
aspect. There was a positive desire to maintain a degree of group to-
getherness which busing would to some degree dissipate. The Chinese
pointed out their system of afternoon schools in Chinatown would

suffer if their children were widely dispersed. Many argued that all groups owed to the blacks an integrated school setting, and to provide it their children were needed. But more and more of us, as I said, believe we—as members of groups—owe something to ourselves. What groups owe to themselves in San Francisco—their desire to maintain themselves, their desire to freely select an option which permits group maintenance—was denied because it was insisted the interests of one deprived group was paramount. Now, if it is true that there was one and only one way in which the education of black children could be improved—and that was to distribute them evenly among the children of other groups—then conceivably some aspect of desired group maintenance had to be given to overcome a greater evil. But there is no clear and unambiguous demonstration of this fact in our research. Even if there were, there were ways of achieving this aim without the destructive, and it appears to me narrow-minded, insistence that whatever elements of group homogeneity existed, because of residential concentration and free individual choices, should be disrupted.

Once again, the tragic fact is that these impulses to group maintenance were denounced as racist, and those who defended them did not have the language or the ideology or sophistication to explicate their desires and to put them in a framework in which the charge of racist could be lifted. I think it is critical to explicate such a point of view, one which indeed takes into account what we owe to each other—to deprived groups—but which also takes into account what each group owes to itself, and which finally takes into account what we owe the nation. Let me suggest the framework for such a point of view. This framework is drawn from the distinctive American experience in forging a single nation from many groups, which still has a great deal to teach us.

1. *I think the first principle in the framework is that the* individual *is paramount, not the group.* The group has no claim on the individual if he does not want to be a member of the group. It can levy no tax on him, though he may give voluntary contributions. It may levy no loyalty, though he may give voluntary loyalty. Government recognizes the individual, not the group. Only the individual has rights, not the group.

2. *In the light of this reality of individual freedom, the society maintains primary institutions which have no ethnic or racial coloring.* Its civil service must be open to all, its schools must be open to all, its residential areas must be open to all, its jobs—at least in the major employing institutions—must be open to all, color blind, and indifferent to group affiliation or group origin.

3. *If ethnic and racial groups maintain themselves, they must maintain themselves voluntarily.* Their schools, churches, political organizations are voluntary organizations. Their residential concentrations are voluntary concentrations. Just as government does nothing to

foster them, it does nothing to destroy them. It is not the task of government to disperse a residential concentration or a school concentration or even a job concentration, if there is no sign of discrimination, and if opportunities are available to every group.

4. *But government and public authority is benign in relationship to group formation, as long as this group formation does not harm the interests of other individuals.* Government accepts that in a large and complex and plural society group affiliations serve many purposes. It accepts and endorses Tocqueville's description of America as a society of multifarious associations—and among these associations are ethnic associations. It may even to some extent offer aid and assistance to associations in the form of tax relief or some public facilities. But it must balance this benign attitude toward association with principle one, the primacy of the individual, and principle two, the need to maintain public, supra-ethnic institutions.

5. *Just as government is benign in its relationship to voluntarily formed ethnic associations, without giving them any formal public recognition, so it must be prudent in acting to redress situations in which groups, even with the fullest enforcements of individual rights (principles 1 and 2), end up poor and powerless.* This will inevitably lead to instability, and special measures are necessary to overcome radical group imbalance in wealth and power. But these measures must be addressed to the *individual.* Government cannot accept the formal partnership of formally organized ethnic groups. To do so is to damage the minimal requirements for common political and social action that the nation requires, and to damage the interests of those—undoubtedly a majority of the country—who seek no ethnic group affiliation and want to be forced into none. To give benefits to groups is to give incentives to encourage individuals to maintain group affiliation. This is both a restriction on individual freedom, the paramount principle, and damaging to efforts to achieve a minimally necessary level of common action.

6. *What is most neglected in the present situation is what we owe to the entire society of which we are a part.* Some minimal degree of a common culture, a common language, a common loyalty, is necessary to create a common society. There was some justice even in Americanization. If German Americans in World War I and II had the view of loyalty that so many members of minority groups hold today, undoubtedly there would have been civil war in this country. If the view that justifies group self-interest had been as prominent some decades ago as it is today, I do not think we would have a better society today, but a worse one. I believe we must all agree the country cannot be dissolved into air-tight constituent parts. This would not only make it impossible for it to function, to all our detriments, but would be unjust to all those who do not want to see themselves as bound to and by any ethnic or racial group, but as free individuals determining their own associations and selecting their own values.

We have been so involved so long in the rhetoric of what we owe deprived groups, and what we owe ourselves, that we are left tongue-tied by these larger questions. Even when our instincts are right, we are often inhibited because of group loyalty in defending what is right. We now have to decide whether we are really serious about various groups living in peace in a good society. If we are, we all have to change a lot of rhetoric, judge the weight of interests, and decide whether there is indeed a decent American pattern for a multi-group society.

resources

CENTERS, INSTITUTES AND RESEARCH PROJECTS ON WHITE ETHNIC AMERICANS

A growing number of centers, institutes and research projects are currently investigating many of the questions raised in this book concerning white ethnic Americans. Most of them have explanatory materials and other publications available at nominal cost. The three largest, national centers are presented first with brief descriptive statements; other centers follow after them.

CENTER FOR THE STUDY OF AMERICAN PLURALISM. Rev. Andrew Greeley, Director. National Opinion Research Center, 6030 Ellis Ave., Chicago, Illinois, 60637.

A continuing sociological study on the nature and role of ethnicity in American life. The study seeks to determine to what extent the ethnic variable persists in our society, and to what extent it is an indicator of behavior. Random sample survey data are used extensively on selected ethnic populations to discover answers to the complex questions surrounding ethnic identity. The Center publishes a quarterly magazine, *Ethnicity,* and has other research materials available. The Center receives funding support from the Ford Foundation.

NATIONAL CENTER FOR URBAN ETHNIC AFFAIRS. Msgr. Geno Baroni, President. 4408 Eighth Street, N.E., Washington, D.C., 20017.

This is an independent center affiliated with the U.S. Catholic Conference. It was initially established in response to the intensifying urban crises and the needs of working class Americans. The Center has developed cooperative relationships with numerous northern cities through technical assistance to neighborhood based community organizations. It attempts to develop models for other urban ethnic and working class communities, demonstrating the kinds of organizations and programs which will improve the quality of life for such communities. Literature available includes periodical reprints, case studies and workbooks such as "Working Class and Ethnic Priorities." The Ford Foundation, among others, provides funding support.

NATIONAL PROJECT ON ETHNIC AMERICA. Irving Levine, Project Director. Judith Herman, Project Coordinator. American Jewish Committee, Institute of Human Relations. 165 E. 56th Street, New York, New York, 10022.

A pilot depolarization project launched in 1968 to help develop more positive approaches and responses to the needs of lower-middle-class whites and to defuse tensions among white and other minority ethnic groups. The Project has been funded since 1971 by the Ford Foundation. It relates to "middle America" phenomena in such areas as mental health, education, work, neighborhoods and other topics. While concerned generally with lower middle class life styles, it specializes in the problems of working class youth and women. Available literature includes the Middle American Pamphlet Series, periodical reprints and a bibliography on ethnicity.

Other centers and institutes participating in research on white ethnic Americans are listed below.

CENTER FOR IMMIGRATION STUDIES. Rudolph Vecoli, Director.
7925 Sapher Street, St. Paul, Minnesota, 55113.

CENTER FOR MIGRATION STUDIES. Fr. S. M. Tomasi, Director.
209 Flagg Place, Staten Island, New York, 10304.

CENTER FOR URBAN ETHNOGRAPHY. John Szwed, Erving Goffman, Dell Hymes, Directors.
University of Pennsylvania, Philadelphia, Pa., 19104.

CROSS-CULTURAL SOUTHWEST ETHNIC STUDY CENTER. Z. Anthony Zruszewski, Co-Investigator.
University of Texas, Box 13, El Paso, Texas, 79968.

ETHNIC HERITAGE AFFAIRS INSTITUTE. (No first name used) Jaipaul, President.
260 South 15th Street, Philadelphia, Pa., 19102.

MULTI-CULTURE INSTITUTE. Ms. Frances Sussna, Director.
693 Mission Street, San Francisco, California, 94105.

NEW YORK CENTER FOR ETHNIC AFFAIRS. Ralph Perotta, Director.
11 W. 42nd Street, New York, New York, 10036.

PROGRAM OF ITALIAN-AMERICAN STUDIES. Richard Gambino, Director.
Queens College, Flushing, New York, 11367.

SLAVIC AMERICAN STUDIES. Professor Peter Goy.
City College of New York, New York, N. Y. 10031.

SOUTH EAST MICHIGAN REGIONAL ETHNIC HERITAGE STUDIES
CENTER. Professor Otto Feinstein.
111 East Kirby, Detroit, Michigan, 48202.

bibliography

Abramson, Harold J. *Ethnic Diversity in Catholic America.* New York: Wiley & Sons, 1973.

Bailey, Harry A. & Ellis Katz, eds. *Ethnic Group Politics.* Columbus, Ohio: Merrill, 1969.

Balch, Emily G. *Our Slavic Fellow Citizens.* New York: Arno Press & *The New York Times,* 1969.

Banfield, Edward & James Q. Wilson. *City Politics.* Cambridge, Mass.: Harvard U. Press, 1963.

Barron, Milton L., ed. *Minorities in a Changing World.* New York: Knopf, 1967.

Berger, Bennet M. *Working-Class Suburb.* Berkeley: U. of California Press, 1968.

Binzen, Peter. *Whitetown, USA.* New York: Random House, 1970.

Brown, Francis J. & Joseph S. Roucek, eds. *One America: The History, Contributions, and Present Problems of Our Racial and National Minorities.* Westport, Conn.: Negro U. Press, reprinted, 1970.

Capek, Thomas. *The Czechs in America.* New York: Arno Press & *The New York Times,* 1969.

Carlson, Lewis H. & George A. Colburn. *In Their Place: White America Defines Her Minorities, 1850–1950.* New York: Wiley & Sons, 1972.

Coleman, John R. *Blue-Collar Journal.* New York: Lippincott, 1974.

Coles, Robert & Jan Erickson. *The Middle Americans.* Boston: Little, Brown, 1971.

Covello, Leonard. *The Social Background of the Italo-American School Child.* New Jersey: Rowman & Littlefield, 1972. (First published in 1967: Leiden, Netherlands: E. J. Brill.)

Dahl, Robert A. *Who Governs?* New Haven: Yale U. Press, 1961.

Dinnerstein, Leonard & Frederick Jaher, eds. *The Aliens.* New York: Appleton-Century-Crofts, 1970.

Fackre, Gabriel. *Liberation in Middle America.* Philadelphia: Pilgrim Press, 1971.

Feldstein, Stanley & Lawrence Costello. *The Ordeal of Assimilation.* New York: Doubleday, 1974.

Fenton, Patrick. "Confessions of a Working Stiff," *New York*. Vol. 6, No. 14. April 2, 1973.

Franklin, John Hope, Thomas F. Pettigrew & Raymond W. Mack. *Ethnicity in American Life*. New York: Anti-Defamation League, B'Nai B'Rith, 1971.

Friedman, Murray, ed. *Overcoming Middle Class Rage*. Philadelphia: Westminster Press, 1971.

Fuchs, Lawrence H., ed. *American Ethnic Politics*. New York: Harper & Row, 1968.

Gambino, Richard. *Blood of My Blood: The Dilemma of Italian-Americans*. New York: Doubleday, 1974.

Gans, Herbert. *The Urban Villagers*. Glencoe, Ill.: Free Press, 1962.

Glazer, Nathan & Daniel Moynihan. *Beyond the Melting Pot*. 2nd ed. Cambridge, Mass.: M.I.T. Press, 1970.

Golden, Loretta. *The Treatment of Minority Groups in Primary Social Studies Textbooks*. Ann Arbor, Mich.: Doctoral Dissertation Series, University Microfilms, 1964.

Gordon, Milton M. *Assimilation in American Life*. New York: Oxford U. Press, 1964.

Gossett, Thomas F. *The Idea of Anglo-Saxon Superiority in American Thought, 1865–1915*. Ann Arbor, Mich.: Doctoral Dissertation Series, University Microfilms, 1953.

Greeley, Andrew M. *Why Can't They Be More Like Us?* New York: Dutton, 1971.

Greene, Victor R. *The Slavic Community on Strike*. Notre Dame, Ind.: U. of Notre Dame Press, 1968.

Handlin, Oscar. *Race and Nationality in American Life*. New York: Doubleday Anchor paperback, 1957.

———. *The Uprooted*. Boston: Little, Brown, 1951.

Hansen, Marcus L. *The Atlantic Migration, 1607–1860*. New York: Harper Torchbooks paperback, 1961.

———. *The Immigrant in American History*. New York: Harper & Row, Harper Torchbooks, 1964.

Hartmann, Edward G. *The Movement to Americanize the Immigrant*. New York: U. of Columbia Press, 1948.

Hawkins, Brett W. & Robert A. Lorinskas, eds. *The Ethnic Factor in American Politics*. Columbus, Ohio: Merrill, 1970.

Herberg, Will. *Protestant-Catholic-Jew*. New York: Doubleday, 1955. Anchor paperback, 1960.

Higham, John. *Strangers in the Land: Patterns of American Nativism 1860–1925*. New York: Atheneum, 1968.

Howe, Irving, ed. *The World of the Blue Collar Worker*. New York: Quadrangle Books, 1973.

Howe, Louise Kapp, ed. *The White Majority*. New York: Random House, 1970.

Jenkins, David. *Job Power: Blue & White Collar Democracy*. New York: Doubleday, 1973.

Kallen, Horace M. *Cultural Pluralism & the American Idea*. Philadelphia: U. of Pennsylvania Press, 1956.

Kane, Michael B. *Minorities in Textbooks*. Chicago: U. of Chicago, Quadrangle Books, 1970.

Kantrowitz, Nathan. *Ethnic and Racial Segregation in the New York Metropolis.* New York: Praeger, 1973.

Killian, Lewis. *White Southerners.* New York: Random House, 1970.

Komarovsky, Mirra. *Blue-Collar Marriage.* New York: Random House, Vintage Books, 1967.

Lasson, Kenneth J. *The Workers: Portraits of Nine American Job Holders.* New York: Grossman, 1971.

Laumann, Edward O. *Bonds of Pluralism.* New York: Wiley & Sons, 1972.

Lemon, Richard. *The Troubled Americans.* New York: Simon & Schuster, 1970.

Levitan, Sar A., ed. *Blue-Collar Workers.* New York: McGraw-Hill, 1971.

Levy, Mark & Michael Kramer. *The Ethnic Factor: How America's Minorities Decide Elections.* New York: Simon & Schuster, 1972.

Lieberson, Stanley. *Ethnic Patterns in American Cities.* Glencoe, Ill.: Free Press, 1963.

Litt, Edgar. *Ethnic Politics in America.* Glenview, Ill.: Scott, Foresman, 1970.

Lopreato, Joseph. *Italian Americans.* New York: Random House, 1970.

Marden, Charles F. & Gladys Meyer. *Minorities in American Society.* New York: Van Nostrand, Reinhold, 1968.

Moquin, Wayne, ed. *Makers of America.* 10 vols. Chicago: Encyclopaedia Britannica Educational Corp., W. Benton, Pub., 1971.

Newman, William M. *American Pluralism: A Study of Minority Groups & Social Theory.* New York: Harper & Row, 1973.

Novak, Michael. *The Rise of the Unmeltable Ethnics.* New York: Macmillan, 1971.

Parenti, Michael. "Ethnic Politics and the Persistence of Ethnic Identification," *American Political Science Review.* September, 1967.

Parker, Richard. *The Myth of the Middle Class.* New York: Liveright, 1973.

Portal, Roger. *The Slavs.* New York: Harper & Row, 1969.

Rainwater, Lee, Richard P. Coleman & Gerald Handel. *Workingman's Wife.* New York: Oceana Pub., 1959.

Rose, Peter I., ed. *Nation of Nations: The Ethnic Experience & the Racial Crisis.* New York: Random House, 1972.

————. *They & We: Racial and Ethnic Relations in the United States.* New York: Random House, 1964.

Schermerhorn, Richard. *Comparative Ethnic Relations.* New York: Random House, 1970.

Segal, Bernard, ed. *Racial & Ethnic Relations.* New York: Crowell, 1966.

Seifer, Nancy. *Absent From the Majority: Working Class Women in America.* New York: Institute of Human Relations Press, The American Jewish Committee, 1973.

Sennett, Richard & Jonathan Cobb. *The Hidden Injuries of Class.* New York: Knopf, 1972.

Sexton, Patricia C. & Brendan Sexton. *Blue Collars and Hard Hats.* New York: Random House, 1971.

Shostak, Arthur B. *Blue-Collar Life.* New York: Random House, 1969.

Simpson, George E. & J. Milton Yinger. *Racial and Cultural Minorities.* New York: Harper & Row, 1965.

Suttles, Gerald D. *The Social Order of the Slum: Ethnicity and Territory in the Inner City.* Chicago: U. of Chicago Press, 1968.

Terkel, Studs. *Working: People Talk About What They Do All Day and How They Feel About What They Do*. New York: Pantheon, 1974.

Thomas, William I. & Florjan Znaniecki. *The Polish Peasant in Europe and America*. 2 vols. Chicago: U. of Chicago Press, 1918, and New York: Dover Publications, 1958.

Tomasi, Lydio F. *The Ethnic Factor in The Future of Inequality*. Staten Island, N.Y.: Center For Migration Studies, 1972.

———— & Madeline H. Engel, eds. *The Italian Experience in the United States*. Staten Island, N.Y.: Center For Migration Studies, 1970.

U.S. Department of Commerce, Bureau of the Census. "Characteristics of the Population by Ethnic Origin: November, 1969." Washington, D.C.: U.S. Government Printing Office, April, 1971.

U.S. Department of Health, Education and Welfare. *Work in America*. Cambridge, Mass.: M.I.T. Press, 1972.

Warner, W. Lloyd and Leo Strole. *The Social Systems of American Ethnic Groups*. New Haven: Yale U. Press, 1945.

Weber, Max. "The Ethnic Group." In Parsons, Talcott, ed. *Theories of Society*. Vol. I. Glencoe, Ill.: Free Press, 1961.

Weed, Perry L. *The White Ethnic Movement and Ethnic Politics*. New York: Praeger, 1973.

Wenk, M., S. M. Tomasi & G. Baroni, eds. *Pieces of a Dream: The Ethnic Worker's Crisis With America*. Staten Island, N.Y.: Center For Migration Studies, 1972.

Whyte, William F. *Street Corner Society: Social Structure of an Italian Slum*. Chicago: U. of Chicago Press, 1955.

Wytrwal, Joseph A. *America's Polish Heritage*. Detroit: Endurance Press, 1961.

Yinger, J. Milton. *A Minority Group in American Society*. New York: McGraw-Hill, 1965.